What Ever Happened to My White Picket Fence?

My Brain Injury from
My Massive Brain Tumor

3/6/18

To: John
Thank you
for reading!

Janet Johnson Schliff, M.S.Ed.

Janet Johnson Schliff

outskirts
press

DEDICATION

First, I dedicate this book to the brain-injured, and all the exceptional caregivers who unselfishly nurture them each and every day, though it's not an easy task.

Second, I dedicate this to my late cousin Heather Johnson, who was my inspiration for becoming a special education teacher, my true calling.

And, most important, I dedicate this to God, Who I know holds me in His loving hands.

TABLE OF CONTENTS

DISCLAIMER

This book does not offer advice on the medical treatment of patients, which is only appropriate for specially-trained medical professionals who have a detailed knowledge of the patient. Do not rely on information in this book in place of requesting professional medical advice. Please remember that medical information is frequently changing.

This book is the product of my experience and exhaustive research. I assume no liability for the information provided here. Use of the information in this book releases me from any responsibility for any loss or other liability incurred by the reader.

[I hope that the necessary legalism of this disclaimer does not bother the reader as much as it bothers me having to put it here. JJS]

Editor's Note

In the nearly three years I have worked together with Janet Schliff as editor and coach for her memoir, I have been fortunate to get to know an exceptional woman with an unusual story that contains lessons for us all: brain injuries, such as hers, are invisible, yet they produce often puzzling behavior that can alienate victims from friends and families just when the afflicted most need the love and caring of these former intimates.

Imagine having to relinquish the career that you love, due to a growing morbid fear of germs. Imagine being cured of that by a radical brain operation that removed a tumor the size of an orange, leaving the part of the brain in the immediate vicinity of the excision damaged both by the previous pressure from the tumor and by the loss of brain matter due to the operation.

Writing this book has required unusual perseverance. Janet persisted despite severe back pains (requiring a back brace), skin cancer surgeries, ulcers, liver problems, tendinosis (requiring a boot), cardiovascular issues, painful urinary tract infections, her dog Happy's canine medical issues, and relationship disappointments…yet, weekly she came to our meetings with her writing and correcting done, often lugging in back-up material, besides.

Janet has been left both hyper-sensitive to the world and less able to self-censor her comments about what she experiences.

We have joked, though Janet finds joking uncomfortable because it can be hurtfully ambiguous, that she should wear a button, "Handle me with care…I'm brain-injured." Yet, she and others like her want not to be treated as so very different from the rest of us. Just given a bit more slack, a bit more care, a bit more love. So much hurt and misunderstanding could be prevented if people were a bit more careful. Those who read Janet's story will want to do just that from now on.

I believe you will find Janet's story intriguing, inspiring, and enlightening.

Douglas Winslow Cooper, Ph.D.
douglas@tingandi.com

Foreword:
In the Eye of the Storm

"If you have seen one brain injury, then you've seen ONE brain injury!" Sadly, this statement is not heard often enough in the world of brain injuries. There is too great a tendency to typify behaviors and possible outcomes. While there are some impacts commonly experienced, **many factors are important to consider: the person's pre-injury functional status, the cause of the injury (trauma, stroke, or tumor), the area affected, the post-injury rehabilitation treatment, and the natural supports in each individual's life.** These all play significant roles in the recovery process and long-term outcomes.

Brain injury effects are invisible until a deficit area is stimulated, resulting in an observable behavior that can be cognitive, emotional, behavioral, or social. There are areas of the brain that help to regulate behavior and allow for controlled responses. These areas allow us to think things through and then respond. Other areas of the brain are more reactive, in that they respond without our thinking, based on body signals received that are related to anger or stress. Brain injury can result in structural, neuronal, and/or chemical changes in the brain's functioning. **When the responsive area of the brain sustains damage, there is less thinking things through, and more impulsive, acting-out reactions.** This can result in a range of emotional upsets, including aggression, depression and anxiety. **The observable responses may include attention deficit, impulsivity, disinhibition, poor insight, impaired judgment, and anger-management struggles.**

Such is the impact of the storm that wreaks havoc on what was once a person's previously well-controlled life. A low frustration

threshold, high intolerance, and exaggerated reactivity can affect both the individual and the individual's interpersonal relationships. A vicious circle of increased occurrence, decreased control, and increased difficulties may result. Feelings of resentment, insecurity, inferiority, and isolation may begin to take control of social activities. **Because the affected person appears unchanged, those around the person who is within the storm** question the validity of the issues, or question the person's ability to exercise control, **wrongfully believing that if the person really wanted to, or just tried harder, he or she could manage and control the behavior.**

This is the storm that Janet Schliff navigates daily. In the years that I have known Janet, I have watched her struggle with how the impact of her brain injury, resulting from a cerebral tumor and its removal, has caused deviations from her pre-injury pattern of behavior; I have seen her frustration as she has tried to recognize and derail her negative reactivity; and most of all, **I have known also that she suffers the deep emotional heartache of having people in the various circles of her life question the honesty of her struggle and pain.** I have become aware, sadly, of their inability, or unwillingness, to acknowledge the self-imposed regimen she follows in seeking assistance through traditional and alternative medical practices, as well as by attending multiple support groups, in her attempts to utilize any and every treatment or strategy to exorcise that which she wishes she could remove from her life.

Janet could have easily succumbed to the weight of this invisible, residual, and chronic impact of her brain injury, this permanent damage to both her frontal and temporal lobes, but that is not who Janet is. The same tenacity that inadvertently sometimes fires off her brain's overreaction is what also keeps her fired up to work on these areas of her life. It is a daunting task to keep aiming for a moving target that arises and detonates without warning. **Yet Janet pushes herself to learn what it's made of, and to face it head-on. Janet has come further along than even she realizes…**because she lives in the eye of the storm. **Her unwavering determination, and the support of those who genuinely care enough to weather the storm right beside her, will continue to ensure positive outcomes in her life.**

Adaptation to the "new normal" of post-brain injury is about **progression, not perfection.**

Dr. Lois P. Tannenbaum
Psy.D. in Clinical Psychology
Master of Science in Education
Certified Brain Injury Specialist
Former Director, Mid-Hudson Brain Injury Center
Board President, Brain Injury Association of New York State
(2013-2016)
DrLPT03@aol.com

[Just to let you know: Lois has emailed and texted me the sweetest words to thank me for cards I sent, things I do for her and others in our support group, and more. She is so smart, sweet, and just, plain good, and I LOVE her for that!]

THE MIRROR OF BRAIN INJURY

by Dr. Lois P. Tannenbaum

Life's difficult moments, so hard to pen
Sitting alone, absent of family or friends
Beyond the road traveled with all of its bends
In the silence of struggle, life must transcend
Memories refocused in my mind's lens
Thoughts reflected, honored, negativities cleansed
Light slowly returning, hope rising again
Determination, rebuilding, timeframes without end
Rewriting my life's script
Unsure how it will end
Living fully each moment
Allowing my soul to mend

ACKNOWLEDGMENTS

I have a long list of people to thank for getting this book out, but I have to begin with my editor, Dr. Douglas Winslow Cooper.

Not only has he typed this from my long, weekly scribbles and spent lots of time teaching me how to be a better writer, he also provided much love and concern when I was struggling either with writing or life in general.

There were many Friday mornings (our usual meeting times), that I had to vent about something before I could actually concentrate on the work that we had to do at that appointment.

He sat there patiently, listening to what was bothering me that day (problems with "Aiden" – an ex you'll read about later – my mother's ailments, my dog's health, my health, and on and on and on).

After I was done with this venting, he'd carefully help me feel better about it all. Sometimes, he'd "take Aiden's side" and others, he would agree with me, that whatever Aiden had done or said was hurtful.

Dr. Cooper would also help me calm down if I was upset about not being able to take better care of my mother, or if I was scared about something regarding my dog Happy.

He helped me relax when I'd get bad news from various doctors (ulcers, skin cancers, back pains, bladder problems, tendinosis, *etc.*).

All of this going on at the same time was sometimes just too much for me. But, his gentle soul always brought clarity and calmness to our meetings (and he even allowed my dog Happy to accompany us at his house and at the office where we met), and so I got it done. I'll always be thankful to him for that.

And I will forever say, he's the ONLY man, since my childhood, that I allowed to correct me! All others before Dr. Cooper tried and failed!

As for everyone else, the list is too long to present. The people that have helped me are written about in here. There are just too many to count, and anyway, I want you to get started reading my story!

Finally, I have to thank God. If not for Him saving my life, I wouldn't be here to write a memoir. To Him be all my gratefulness....

PREFACE

To copy a sentence from my editor's memoir – why am I writing this memoir? So, why am I?

The answer for me is pretty simple. If I, a former special education teacher, who taught more than one child with a brain injury, knew as little about brain injury as I did before my own (damaged temporal and frontal lobes), then more work had to be done to get the information out there.

I am no expert when it comes to research or technology as far as the brain is concerned. What I am an expert in is what happened to me, what is still taking place to this very day, and what I have learned from many others with brain injuries. And I know there are many others with brain injuries like me. From 2007-2013, the rate of brain injury increased 50%, hitting a record level, according to the Centers for Disease Control and Prevention.

According to the New York State Department of Health, "In New York State, **more than 500 people** sustain a brain injury each day. **Prevalence is estimated to be 50% higher than reported.**"

According to other sources I've read, elderly people are particularly vulnerable, as they have a high likelihood of falling, possibly causing a brain injury.

And as a side note, more and more famous people are being diagnosed with brain tumors and diseases. The ones that have been reported at the time of this writing (summer, 2017), include: ice skating champion Scott Hamilton; U.S. Senator John McCain; TV host Maria Menounos; comedian Jim Gaffigan's wife, Jeannie, a comedy writer; and former New York State Congressman, Maurice Hinchey. I wish all of them, and everyone else with these scary diagnoses, the best of health.

As for me, I know how easily "bruised" I become with others' careless wording. I know how triggered I am by thoughtless questions (such as, "Why are you wearing sunglasses inside?" to name one of the too-many examples that take place daily; you'll read why I do here).

I realize that I'm very high-functioning as far as brain injury comparisons. However, there are many of us that, though we "walk-the-walk" and "talk-the-talk," there is much going on inside of our brains that gets us "off course" and thus, bothersome to certain other people who don't "get it" and therefore steer clear of us.

That's why I had to do this: so, hopefully, caregivers, family members, loved ones, friends, colleagues, and/or former colleagues, fellow church-goers, and everyone else, can try to help those of us with this condition to navigate life as well as we can, now that our lives will never be the same, after this injury.

I don't expect this book to be a bestseller. I know it's not in chronological order. Within chapters, stories go back and forth. Some stories and/or information is repeated. My memory is choppy. Some details are sharp, others vague or missing. Even so, what I do hope is that people will learn how to take better care of someone who has a brain injury.

As I compiled this preface, I met someone for the first time who told me how her doctors told her to "steer clear" of a family member of hers whose brain was injured in a car accident, because of how much of a toll that brain-injured family member was taking on this person.

I really gave that story a lot of thought, and that's why it's here in my preface. If a doctor is counseling his/her patient to "steer clear" of a family member with a brain injury, then who is going to help that brain-injured person in need of love and warmth, when it's needed most?

Shouldn't the doctor help find solutions to the problems within the family that are due to someone's injured brain, rather than take the easy way out and just advise the others to avoid the person?

As the highly knowledgeable Dr. Travis Stork stated on his television show *The Doctors*, "…brain damage, particularly in the frontal region…can control…judgment, impulse control, memory, social behavior…." [My brain damage includes this frontal region, and I have problems with everything he listed.]

As a brain injury expert from New York's Mt. Sinai Hospital, Wayne Gordon, said with respect to treating prison inmates, "You need to train the correction officers to understand brain injuries so that when somebody may be acting rude or answering back or forgetting what they're supposed to do, it's not a sign of maladaptive behavior or disrespect, it's a sign of a brain injury."

We all need love, whether we're healthy or not. People with brain injuries, mental health issues, and other behavior problems need just as much attention as (if not more than) those without such problems because their behaviors can lead to detrimental societal issues, on a large scale, and to terrible family disruptions, on a smaller scale.

So, please, show some love right now to someone you know that is not well emotionally. Whatever the reason, just be there for them, even if it's just simply saying, "I love you." Words that are warm can truly lift someone's spirit when that person is in a dark place.

And the dark place is where our brains take us if we're not careful. We, the brain-injured, need help getting on with our lives in as positive a way as possible. Please lead us there in a calm and gentle way. Show us the love even though sometimes we can be very difficult to be around.

I can't believe I'm about to suggest this, considering I was mysophobic (which is explained in great detail here in this book), but how about a simple hug now and again? Hugs can really help calm the inner turmoil that is bubbling and brewing below the surface in the brain-injured's mind.

I know one day I received three hugs from a woman named Hilary that I had just met because I was volunteering at church with her little four-year-old son. Those hugs helped me mentally later on in the day when I dealt with one more doctor's appointment. It's amazing what may seem a small gesture to you might leave a big impact on the receiver. [But always remember to ask if the person would like a hug. I shrieked when others tried to touch me when I was afraid of germs. You'll understand that as you read my book.]

Now – about my fear of making enemies since I decided to write this candid book. Author Judith Barrington in her *Writing the Memoir: From Truth to Art* stated sentences that I'm going to use because I'm sure that some of the things I told in my chapters are not how others remember them. I did my best to tell it all as I remember it taking place, but there will be one (or more than one) story that someone doesn't remember quite like that. But, I did my very best in truth-telling.

So – here's Ms. Barrington's paragraph. It could not be better stated than this, and I knew when I read it the first time (January 2016) it would end up here to be repeated: "As soon as I started to write about my own life, I understood that to speak honestly about family and community is to step way out of line, to risk accusations of betrayal, and to shoulder the burden of being the one who blows the whistle on the myths that families and communities create to protect themselves from painful truths. This threat was like a great shadow lurking at the corner of my vision, as it is for anyone who approaches this task, even before the writing leads them into sticky territory."

And "sticky territory" it was. I threw my pen more than once when I was remembering a story from my life and then writing it here, because the floodgates opened in my head of various bad and/or sad memories. One gut-wrenching aspect of my life story is the domestic violence I've experienced on and off throughout my life. (I've chosen not to go into detail about that here – this book is about brain injury.)

Despite how upsetting to me it was sometimes in writing this memoir, I hung in there, and here it is. I hope you enjoy it, learn from it, and best of all – treat others better because of it.

I'm 100% positive that I've forgotten things that I originally wanted to include in my book. I tried to scribble all ideas down, but some scribbles got lost along the way.

I'm pretty sure there were people I told that they would be in my book, but then they are not because of my forgetfulness, or, that my editor and I HAD to streamline some stuff because this adventure became too large, long, whatever…. I'm well aware that this book cannot be perfect. I know there are mistakes in virtually every book that is printed. There will be mistakes, either of grammar, punctuation, *etc.*, and even some facts. Remember – I have permanent brain damage. As Dr. Barry J. Gibb wrote in his book, *The Rough Guide to the Brain*, "… the brain can create false memories to embellish its version of reality – just as it can suppress memories of events it found unpalatable."

I just hope and pray that I offend no one. That was not my intention. I just had to tell my story to, hopefully, help some others with what I learned in the struggle I survived. Writing about what I did remember, the way I remembered it, was very difficult at times. But I pushed myself through it.

All the comments from others:

"Your book's not done yet?"

"You missed your deadline?!"

"What's taking so long with that book?"

"Are you ever going to be done?"

And MANY more frightening comments like these actually slowed me down because I would get upset, and take a break.

That is, until my psychologist, Dr. Robin Scherm, gave me an excellent idea: "finish when you're finished" and just say, "oops" to the pre-determined schedule.

I heard these pieces of advice (that became my "script" when more comments came my way) at the same time I learned from one more endoscopy that I had multiple ulcers.

My gastroenterologist, Dr. El-Schaer, told me, the day after I saw Dr. Scherm, that I had to relax, step back from working so hard to complete the book, and take better care of myself.

So, on this day, I say this: the work will go to print when I'm done.

What's a truly sweet ending to this, since just hours after I wrote the preceding paragraph, I attended a book-signing for the *New York Times* best-selling author, Elizabeth Lesser, at one of my favorite bookstores (Oblong Books in Rhinebeck, NY).

I quickly spoke to her before her excellent presentation about her book, *Marrow: A Love Story*, and told her about my book, that I watched her intently when she was on Oprah's "Super Soul Sunday," and about my deadline stress. I asked her how long it took her to write her very first book.

"Three years."

I smiled a huge smile for the first time in a long time because I stopped feeling too much pressure trying to wrap this up by 2016 (the year printed on my first author business card stating when my memoir would be published).

Then, there are the words she wrote on the title page of my purchase of the beautiful story she wrote about donating her bone marrow to help save her sister's life: "To Janet – take your time. Your heart will know when it's time. [heart] Elizabeth"

Thank you so much, Elizabeth. The heavy weight I had been carrying on my shoulders was lifted as you slid that book back to me!

I know that I am being calmer now as I conclude this book (2017), than I was when I began it three years ago. I thank you for reading it, and I hope it helps your life in some positive way....

Janet Johnson Schliff
Lake Katrine, NY

PROLOGUE

"Janet, say something! Janet, say something!"

Stunned, I stared at this doctor whom I had just met. She, too, was alarmed, having just examined my MRI, which revealed I had a massive brain tumor. She ordered me to go to New York University's Medical Center to be operated on right away.

Brain tumor? Operation? I was silent, which is very rare for me!

Then, only half-joking, I replied, "First, I'm going to McDonald's to get a Big Mac and fries, because if I am going to die, my last meal is not going to be a fat girl's diet salad."

That doctor, Dr. Tamai, whom I primarily credit with saving my life, giggled, and the medical residents with her laughed, too. Laughter made this terrible news a bit better.

The couple of days I had between being told I had a massive brain tumor, and the trip to NYU for surgery, boyfriend-at-the-time, Aiden, and I wrote my eulogy in case I didn't survive.

One part of that eulogy was actually pretty funny. Aiden was going to state that three stocks went down the day I passed: Disney, Hallmark, and bacon.

To this day, I laugh at that joke because it's probably accurate. I love that smiley Mickey Mouse, sending cards, and eating bacon with eggs, waffles, pancakes, peanut butter, chocolate or practically any other food item. I'm VERY glad I get to write about it here versus Aiden's delivering it at my funeral.

As frightening as the diagnosis was, learning I had a brain tumor actually brought me some relief, as it explained much that had puzzled me for so long. You will understand when I explain my saga....

And, I just need to write this: a wonderful woman, a stranger, whom I can only picture but cannot recall her name, came over to me as I cried, trying to eat that Big Mac right after I was told about my huge tumor. She touched my shoulder, and I jumped (because of my mysophobia – fear of germs). She asked why I was crying, and I told her my tumor diagnosis. She told me to go home and call my mother and father, as well as my boyfriend. I told her none of them talk to me anymore. She said they would all want to know about this.

Then, she called her family over to pray for me. I thanked her and have always considered her an angel. I hope she reads this someday and remembers this story from June of 2009 at McDonald's in Kingston, NY.

Chapter 1

TEACHING UNTIL I COULD
NO LONGER TEACH

I GREW UP along the Hudson River, in upstate New York, the Rhinebeck and Red Hook region, about 100 miles north of New York City, graduating from Red Hook Central School in 1978. To be more precise, I grew up in Rhinebeck's Forest Park. The house my father and mother had built for us had a Rhinebeck address and telephone number, but my two sisters and I went to the Red Hook schools, as did all the other kids in Forest Park.

Writing about growing up in that suburban development brings back a lot of fun memories. At Halloween time, we were in costume contests. In the summer, we had daily kickball games on Cedar Drive. As you will understand more fully when reading later on in the book, I was the boss of everyone outside playing the games.

I still remember lying in my bed with my window open on summer nights and listening to the crickets chirp. Sleigh-riding on a nearby hill was lots of fun in the wintertime.

Sometimes when I'm having a bad day, I drive through Forest Park and try to remember the names of the kids I knew there so long ago. It really was a happy place for me.

When I drive around Forest Park to remember the names of people I once knew, I am doing what my "brain doctors" told me to do to help remember my life, after I had my brain operated on, and I have lots of fun memories to recall. I find it amazing that I can remember some stories from long ago but there are other parts of my life that I have zero recollection of! I know this is true for others with brain injury, and it's one of the many bizarre aspects about my life now....

But, back to that drive around the old neighborhood – I remember:
- the Kruses' daughter Joy, who was our babysitter;
- the Arends family, whom we played kickball with;
- the Plotskys, whom we watched *The Wizard of Oz* with;
- the Silvernails, whom I still have contact with, whose daughters I babysat;
- the Warnimonts' house, where I went to Girl Scout meetings at;
- the Scisms, for haircuts;
- the Engassars' driveway as our bus stop; Mrs. E. as a pseudo-bus-monitor had a system to rotate the best seats among the kids waiting;
- the Salmons, whose son, Gerry, I had a childhood crush on, and when he came to a party I hosted as a little girl, he handed me my present (perfume?) and said, "My mother made me get this for you!";
- the Hendricksons, whose son David and I won a dance contest in seventh grade at Linden Avenue Junior High in Red Hook, NY, dancing to Elton John's "Crocodile Rock" [Rest in peace, David];
- my friend Donna Malloy;
- Kelly Mosher was our paper deliverer;
- the Chupays for piano lessons;
- the Oakhills, where I went to 4-H meetings, because of being

a Forest Park Sew and Dough Girl. I remember winning blue ribbons at the Dutchess County Fair for baking Scottish Shortbread and sewing a green apron. That cracks me up now because I hate sewing, and I'm afraid I'll start fires if I use my oven, due to my memory problems;

- the Bartos, Albanos, and the Randalls, for being friendly neighbors.

I moved on to chilly SUNY [State University of New York] Plattsburgh, where I graduated four years later with a Bachelor of Science in Special Education. My time at P-burgh was the happiest four years of my life, though I didn't know it at the time. I still remember swaying to Billy Joel's "Piano Man" every Friday night before going downtown. That trip to the bars came after some dorm party. That was really the only time I partied in college. I stayed in lots of Saturday nights so I could be up early and doing classwork at the library on Sundays with the handful of other nerdy students. Looking back now, I wish I had had more fun and less studying time. I tell all young people that I meet nowadays to enjoy their youth. None of us knows what's coming....

Returning southward, I earned my Master of Science in Education degree from SUNY New Paltz, and then taught N.Y. special education classes for 25 years: Pine Plains Central School District, Ulster County BOCES [Board of Cooperative Educational Services], and Rondout Valley Central School District.

From the very beginning, my job was my very life! I loved those students as if they were my own children. I never gave birth to babies of my own, so I bought "my kids" needed things like breakfast, socks, school supplies, and on and on and on...to the point that my tax accountant, Alex Vargas, one year said he would fire me as a client if I brought him that many receipts (over $5000) ever again. After Mr. Vargas passed away, his associate Chip referred to this story as "The Ghost of Taxes Past."

Being in special ed. was in my blood. On my father's side of the family, one cousin, Heather, was born with Sanfilippo Type A Syndrome, a heritable physical and neurological disorder. Sadly, she never made it to adult life, but when she was young, I bonded with her intensely. While she still could, we danced to Simon and Garfunkel's song "Cecilia" over and over again. But when the song was about to reach the line "making love in the afternoon," my dad ran to turn down the volume on the stereo. Whenever I hear it, I remember my too-short time with her, and it brings tears to my eyes. She had the prettiest smile. I know she is in Heaven now with God, but I still miss her. Every January 16th, her birthday, I tell her of my love in my prayers. I cherished being with her for that short time we were able to be together.

On my mother's side, I had an Aunt Margaret who was an aide in special needs classrooms in Brooklyn and in Florida. She was so patient with these kids! She even took one of her students to live with her, almost as mother and child, a child lucky to have my aunt in her life. Aunt Margaret and that child have passed away, but I think of them often. I also took one of my students into my home as a foster son… but I will tell that story here later on.

I cannot state strongly enough how much I loved being a teacher! I was organized and prepared. Most Sundays were spent going to church and then writing lesson plans for the upcoming week during the rest of that day. My classroom was loaded with decorations (some educational, some thought-provoking, and some just for fun).

I'm a major Mickey Mouse memorabilia collector, and so we did lots of special activities to commemorate his birthday. November 18, 1928, was when MM premiered in *Steamboat Willie*. On November 18th most of the years I taught, we prepared MM pancakes and played with MM dice for our math time. We dressed up in all of the T-shirts that I collected on my too-numerous-to-count trips to Disney World in Florida.

On those trips to Disney World, I loved buying my students souvenirs from the gift shops. The first day of school in September or the first days back from our winter and spring breaks, the class would find on their desks MM pencils, erasers, notepads, candies, and, oh, so much more!

Carrying the Disney shopping bags around the theme parks became so cumbersome, my family helped me…until one year when my mother put both of the huge bags over my shoulders and told me she was done!

I had unique ways of teaching routine topics. When the kids needed to learn the months of the year, for instance, instead of merely reciting from a chart with January through December, we would dance and sing to the song "September" by Earth, Wind & Fire and replace some of the words in it with the other months' names. Instead of just reciting the alphabet, we'd dance to the Village People's "Y.M.C.A.," and use our arms and legs to form those four letters, as lots of folks still do while dancing at wedding receptions.

I met the Village People once, when we stayed at the same hotel while they performed a show with Cher. Being very good at telling others exactly what to do, I told the Village People that they do the letter "M" wrong. They told me that it's **their** show! Silly me.

I was very active in Special Olympics. I coached, volunteered, and sat on many committees over the years. These games were so eagerly anticipated by my students that they hardly slept the night before. Many of these kids, as adults, still display in their homes the medals they won as Special Olympians. I cannot say enough about how wonderful that organization is for special needs people! I reference an excellent book about it in my reading recommendations.

I spent extra hours and hours on my teaching job. I went in early and stayed late. I brought tons of paperwork home with me. I visited the homes of many of my students. I planned numerous field trips to both fun and educational places. Despite the extra effort involved, these outings were well worthwhile.

I can still remember some of the great places I took my students to. At a water park one day in Summer School, Danielle, a former student who is now in her 30s, but very young then, flipped over into the water while sitting on a floating inner tube. When the lifeguards did not see this happening, I jumped in and pulled her out of the water. I still visit her, and she tells that same story with the refreshing enthusiasm of a youngster almost each time we get together at local restaurants. [I have permission from her parents to use Danielle's name.]

Some of my students had never eaten lobster, so we took trips to Red Lobster. The kids loved wearing the plastic bibs as they sampled dipping their lobster meat into melted butter. Recently, a former student who was moving out of the state with his family asked me if we could get together to say our good-byes. I couldn't wait to see him again…and he picked Kingston, New York's Red Lobster as our place to eat, as that was his favorite field trip destination long ago.

Because of my memory problems caused by the brain injury, I can't remember all of the places we went to on field trips. That's why I'm glad that I took tons of pictures over those years. The pics are not organized, so they sloppily fill several suitcases. Yes, suitcases! But when I need to feel better about my life, I go to my "teacher room" in my condo, and I look at those pictures. The fun of the class trips is easy to see on the faces of those kids!

I taught after-school and evening classes to other teachers. It makes me feel so good when I bump into some of those professionals and they tell me how they're continuing to use the methods they learned from me years ago. I was on many different committees and attended lots and lots of meetings. Anyone who criticizes teachers for their "short" hours should just watch a teacher for a week and then they'll know there's so much more to teaching than just the hours spent at school. I applaud anyone in this field because I know how hard it can be sometimes. I also know it is incredibly rewarding!

If I knew then what I know now, I would have cherished teaching even more. Not going to work each day breaks my heart.

The damage from my long-undiagnosed brain tumor is permanent, as one might expect from something that grew to be the size of an orange. My behavior nowadays is sometimes "off the charts." I need to learn each day how to watch my impulsivity and irritability. What's particularly ironic is that I now do behavior modification for myself just as I once did for my students. On my "good behavior" days, a wee bit of milk chocolate at the end of the day is my way of rewarding myself. On my "bad behavior" days, I reflect on how to improve so I can merit some more chocolate.

I always had a feisty personality. I spoke my mind loud and clear. When that behavior decreased, it should have been a warning sign that something was wrong with me. I became quieter and quieter. When I did speak, I slurred some words, even though sober.

I began to have serious problems with a morbid fear of touching doorknobs and anything else that might harbor germs. This mysophobia (fear of germs) became truly obsessive! I could not sit in movie theaters or in church because I once heard a DJ on the radio state that those places are never cleaned. I had a very difficult time in restaurants whenever I witnessed what I considered to be unsanitary practices. I needed help in restrooms because I couldn't touch the latch or faucets or doorknobs....

At my local McDonald's I was affectionately dubbed "Myso Girl," because I needed help with handling my money, and I expected the workers to be extra careful when using gloves when preparing my meals. I'll bet my local McDonald's spends less on plastic gloves now since I'm over this OCD [obsessive-compulsive disorder] behavior.

This time of my life was very dark for me. I spent $1000 a month on items like hand sanitizer, disinfectant wipes with bleach, vinyl gloves, etc. I lost the skin on the back of my hands because I scrubbed my hands with so many chemicals! At school, I went into my classroom at 6 a.m. every day and scrubbed the doorknobs, the seats I sat in, the chalk I touched, the classroom's phone, and so much more. It was exhausting!

I was teaching children who were chronologically seventh and eighth graders at my last job. Academically, they were several years below these grade levels. I felt so much guilt about being less of a teacher than I once was. I had earned many awards over the previous years. In 1992 I had a medal draped around my neck by the New York State Commissioner of Education at a ceremony at the Hotel Thayer at West Point. I tumbled from that type of recognition to crying each day as I scrubbed the classroom down.

Some folks laugh about being a "germ freak," being a "germaphobe," but for millions of us, it is not a laughing matter. It ruled my existence.

One spring day in 2007, two years BEFORE learning I had the brain tumor, I had just taught a math lesson. The students were working on a worksheet, and I went to my desk to scrub myself with hand sanitizer. I had bottles of the chemical all over my room. The classroom phone rang at the same time that someone knocked on the door. My student Ned [some student names have been changed in this memoir for protection of their privacy] went to answer the door, as they all knew I couldn't touch it, and my student Barbara ran to the phone, which the kids knew I wouldn't touch, and said, "Ms. Schliff's class. How can I help you?"

Both of these tasks should have been mine to handle. Instead, I sat at my desk scrubbing my hands as if I were preparing to perform surgery. I looked up and began to sob. These poor kids were doing my job, when they had so many difficulties of their own. I looked at my assistant and said, "Lorraine, I have to go." Lorraine Iocovello was a present from God at the darkest time of my life. She was my assistant at this, my last job. She helped me in so many ways when I couldn't do a good job anymore.

I went down to the first floor and into the Union President's room and began the process of resigning from the profession I loved.

Chapter 2

My Family

By far, this is the hardest chapter to write. As of this writing (spring 2017), I've had few meaningful conversations with practically anyone in my family in quite a while.

Things have been rough for many years, on and off. But, when my tumor was discovered and removed, things improved – for a while. But, then it all unraveled again. I'm sure most of my relatives think it's because of my instabilities, but I think it's due to a combination of many factors....

My two sisters and I have three very distinctly different personalities. I am the oldest, and so, of course, they were compared to me at home, in school, church, and other places. I was the skinny one, the one with the best grades (National Honor Society), the most athletic and on and on. That had to be difficult to "compete" with. I love my sisters, but we don't really have anything in common, other than we "popped out" of the same mommy (with the same daddy). My sisters are also gifted. Joyce is an excellent chef and baker. Jayne is an excellent educator.

My mom and I go back and forth. Sometimes we are close, and other times we avoid contact, since we sometimes agitate one another. This has been true since I left for college many moons ago. We have some things in common (like our outspokenness) and many things not in common (like her domestic capabilities in the kitchen and throughout the house compared to my incapacities like that). I recall her happily ironing my dad's handkerchiefs, but at the spot where my ironing board is in my condo, my sign says, "Ironing Bored," and that's NOT a spelling error. I actually have another sign that says, "The only thing domestic about me is that I live indoors." Very true!

Unfortunately, I did not inherit the "clean gene" from my mom. She kept an impeccably neat and tidy home for us all. My sisters and I had to clean up our bedrooms every Saturday morning. [And I mean clean – dust, vacuum, change the sheets....]

Now, I don't want to label myself a slob, but I sure know vacuuming, dusting, etc. are too annoying for words. I only do them when I absolutely have to. My kitchen and bathrooms are moderately clean, at best.

Because of this, only a selected few people are allowed into my "inner domain." And, I like it like that.

I'm not saying that my mom and I got along perfectly before I went to college, but we did better when I was younger. However, I do remember a big fight we had over what words should be underneath my senior picture in my high school yearbook.

I wanted the words from Fleetwood Mac's song that goes, "Don't stop thinking about tomorrow...." She wanted some mushy-gushy love words. She won, and to this day, every single time I browse through the pictures of the graduating class of 1978 from Red Hook High, I'm not nostalgic as much as I am annoyed that I gave in on that one. It's a black-and-white example about the fact that the words you choose can haunt you forever – even if in a yearbook. To that same end, when I hear that Fleetwood Mac song on the radio, it also agitates me that I didn't stick up for my opinion enough.

My mom has had it rough medically and emotionally for a few years now. She was diagnosed with a brain tumor about one year after mine was removed. She had some similar symptoms to mine, and that's one of the ways it was discovered. Luckily – hers was much smaller, since it was caught way sooner. Then, she was diagnosed with Parkinson's. This has truly been a hardship, and I respect all caregivers who help their loved ones with this debilitating disease.

Then, my dad passed away from esophageal cancer. Their relationship had a warm ending, which was unfortunately short-lived, because they had been separated right before his diagnosis. After that, she had colon cancer. And then, hip surgery because she fell. All of what I just wrote about for her took place in only about six or seven years. That's too much for anyone to handle!

My dad was a true IBMer. When he died, I gave his eulogy two times – once in the Daytona Beach, Florida, area, where he lived at the end of his life, and once in Poughkeepsie, NY, for a Hospice service, since many of his New York State friends could not attend his first service. I made the other IBMers laugh when I stated, "He died in true IBM fashion – 5:55 a.m. on 12/12/12."

Dad worked for IBM in Kingston, NY, and then in Boca Raton, Florida, for many years. Growing up, I remember going to the IBM Country Club on Kukuk Lane in Kingston for swimming lessons, picnics, BBQs, and so much more. That was a very happy time of my life. I still remember the excitement of going over the Kingston-Rhinecliff Bridge to enjoy a day there. My dad's being a "Beemer" really had its perks!

My father had high expectations for me. He expected excellent grades. When I didn't get a 100% on a spelling test, for example, we "discussed" the words I spelled wrong versus celebrating the ones I got right. This led to years of trying to be perfect, which is never reachable, but this did make me a better teacher later on, congratulating my students for their right answers, rather than criticizing them for the wrong answers on the spelling test. As a side note, he became very upset with me the first time I told him that I wanted to be a special education teacher because he wanted me to follow in his footsteps and work for IBM, too, or become a lawyer.

My dad and I had lots of arguments over the years. The biggest was when he cancelled my wedding reception with my first fiancé, because during our engagement, we discovered my fiancé had retinitis pigmentosa. My dad was worried about my future, as most dads would, but he handled it badly and apologized profusely for all of it on his deathbed. He realized that the failure of that marriage had a lot to do with the rocky start that marriage had, due to him. That marriage's failure led to a long, hard road of other failed relationships in my life. I truly believe that a little girl's relationship with her dad has a lot to do with the choices she makes as she grows up. I know that was true for me!

I miss my dad every day. I talk to him when I see his picture somewhere in my condo. I know he made mistakes, but I also know he got a lot right. I wish there were some conversations and arguments I could "take back," but I can't…. So, I try to focus on what he got right instead of the negative. Fathers of girls have a special place in heaven.

I will be eternally grateful to my parents for the camping trips they took us on. We had a pop-up "Skamper Camper" that we used for our cross-country trip. Most of the sights I saw when I was only 13 years old I have never seen again. But, when I hear John Denver's song "Country Roads," I remember my dad popping that tape into our station wagon's cassette player, and listening to that song's words as we drove to California and back from our driveway at 18 Cedar Drive, Rhinebeck, NY.

As I've stated earlier, I have two sisters, Joyce and Jayne. Since our last name was Johnson, all three of us were JJs. That nickname was not fun for very long. And to make matters worse, all of our middle names began with the letter A: Janet Ann, Joyce Aileen, and Jayne Alison. (Or is it "Allison"? I can't find out, because my sister and I really aren't speaking at the time of this writing. I hope that will change.) For some reason, my parents thought this was a good idea. I can't speak for my sisters, but I think naming your children similarly (either on purpose or just because it works out that way) is kind of silly. But – those similar initials are really one of the only similarities we share….

We were each born a couple of years apart, five years from the eldest to the youngest, but it seems like a bigger separation than that. When we were young, I was the "Miss Priss." My clothes were always neat and tidy. When she was young, Joyce was the "tomboy." She loved mud puddles, among other things. Jayne, the youngest, had a bit of both of Joyce and me in her at different times, and at other times… hardly at all.

But, now that we're all in our 50s, I'm no longer too concerned about my wardrobe. I wear wrinkled clothing, and most of my outfits are out of style or the wrong size, depending on whether I am dieting or overeating. I wear T-shirts more than anything else. Guess what? I'm happy with all of that!

Now, Joyce, on the other hand, is the opposite of that, or at least she was at the last time I saw her. The last time I saw Joyce (2011), she looked well-dressed and was concerned about her hair. The only days my usually unkempt hair looks good is when I step out of the salon!

Joyce has changed into a woman who genuinely cares about her looks. I turned into the tomboy she once was. But, that's not the only big difference between us….

Joyce can cook! She is also an excellent baker. She sure can mess up a kitchen, but the results are phenomenal! My messes in that room are more on the paperwork side (piles and piles of chapters for this book are stacked on my kitchen table as I write this). There is NO room for food in my kitchen – other than in the fridge or microwave oven. I eat in my living room. My kitchen is truly one of my many workspaces.

Joyce and I have hardly spoken since she left after a visit here in the fall of 2011. Right before that visit, our grandmother had just passed away. Joyce and her husband did not attend her funeral, though she loved Grandma and lived in Florida only a few hours away. Joyce and her husband's visit to New York State had been planned way before we knew we would lose a relative.

I was beyond hurt and angry that she wasn't present at the service that the rest of our family attended in Florida. I was counseled by more than one therapist about how to behave when she arrived here. She stayed at my condo while her husband visited his family in nearby Red Hook.

At first, I was able to squelch my opinions and questions about why she didn't attend the funeral. But at a lovely local restaurant, with a lobster bib still on, I "lost it," and became enraged when she spoke of our parents in a negative way. Her relationship with them is why she skipped the funeral. I was so livid, I walked out of that restaurant mid-meal with the bib still dangling around my neck. Some woman at the bar told me that it was still on me, as I was running for the door.

My boyfriend, Aiden, literally had to separate us that night because it was so volatile. The next day, Joyce and I cordially said goodbye. I vaguely remember talking on the phone somewhat after she and her husband arrived back home in Florida. But, we have completely left each other's lives since Dad passed away.

Joyce didn't attend Dad's funeral, either. Though I've spent countless hours discussing forgiveness at various doctor and therapy appointments (as well as at numerous *Bible* study groups), I have yet to let this one go. I don't know if I'll ever be able to understand her choices. Therefore, it's better that I'm not around her so I don't say or do something worse than the silence between us already is.

It is truly amazing to me how siblings from the same parents can see certain things so differently. Her version of our childhood situations is one way and mine is another way. That doesn't make one wrong and one right. It just makes us separate.

My sister Jayne did attend the funerals I'm discussing here. But, just like Joyce and me, we don't have much else we do (or did) in common either. She's the mother of two girls. I haven't spoken to either of my nieces for a very long time. I was very close with the older one when she was a little girl, but now she doesn't like me. I've never been told by anyone in my family exactly what I did to cause a rift with her, so all I do is speculate.

That speculation led to more problems between my mother and me because she would constantly speak of her two granddaughters with me as if I wasn't affected by all of their stories and how I wasn't included in any of them. My nieces ignored me for birthdays and holidays when I was still acknowledging them with cards. But, my mother would rattle on and on about occurrences in their lives. When I asked her to please stop, which I did at the suggestion from my doctors, she stopped talking to me altogether. I firmly believe that everyone has the right to say what subjects are the ones that are off limits to discuss.

At first, I had asked my mother politely not to talk about my nieces, L. and G. But, phone call after phone call, she continued to do so. My doctors helped me to write a script, keep it near the phone, and then read it to her if she brought them up one more time.

Of course, she did bring them up. I was silent and listened to five or more minutes of it all, and then I read the words that had been prepared. She became furious with me, and the call ended very badly. At the time of this writing, we speak for a few minutes to thank one another for the "obligatory" birthday/holiday flowers or cards. We also are sometimes able to talk about our various health conditions.

What I have never understood about my sister Jayne is why she didn't help repair my relationship with her daughters. My mother taught us to respect and appreciate our aunts when we were children. I miss terribly the relationship I once had with the elder niece, L., and I never really got to know the younger niece, G., very much.

The little bit I did learn is that G. really disliked me. I've never been spoken to by any other child the way she did when I used to gather with my family. I stopped sending cards with money to my nieces and then just cards altogether after I was ignored for so long.

My sister Jayne sent me one lovely card after I did recognize her 50th birthday by sending her one of those booklets about the year she was born. It had facts and fun information about the year 1965. Though I had done the same thing for Joyce two years earlier when she turned 50, and I never heard from her, I wanted to let Jayne know I was thinking of her.

Jayne's thank-you card was very sweet. She addressed how messed up our family relationships truly are. About this, I couldn't agree with her more!

It's truly sad that I have a very poor relationship with almost everyone in my family. Once, when I had Aiden drive me to Florida to help my aging mom, and I hadn't seen my sister Jayne in over two years, she met up with my mom and me at a mall for only about one and a half hours.

When Jayne first saw me, all I got was, "Hi, Janet." No smile, no hug, no warmth whatsoever.

For a very few minutes, we discussed "business" (i.e., Mom's doctor appointments and such). We never asked each other one thing about each other's lives. I just mimicked her. You get what you give. If she had a hint of a friendly face when she first saw me, I would have joined in. Instead, I just bit my tongue.

Then, as we walked in the mall, she bumped into someone she knew. That woman introduced Jayne to her sister. Jayne did not introduce either my mother or me, so I just moved my mom onward. I was so crushed by this, I talked out loud to God as we rolled along.

My mom was facing me since I was pushing her in her walker. (She brought it to the mall instead of her wheelchair because she thought she would be able to get herself around.) However, she was too sore to do that, so I did it. She just sat facing me and watched me crumble with this most recent hurtful gesture.

Mom's eyes could read into my soul and see how absolutely devastated I was that my own sister cares so little about me. I have no idea what I've done, since Jayne and I hardly communicate, but it really must be something!

As I pushed my mother towards the next store, she asked if I was okay.

"No, Mom. I'll never be okay with siblings that dislike me so much."

She patted my hand. When we were joined again by Jayne, I left Jayne with our mom so I could go take my calming-down medicine. How sad that family members cause so much heartache for other family members! To this day, it's never been explained to me why they harbor so much distaste for me. And by "they," I mean my sisters and my nieces. If I had been told, I think I would remember it.

I've asked my mother to intervene too many times to count. She says that when she brings the subject of me up, no one wants to talk.

This is so gut-wrenching for me that Pastor Wes, a wonderful man who guides me at my church, prayed with me before this trip, because I knew ahead of time that my mom was not doing well and that I'd be ignored by other relatives there. He also gave me specific Scripture passages to read about self-control, which also helped.

And I was right about being ignored. I was there for six full days but never heard from anyone (except for Jayne's brief mall visit). Pastor Wes told me to label this trip "MM" for "Mission Mom" (vs. what "MM" usually stands for in my life – "Mickey Mouse"). As I struggled with being ignored, I just kept telling God that I was there for my mom, and the rest didn't matter.

But, of course, it did matter. If I knew what was wrong, I could try to repair it. But, I don't know, so I just struggle trying to be nice and as polite as possible. This is no easy task. And, there are many times that I don't get it right.

After our short mall visit was over, I initiated the hug goodbye to Jayne.

She said to Aiden and me, "It was nice seeing you."

It was??? We barely talked, and you never asked why my back was in a brace, how our trip went, how my book is coming along, etc. Because she won't talk to me, I shy away from all conversations other than ones involving Mom. Since Jayne allows her daughters to completely ignore me, all respect is gone. I pray that someday it returns.

I think Don Henley's song "The Heart of the Matter" says it best (even though I believe this is a love song, it applies to family heartache as well).

So – let me wrap up this section about my family. To end on a better note, I will be eternally grateful to my two sisters for coming to New York State the week I was at the NYU Medical Center. They cheered me up by their brief visits (with chocolate) as I recovered there from brain surgery. They didn't have to leave their busy lives to help care for me that week, but they did.

My parents came to care for me when I got back home. The month of August 2009 was filled with delicious meals prepared by my mom or at their favorite restaurants in towns from long ago when they lived here. I enjoyed the drives around the various towns so they could visit with friends they hadn't seen in years.

My mother helped me with the wraps that I wore around my head to cover the huge, ugly scar where some of my hair had been shaved off to prepare for the surgery. My dad enjoyed going to watch Aiden pitch a game or two for his softball team. All four of us got along because we were all so grateful that I survived. Little did any of us know that, though we were back together, it wouldn't last for very long....

I have some cousins whom I once stayed in better touch with than we do nowadays. I hope when I put this pen down, I get to see my cousin Craig's family, because they live the closest to me. (Elsewhere in my book, my other cousins are mentioned.) I was at one time very close with their parents, Aunt Valerie and Uncle Bobby. Though my uncle's personality was almost opposite to his brother's, my dad's, I have loved him very much. My mother and her sister-in-law Valerie had their ups and downs, but their relationship has improved tremendously.

I still remember when these members of my father's family lived on Long Island and I went to visit them each Thanksgiving after my immediate family moved to Florida. I can still smile about the times I would watch the annual Macy's Thanksgiving Day Parade in their living room, go shopping the next day for Black Friday with my aunt, and then help them cut down a live Christmas tree the next day for them to decorate after I left.

Those Thanksgiving weekends were some of my fondest adult-life memories of Turkey Day. I miss that whole family now and again throughout the year, but at Thanksgiving time, tears come to my eyes when I recall when we were all so much closer. Nowadays, I just send cards to my cousins' kids for birthdays and holidays. I wish I could see them more, and I wish I heard from them more.

In the fall of 2016, I watched a "Dr. Phil" episode about a 74-year-old grandmother whose teenage grandson was afraid of her due to her outbursts.

This woman had long ago suffered a brain injury from an aneurysm, as well as having many other problems in her life. I connected with her so much as I watched her angry behavior. Our similarities were frightening:
- public outrages
- temper tantrums
- resistance to change
- bossiness
- poor judgment.

Though the term "brain injury" was not stated, I know from all of my research that an aneurysm is one form of acquired brain injury.

Her life's circumstances had torn her family apart. One of her daughters had contacted Dr. Phil, and then the grandmother, named Sonia, and her two daughters were on his show.

At the beginning of watching it, I kept thinking two things:

1) my editor's "no more additions – your book is getting too long" and

2) Dr. Phil better really help this woman.

Dr. Phil seemed aggravated with her rude behavior for a while, but then, he didn't. Dr. Phil stated that a brain aneurysm alters the way you function. He truly helped this family by offering her treatment in places specializing in care for people needing special attention.

When the show was almost over, her two daughters got out of their seats, and hugged their sobbing mother. They all were so angry in the beginning of this episode, and by the end, the family took a turn towards repair.

I sobbed the first time I watched it and each time since (it's saved on my DVR list).

Thank you, Dr. Phil, for giving her the help she deserves, and thank you, Dr. Cooper, for allowing this entry. I pray my family comes together like Sonia's did!

So – that's it for my family chapter. I'm quite sure some of the details I've told here will be disagreed with by whoever reads this book who is in my family. But that's okay, because this is how I remember it. I just pray that we do all come together before it is too late.

Rest in peace, Aunt Jen, Cousin Heather, Grandpa Johnson, Grandma Johnson, Grandpa McColl, Aunt Margaret, April, Grandma McColl, and Daddy….

As one writer put it: "I believe the hardest part of healing after you've lost someone you love is to recover the 'you' that went away with them."

[And, Daddy, I am trying my best to live up to your last words to me, "Be nice to others, Janet."]

Chapter 3

MYSOPHOBIA AND ME – THE GERMOPHOBE GIRL

As I STATED at the beginning of my book, this debilitating fear of germs can practically ruin your life. I embarrassed myself, family members, and other loved ones when I behaved the way I did with this aspect of Obsessive-Compulsive Disorder (OCD).

I recently watched a documentary called "Howard Hughes Revealed" on the National Geographic channel. This show was excellent in making me feel better about my peculiarities around my past fear of germs.

It discussed Mr. Hughes's multiple concussions and head injuries from plane crashes. It explained his many OCD behaviors that were exactly like the ones I experienced.

It brought tears to my eyes when it showed the times he had to layer tissues to be able to touch a doorknob…because there is a relative of mine who rarely speaks to me anymore, and I think it has to do with my bothering her in a public restroom in New York City when I couldn't touch anything without her help, many years ago.

I'm sure there's way more to her dislike for me than that, but seeing Howard Hughes struggling like I did brought back all the times I used to take her to Disney World and have so much fun with her. Now, I'm not even invited to big events in her life. My brain tumor changed our relationship. Forever?

As someone stated in this documentary, "The head injuries would tend to just make the OCD worse."

My brain tumor caused this strange behavior of mine. The brain injury I now have due to that tumor causes other behaviors I have written about at length in this book.

I hope and pray that whoever loved Mr. Hughes was able to forgive him for what he suffered from. I hope and pray the same for me.

I need to list the many things I could not do and the new behaviors I did do because of this horrible brain tumor. I thank God every day that these behaviors are over for me, and I pray for the millions who suffer from them still…

Of course, having mysophobia does not mean that you have a brain tumor, but a brain tumor caused my fear of germs. Though my list of symptoms is due to an undiagnosed brain tumor, this list can apply to many others who have no tumor but have to live this life anyway. There are strains of this phobia. Some people wash their hands just a little more often than most people do. Others demonstrate many, or all, of the behaviors listed next. And sadly, I am pretty sure there are behaviors I cannot remember anymore or ones that affect other people, but did not affect me. Here's MY list:

- **Doorknobs:** I wouldn't touch them with bare hands – always needed someone else to turn them for me or I had to find a tissue/paper towel/toilet paper to use. I even had to do this in my own home! Sometimes, outside my home, I had to kick some doors open, if I had nothing to touch the doorknobs with or no one to help me.
- **Toilet seats:** I could not sit down anywhere except my own home, and even there, only sometimes. I used chemical wipes

from my purse to clean all seats. I became a master at hovering!

- **Movies/church:** I heard a DJ on the radio say there are two places that are never cleaned, so I stopped going to the movies for four years, and I stood at the back of my church until a sweet woman, Sandy, helped me by laying my coat down for me to sit on, a simple thing, but one I could not think of on my own back then. By the way, the church I go to – Grace Church in Lake Katrine, NY – does clean their chairs and pews, as does the Lyceum Theater in Red Hook, NY.

- **Clothing try-ons**: I could not try on clothes of any sort that had been tried on by someone else. One store in my mall opened the gates early for me so I would go in the back room to try on clothes fresh from the sealed plastic bags.

- **Bras:** speaking of clothes – the only bras I would buy would be sports bras because I sort of knew my size, and I would wash them in hot, soapy water with bleach before I wore them. Right after the brain surgery, my mother took me shopping for real bras, and we made the other women in the try-on room laugh when **I shouted, "Mom, my boobies are touching a dirty bra that someone else tried on!" I was so happy I was cured.**

- **Hotels:** if I had to go out of town for something, I packed an entire suitcase full of chemical wipes, hand sanitizer, toilet seat covers…. I even packed towels to cover carpets because I couldn't step on their carpets or even use their towels. [One of the too-many-to-count fights I had with Aiden was on the train trip to NYC when I packed this type of suitcase to clean my hospital room when I got there. Who gets mad at their loved one as they're about to have brain surgery???]

- **Hot tubs/bath tubs:** speaking of hotels — and even in my own home — I couldn't go into those because once I heard someone call a hot tub "a giant cesspool." We all know how relaxing they can be, so this was a big loss.

- **Beaches:** I could not go barefoot on the beach. This was terribly sad because I grew up going to the beach in Hampton Bays, Long Island, because both sets of my grandparents had houses there. I missed that so much!

- **Envelopes:** I could not lick envelopes. I had to use a small dish of water with a paper towel to pay my bills, send birthday cards, etc.

- **Haircuts:** I couldn't rest my neck on the sink at my hair salon. God bless Lisa Smith, who helped me through this, visit after visit, at J.C. Penney. Lisa is also the first person who washed my hair when I had this huge scar on my scalp after the 42 staples were removed from my head following brain surgery.

- **Doctor appointments:** I had to have doctors' tables covered completely in order that I could sit down undressed on them. Those thin pieces of white paper were never wide enough, so nurses in various offices had to help cover the area completely. I made doctors wash their hands in front of me and to use gloves to touch me. I thank Dr. Keller at Hudson Valley Foot Associates because he was so sweet about this annoying request. Another doctor – who will remain nameless – laughed at me and refused to do it. Any doctor who can laugh at a sick patient is heartless. Another doctor, who will also remain nameless, didn't wash his hands after he used his restroom that was right near his waiting room. I had heard him urinate, flush, and open the door. I told him to go back in and wash his hands. His staff clapped and smiled at me when he did what he was told to do by this patient.

- **Floors:** I mentioned floors in hotels before, but I even had trouble in my own home. I could never go barefoot. I wiped my feet down with wipes before I got into bed each evening. When workers came to the condo to repair heaters and washing machines, etc., I made them take off their shoes and walk on the plastic I had put down before they arrived. The guys from Lowe's Plumbing and Heating and Air Conditioning in

Kingston, NY, were extremely considerate and cordial to me.

- **Cars:** after each trip, I wiped the entire front two seats of my car down, using the chemical wipes. I also cleaned the steering wheel and the shift lever after each time I drove. I had to sit on a towel whether I was in my car or in someone else's car. This became truly necessary when the undiagnosed brain tumor caused frequent wetting "accidents" while sitting. Again, these wetting incidents were blamed on my meds, but I found out later they were another sign of the undiagnosed tumor.

- **Friends' visits:** I rarely allowed anyone into my condo. This wasn't because I was messy. It was because of how exhausting it would be after they left, as I would have to scrub down everything they had touched. My friend Marian would lay paper towels everywhere in her house for me to sit on when I visited there.

- **Shopping carts:** nowadays when you go to many stores, there are wipes available for you to use to clean the cart before you load it up. I feel sometimes as though I helped that idea along because I did this long before stores offered those wipes. I carried my home wipes into each store and wiped my carts right away. Because I had memory problems due to the tumor, I sometimes forgot the wipes. Then I would hold my sleeves down from my shirt or coat and hold the cart handle with my sleeves instead of with my bare hands. Also – I NEVER put anything into the spot where babies are put, because of what "remnants" might be left there from a dirty diaper.

- **Shared pens:** when I was at a bank, doctor's office, or anywhere else where pens are shared, I always had to dig through my heavy purse for MY pen. If I forgot it somewhere, I had to find a tissue or napkin to hold a pen touched by others.

- **Soap:** I could only use soap that was from a pump dispenser. I could never touch a bar of soap, even a new one.

- **Microphones:** I could never hold a microphone. When I sang karaoke when I first met Aiden, I had to wrap napkins around the mic so I could focus on the song.

- **Straws**: I could never sip a drink from a glass, cup, can, or bottle. I HAD to have a straw for each thing I drank. That was very dangerous with hot tea or hot chocolate!
- **Faucets:** I could not touch any faucets either at home or out and about. I turned them on with a tissue, paper towel, hand towel, or toilet paper, and then did the same to turn them off.
- **Phones**: all telephones had to be wiped with chemical wipes before and after each use.
- **Remotes:** if I was home or at a friend's house, I used a remote control for the television with a paper towel, so I could touch the buttons. If I was in a hotel, I wiped it down repeatedly with chemical wipes.
- **Escalators:** when I went places like malls, airports, and others where I needed to ride on the escalator, I couldn't hold the hand rail, so I had to be very careful not to lose my balance. I had – and still have – balance problems.
- **Elevators:** I could not touch the buttons in an elevator, so I would ask someone else to do it for me, if there were others riding at the same time. If I was alone, I touched the buttons with my knuckle. After I did that, I scrubbed my hands with sanitizer, which was always attached to the outside of my purse or was in a pocket of my clothing. I lost the skin on my knuckles because of the overuse of hand sanitizer. I had to use layers of Band-Aids to cover my exposed skin.
- **Church**: I already explained about not being able to sit in a chair or pew without help. But, I also was not able to take communion. When the communion basket was passed, with the symbolic body of Christ, I took one wafer to look as if I was participating. As the ushers went around the whole church distributing the wafers, I talked to myself silently and tried to convince myself the hands that laid that wafer into the basket

were clean, so I should swallow it when the pastor indicated. I never could.

Also – I wrote earlier about "licking" envelopes by using water and paper towels at home. At church, I would put my money in the offering envelope but then would ask whoever was sitting next to me to lick it closed for me. If I was alone, I put an open envelope in the basket and didn't worry if my money fell out, as long as I hadn't had to lick the envelope closed.

- **Laundromats**: before I lived in the condo where I live now, which does have a washer and dryer, I rented an apartment that did not. I had to bring my laundry to various public places to wash and dry my clothes. I brought my chemical wipes and wiped down each machine I was about to use, so no one else's germs would get on my clothes. This caused a few stares by others, probably wondering what was going on with me.

- **Shopping:** I spent approximately $1000 per month on cleaning supplies. Some of those supplies I used to wipe down the packages holding those exact same supplies I was going to use. I couldn't touch any container of anything from the store before I scrubbed it over and over with the wipes. I shopped at Stop & Shop in Rhinebeck, NY, where the staff there was very sympathetic when they observed me load an entire shopping cart full of cleaning supplies each week onto the conveyor belt to be scanned. When I was cured of this nonsense after my brain surgery, I went to the store and told them what had caused it all. I got smiles, hugs, and warm comments from the various people who worked there then. To this day, I get asked how I'm doing whenever I shop there (now called TOPS) for the "normal" shopping cart items.

- **Condiments:** I was unable to touch salt and pepper shakers, sugar dispensers, etc., in restaurants. Whoever was eating out with me was asked to do that for me. If I was eating out alone, I skipped using anything I typically enjoyed. At home, dispensers were washed oh-so-frequently. [I was reminded by my friend Marla that I wiped down things in restaurants with hand sanitizer.]

- **Shelves:** in my own home, I could not lay food, plates, clothing, and/or towels on bare shelves. I had to scrub them down with chemical wipes and then lay coverings on all shelving. To this day, some of those coverings are still on my shelves only because piles of stuff are on top of them now. When I move out of my current place, I'll smile when those coverings get thrown in the garbage, rather than taken with me to a new place.

- **Gasoline pumps:** I was unable to pump my gasoline without gloves on. If I had forgotten the gloves, which sometimes happened because they were in and out of my car so often to be washed, then I used napkins or tissues to hold the pump. When I got back in my car, I scrubbed my hands over and over with hand sanitizer. To this day, I wash with that after each gas pumping episode, but now it's only to get rid of the smell of gas on my hands.

- **Airports:** though at this writing I no longer fly, because when I do the pain in my head is excruciating when the plane goes up at liftoff and down for descent, I know that before my brain surgery, I had a very difficult time in airport security lines due to the mysophobia. I always had to remember to bring extra socks so that when my sneakers had to be removed and I stepped on airport carpeting in my socks, the clean second pair of socks could be put on after I cleared security. I would not put the socks that had touched the carpet back into my sneakers. They went into the nearest garbage can.

In the airplane, I had to scrub down the seat, seat belt, and food tray with chemical wipes before I could take my seat. Of course, this was annoying to those trying to get to their seats who were in line behind me. I am pretty sure I bothered a lot of people who just wanted to get settled so the plane could be cleared for take-off.

When we first sat down, I had to wipe with my chemical wipes the instruction card in the seat back ahead of me. I always followed along when the flight attendants went over the safety procedures, but until the cards were cleaned, I couldn't touch them. I kept thinking about the dirty hands that had touched those cards before me, instead of concentrating on what to do if there were an emergency. Most of the time, I saw others ignoring this routine, but I am such a teacher, I had to listen.

I always had to have a window seat with Aiden sitting next to me. I could barely tolerate his arm touching mine, so I could NEVER rub elbows with a stranger. We all know how crowded airplane seating can be.

I always had to wear a hooded sweatshirt no matter what the temperature was, because I had to put my head into the hood before I could let my hair touch the headrest.

When the flight attendant came around for our drink orders, I was adamant that I needed a straw with my soda, because I could never drink directly from a can or plastic cup. If she or he forgot to give me a straw, my drink just sat on the food tray in front of me until the clean-up began.

During the flight, I used more chemical wipes to clean the buttons on remotes for the TV screen or for seat adjustments. If the person sitting in front of me moved the seat back to get comfortable, I jumped, because I was so scared of the seat being too close to me.

If, heaven forbid, I had to use the restroom on the plane, my chemical wipes went with me so I could clean off the door latch, toilet seat, and faucet. It's quite an accomplishment to tinkle while hovering over a toilet on a bouncy plane flight, but I could do it. And that saying, "If you sprinkle when you tinkle, please be neat and wipe the seat" was done by me with such finesse.

- **Garbage duty:** I would not take out my own garbage. Many friends came over to help me dump my wastepaper baskets into plastic garbage bags, and then they brought the bags out to the dumpsters.
- **Housecleaning:** I could never go near the vacuum cleaner or dust cloths for fear of germs, so numerous friends helped me with that, also. This seems very odd to me now, because you would think I would have loved to get rid of the dirt and grime. But, I couldn't do it. Thank God for friends!
- **Brushing teeth:** I had to wash my toothbrush each day with soap and hot water before I put toothpaste on it to brush my teeth. I purchased several new brushes often.
- **ATMs**: I couldn't touch buttons on an ATM machine without much deliberation. Sometimes, I did my bank transactions with my knuckles. If my knuckles were covered in bandages due to lost skin from too many chemicals used to clean my hands, then I used a pen or pencil from my purse to push the buttons. All of this caused mistakes.
- **Restaurants**: if a waitress or waiter held my teacup by the part where I would sip from, instead of the handle, then I couldn't drink it at all. Too many staff put their thumbs and fingers where mouths go.

A funny story I can write about is that when I was being checked out of NYU Medical Center (July 10, 2009 – only three days after brain surgery), my sneakers got "lost" in all the confusion of that process.

My sisters were there to say goodbye before they traveled home to Florida. Aiden was there to drive me home (because the doctors said I shouldn't ride a train yet), and Aiden's friend was outside in Aiden's car trying to stay out of trouble with respect to parking regulations.

So, when it was time to get out of the wheelchair that had rolled me to the front door, I walked on a New York City sidewalk in my socks only. I laughed hysterically, since just a few short days before, I lugged an entire suitcase full of cleaners into the hospital so I could clean the room entirely before I even undressed.

Now, I was parading around a filthy city sidewalk with only a thin pair of socks on and loving every minute of it! I was smiling, and getting into Aiden's car, thanking God that the fear of germs was FINALLY over! I had made it to the "other side" and I was so radiant.

Many people have called my story a miracle. What I think is truly inspiring about it is that it's one more example of getting through whatever life hands you. You can do it. Don't give up. God never said it was going to be easy. We all have situations and circumstances that are tough to take. But, getting to the other side of them makes you all the more joyous and fulfilled. I'm glad that I've lived to tell my story.

I know that prayer works. Once, when I traveled to Boston, Massachusetts, for a conference to hear preacher Joel Osteen speak, mysophobia was taking over my life. I couldn't even sit in the bleachers without covering the seats with something because I got upset with myself on the ride there that the pants I wore were made of too thin material and the germies would touch me.

I told all this to a woman working there selling Joel's books. She told all the other workers to stop selling and circle around me, don't touch me, and pray. They did just that, and I was able to calmly return to my seat and listen to God's message from Joel.

I know there are some people who don't approve of God's word being spread in this way. But I believe I've come closer to God because of speakers like Joel. His workers could have just kept on selling, but they didn't. They talked to the Lord. Two or three years later, I was free of this phobic chokehold. Amen.

As I was putting the "last leg" on this chapter, I met a couple of friends for lunch. Of course, we discussed how it was going with this book.

We all had an amusing chat about my peculiar habits years ago when I was petrified of germs. I remembered some of the crazy behaviors they brought up.

But, then one of my girlfriends said something that I don't think I ever knew. She told me that I lost a lot of friends because of my behaviors when I had mysophobia.

That shocked me because I didn't even realize that was so. I was so shook up by that information, I didn't even ask who she was referring to.

So, I decided the way I would wrap up this chapter is to apologize to anyone I may have offended, upset, bothered, etc. when I behaved irrationally. We now know why that all took place (my brain tumor), but hopefully, whomever I've bothered, I hope they can let it go. I have to say, I still have a wonderful amount of friends who have seen me through this. Those of you who couldn't, I get it.

And to those of you who can relate to this list, do absolutely everything you can to get better. Life is too short to obsess about germs!

[A very humorous incident happened as my editor and I were proofreading my manuscript. It took place at a restaurant one night when I "ran away" from the stress caused by all of this work. The waitress had inadvertently thrown away my wrapped-in-foil leftover garlic bread with cheese. When I noticed what she had done, I retrieved it from the bucket of dirty dishes the busboy was about to bring back to the kitchen to wash. I just had to get it back, as it is the best appetizer I have ever had. Obviously, I could NEVER have dug through dirty dishes before the brain operation! So, those of you who suffer from mysophobia, I hope you will have a story like this to tell someday yourself.]

Chapter 4

DOCTORS

WELL, LET ME just say from the get-go here that this is a very difficult chapter to write.

Thanks to my help from God, I've forgiven the two doctors who listened to me complain about headaches for many years but never wrote me an MRI scrip. But, sadly, I have NOT forgotten....

One of these two doctors was my psychiatrist. I had seen him on and off for years. He wrote me several scrips for medications to deal with the mysophobia. We didn't realize that no medication would cure the mysophobia, because the phobia was caused by a brain tumor.

In the end, the psychiatrist was the doctor who wrote the scrip for the MRI, but I think he did it in an agitated way.

"I'm sure you're fine, but you've complained about headaches for so long, so there it is," he declared as he banged his prescription pad on his lap while sitting in a chair next to me while I was crying and holding my head. The headaches were so bad at this time, spring 2009, I could hardly take it anymore.

The general practitioner (GP), a doctor I had gone to for years, to whom I had also complained numerous times about my pain, had not written an MRI scrip because he too believed the headaches were caused by the meds for my germ phobia. Instead, he gave me a scrip for physical therapy head massages, which, of course, would have no effect on a brain tumor. When this GP retired, after my brain surgery, he gave me my medical folder to bring to a new GP. I looked up how many times I had complained about headaches over those years. I counted the complaints, and there were more than ten.

This reminds me of what happened in the comedy movie *Kindergarten Cop*. When Arnold Schwarzenegger, a detective playing a teacher, complained to the kids of a headache, one of his kindergartners says, "It might be a brain tumor."

If anything is to be learned from my story it is this: INSIST on procedures to rule things out when you're not feeling well. Your symptoms may be caused by the meds you're on, but as I learned TOO late, something else could be brewing. The toll of that undiagnosed brain tumor is my life being forever changed!

The psychiatrist apologized to me twice. I know it's rare to get an apology from a doctor, but I did. As soon as I found out about the MRI results, I called his office to tell his staff I was being sent to NYU for brain surgery. I called them when the surgery was over. I wish I could have seen his face when his receptionist told him there really WAS something wrong with me.

The GP was not so apologetic. He never owned up to being any part of this mistake. As a matter of fact, at my last appointment, after he had given me my very thick file folder full of normal doctor notes, but also FULL of headache complaint notes he took, he literally patted himself on the back for being so good with me. This has also been hard to forget....

I have been told over and over again by so many other people that I should have sued both of these doctors. I just couldn't do it. That's not who I am....

I even discussed the diagnosis delay casually with a lawyer once, and his response was, "You're worth millions," but I did not pursue anything.

I just wanted, and still want, to let go and move on.

Here is an edited version of a letter I sent to "Dear Abby" that, to my knowledge, was never printed. Even though I wrote this quite a few years ago, I still feel this way:

Dear Abby,

I hope this is well worth a space in your column, as you stated to "Gentle Reminder" on 2/25/12 about her/his work in a doctor's office and comments about patients. I have to state the things I've observed in SEVERAL doctors' offices since I had a massive brain tumor removed and all I do now is go to doctor appointments near and far. What people who work in those offices need to remember is that, unless we are there for a routine yearly checkup, fear and anxiety are within us because of something possibly wrong within our bodies. Coldness and abruptness by staff is upsetting because we need some form of love and concern. Even though it's their job and they can go home at the end of the day, we might have to leave knowing bad news, so please – be nice, at the very least.

Many offices need TONS of paperwork completed before we arrive or when we do, so when we are taken from the waiting room, why do we have to answer so many questions about the information that we just handed in? Nurses grill us and then the doctors do, too. It would be helpful, if we take the time to fill it all out, that we get it read by all first; along that same line, why do we have to re-state all of the meds we are on, when we just handed you a sheet with all of them listed on it? I've asked both these questions in several offices, and I usually get told it's "routine procedure."

Now I'll move on to the phone calls to the offices: all of the buttons you have to push just to be able to leave a message, but then have to wait and wait for whatever information you need to take care of is very frustrating! Remember the old days when the phone was actually answered by a live person, and phone tag didn't take place, so you got your help in a reasonable amount of time? Similar to that – what about when you try to schedule a future appointment, but their computer can only do a few months in advance, so you have to call back in a few months, instead of doing it the old-fashioned way by turning the large schedule book pages so that you were able to leave the office knowing exactly when you would return?

And what about the HIPAA laws that are not followed? For example – doors left open so you can hear others' discussion and they can hear yours? Or – they ask you private questions as they walk you back to your room, so strangers in the hallway can hear your answers. And – walls so thin in some offices that, as you sit and wait to see your doctor, you can hear them in the next room discussing that patients' issues. I find this completely unacceptable!

Another annoying thing is when doctors complete scrips wrong – misspelling your name; not writing "fasting" for blood work when it is sometimes needed, so that when you arrive to give blood, it has to be rescheduled; or forgetting the doctor's signature, so the pharmacy cannot fill it as written. All of these things happen and make a stressful time more difficult.

And finally – when you try to schedule an appointment at a time you can arrive by, the staff tells you it HAS to be 15 minutes sooner, so you reschedule something else you are involved in, but then when you arrive on time, you wait for a LONG time to be taken in, and you could've come when it was more convenient for you. This happened several times to me in a certain office, and when I finally said something about it, other patients that I didn't even know started to clap when they heard me commenting about it to the receptionist, so obviously others felt as I did. I know some of that could be due to others' being late for their appointments, but some of it could also be over-scheduling.

Well, I think the staff in doctor offices will disagree with things reported here, but since we read one writer's thoughts back in February, I thought the other side was fair to state. That's it for me, though I wonder if other people have more that they could add to my list from their own experiences. I am curious if I am the only patient who feels this way, or do others agree? Thank you for letting me vent, Abby!

"Mickey" in New York

Here are some more thoughts since I sent that letter.

I guess it's because of the HIPAA law, but when I call the doctor's office, often they ask me first for my date of birth. To make a point, I give them my name and then my date of birth, to feel like a human and not a number.

Add to these the annoyance of being reminded by an automated call of the date and time of an appointment, but not which of their several locations they expect you at.

One doctor's receptionist, who knew I was very detail-oriented and whom I had already corrected once, gave me an appointment card reading "Thursday, June 16, 2 a.m." When I pointed out to her that it should be "Tuesday, June 16, 2 p.m.," she jokingly got another office worker to make the new appointment card out, saying it was because she did not want to be in my upcoming book twice!

It's not only the behavior of doctors I object to, I believe our system of health care for the disabled and elderly is so broken in America.

I've witnessed in numerous nursing homes, assisted-living facilities, and homes with paid caregivers, patients being treated too slowly, rudely, or lazily.

When some of these workers are late for work or back from their breaks late, they speed unsafely and run through stop signs to get back on the clock on time. I live near two facilities for which this is a daily occurrence. You take your life in your hands when you're driving correctly near them. I don't understand why they're pulling into their job's parking lot two minutes before their shift.

How about setting your alarm 15 minutes earlier?

I know this late thing happens for all of us sometimes, but there are several workers that get it wrong daily (and by "wrong" I mean driving like a maniac to punch in on the time clock on time). I'm pretty sure this happens at a lot of care facilities, and it's not fair to people who live in the neighborhoods near them.

Another mistake that took place in a doctor's office happened when I was going for an endoscopy.

I had learned a couple of years earlier that, since my brain operation, the medication propofol really gets me "worked up." I learned that after the first endoscopy, and I went "bonkers" in the room after it was all over. So, I had put on my medication sheet the words, "No Propofol."

As I was about to get the needle for this second procedure, I said to the nurse, "That's not propofol, right?" She said that it was. I pulled my arm back and yelled, "Does anyone in doctors' offices read what is written on the notes we fill out and then turn in? I can't have that med!"

Then, the anesthesiologist came in, told me I was wrong and that he couldn't do the procedure without it. I told him to go look it up and come back to tell me what he learned.

He came back sheepishly and admitted that I was right, and he could only use with me a very small amount of it, mixed with some other med (whose name I can't recall) to knock me out, so I would "wake up" in better shape than the last time.

So, it all went better after that, and he met me in the lobby, as I left, to ask if I was okay. I'm sure he was more concerned if I would let others know he instructed his nurses to give me something that, in writing, it stated I wasn't supposed to be given. I'm just very glad that I asked that nurse what was in that injection, because otherwise, even more outlandish behavior could have taken place again.

Patients, for the most part, know themselves better than staff does. Listen to us better if you want our trust, and more than that, our business!

Enough about the doctors whom I had to forgive.

I've had several doctors who have been fabulous with me, both when I had the mysophobia and afterwards....

As I mentioned at the beginning of this book, Dr. Tamai was the neurologist who had to tell me I had a brain tumor. She was on call at the place where I had my very first MRI. She's the first doctor who told me the mysophobia was probably caused by the tumor.

I see her regularly to this day, every three-to-four months, at what is now called Healthquest's Division of Neurology, formerly Kingston Neurology Associates. She has listened to it all, from my stories of my crazy rampages to my in-office bouts of uncontrollable tears, etc. She counsels me as well as gives me neurological check-ups. She is the most sensitive doctor I have ever known, and I tell her that as often as I remember to.

Recently, Dr. Tamai was quoted as saying, "What's most rewarding about my job is being able to really help a patient and know that you've made a difference in their quality of life."

And, she has really helped this patient! My quality of life is improved because she listens to me and helps me figure life stuff out. [And I think her nurse Bridget is fabulous too!]

Each Christmastime, I buy Hallmark's doctor ornament of the year and give it to Dr. Tamai with a card that expresses my appreciation for how wonderfully well she takes care of me. Words in a card and an ornament could never really match the way I feel towards her. She is a present from God for whom I will be eternally grateful. I highly recommend her to anyone in need.

Another doctor who has been wonderful with me is Dr. Pappas, my ophthalmologist. She works for Caremount, formerly the Mt. Kisco Medical Group, and I see her regularly to have my eyes checked. These appointments are very nerve-wracking for me because the tumor was behind my left eye, and I fear it may re-occur.

The mistake I made, back when I had the tumor, was that I went to an optometrist only. I found out later that if I had been seen by an ophthalmologist, he or she would have been able to spot my tumor with the special tests these medical doctors use. Optometrist appointments are not the same, and therefore never detected the tumor, though I went for new glasses regularly.

Once, after my brain tumor surgery, a nurse in Dr. Pappas's office was checking my pupils with a special light. She commented that something was different when she peered into my left eye versus my right eye. She went and got another nurse, and the second nurse used a different light, but said the same thing. I freaked out in the chair because I imagined the worst! Over and over in my head I kept thinking: *the tumor is growing back.*

Once I became uncontrollable, the nurses went quickly to get Dr. Pappas, who left another patient to come into our room and look at my left eye herself. She said that her examination light was better and that everything was fine. I'm pretty sure she spoke to those two nurses in the hallway about treating me with kid gloves because of how overly sensitive I am about the tumor's reoccurring. Dr. Pappas is very sweet and gentle with me.

Another caring doctor who comes to mind is Dr. Keller, who works for the Hudson Valley Foot Associates. Back when I had the undiagnosed tumor and I was so fearful of germs, he would wash up in front of me and put gloves on. I needed him to do this. His staff were friendly and considerate of my special needs. I highly recommend his office for care and concern about one's medical needs.

Another wonderful medical professional is Karl Kruszynski, P.A.-C., a physician's assistant who has helped me with many skin problems in the two offices where he has worked.

Karl is humorous and a great listener. Most staff at his new office, Hudson Dermatology, are very friendly and accommodating to what I refer to as my "award-winning personality" – *i.e.,* I'm a real pain in the butt sometimes.

I am absolutely petrified of needles and, of course, they need to be used when biopsies are taken. I have had several skin cancer episodes, "thanks" to not listening to my mommy as I child, when I was told to put on sunscreen, and then as a 20- or 30-something-year-old using a tanning bed!

Karl always smiles through my "episodes" and is still warm and friendly the next time I come back for more.

In the office where Karl worked at first, I met a doctor before I met Karl. Her name was Dr. Wendy Epstein. To this day, though I no longer see her because she left that office, I have a fond memory of her:

I was in my hospital bed, a couple of days after my brain surgery at NYU. She spoke with me over the telephone to see how I was doing. I was so touched that a doctor who only saw me for my skin conditions was a doctor who took the time to check on me like this. How many doctors can you say that about anymore?

An excellent chiropractor that I have to mention here is Judith Dougan. I met her when I hurt my back (the story in my "Music, Music, Music" chapter). She and her assistants (Vicki, Jackie, and Linda) all helped me feel better too.

And, finally, another great doctor is Dr. Jafar Jafar, the doctor who removed my brain tumor and used it in a class at NYU Langone Medical Center to teach others. Many people have asked me why his first name is the same as his last. I was curious, too, about why his name was like that, but, most importantly, I just cared that he saved my life.

Dr. Jafar is a neurosurgeon with the cleanest doctor's desk and office I've ever seen. At my first appointment after being released from NYU, I was embarrassed when he had to tell me to wash my hair as soon as I got home. Right after the surgery, I had been so scared to touch my head with its 42 stitches that I couldn't do it, but after he said that, I went home and lathered up.

Dr. Jafar will always be the doctor who told me my tumor was the size of an orange. But, more importantly, he will be the doctor who told me I would no longer be afraid to shake hands with him, after he operated on me, since my fear of germs would be over. He was right!

So, what I try to do every day now is to forgive those two doctors who did not listen to me well enough, allowing the brain tumor to grow so large before it was discovered. I try to focus on the good, positive doctors I have met and hang on to the thoughts about them, rather than perseverating [inappropriately not letting go] about the mistakes of others.

Focusing on the positive is truly a struggle for me. I talk to God every time the bad doctor memories become overwhelming, which is way too often. Praying sometimes brings relief. I look forward to the day when I've completely moved on. In the meantime, I take baby steps in the land of forgiveness....

I know God is the Great Healer!

Chapter 5

CHURCHES

I WAS BAPTIZED as a baby in a Bay Ridge, Brooklyn, NY, Presbyterian Church.

After moving upstate, I grew up attending and being confirmed at Third Lutheran Church in Rhinebeck, NY. I sang in the choir, went to youth group, was an acolyte, worked at our food booth at the Dutchess County Fair, and so much more. I was a Sunday school teacher, then the Superintendent, as well as the Christian Education Chairperson. I loved Pastor Torcello.

I left the church for a few years, but then got back on track in the late 1990s when I lived near a church in Fishkill, NY. I have always enjoyed reading the signs that are posted in front of many churches to help one take in life's lessons. I actually nicknamed a church that I was once a member at (Fishkill Baptist Church) the "sign church," because of how the words on their sign encouraged me to come back to church after years of falling away.... I used to deliberately drive by it over and over to read the words posted there. One Sunday, I parked and went in. I hadn't been in a church in years due to a very unpleasant experience elsewhere years before. (Unfortunately, I recently heard from friends that still attend that church that they no longer use their sign for encouraging words. That's too bad.)

This church's carefully selected sign words are what got me back to God. I was baptized as an adult at Fishkill Baptist, helped in the Sunday school, and sang in the choir there too. I learned a lot from Pastor Eckler.

When I moved to Ulster County, in New York, I began attending church where I am a member now, Grace Community Evangelical Free Church, in Lake Katrine, NY. Pastor Wes Smith has helped me through some pretty dark episodes, and I'm a better Christian because of him.

The time spent with children at my church is the highlight of my week. I truly wish that all adults could be as sweet to one another as children can be. I love helping in classrooms there and teaching the kids songs to sing in front of our whole congregation. Watching their enthusiasm (and nervousness, too) when they perform really helped me come to terms with what I used to do decades ago as a teacher when my students would perform at school concerts and productions.

Another person whom I actually listen to and learn from at Grace Church is Craig Paquette. When he opens our service with a *Bible* reflection, he explains stories in real-life terms that I actually can make sense of.

Besides that, his cheery disposition is comforting to be around. He's told many stories in our church, but here's my favorite, and I'll explain why after you read it:

> *The metaphor of the "downward escalator" is one of our spiritual life. Just about every child has tried to walk up a down escalator. So envision yourself going up a downward escalator.... If you stop in the middle, what happens? You start going down. The point of the analogy is that there is no middle ground. If you're not going up, you're going down. The same applies to our relationship*

with God. If we're not constantly exercising spiritual life (by being in steady obedience with God, going to church, being engaged in the Bible, and being in fellowship with "like"-minded people), it will be hard to overcome the downward pull of the world, the flesh and the devil always trying to tether us to this Earth. By doing this, it enables us to move toward a trajectory (God) instead of just randomly going about.

This story helped me because, when I first heard the word "escalator," that reminded me of my unbelievable fear of touching them back when I had mysophobia. But then, I really "got" what Craig was saying and why.

(And, once when he addressed our whole congregation, he talked about bacon. Anybody that discusses bacon, I listen to!)

So, if you've never been to a house of worship, why don't you try it? If you are not comfortable, try another one. Just go to learn more about God, and how He can help you take on life's challenges.

And, churches can also be fun places. A boy named Jacob in my church made me laugh when he saw a cancer surgery scar on my face and said, "You look like you have a giant exclamation point on your face." Boy, was he correct!

I will be eternally grateful to Pastor Torcello (*R. I. P.*), Pastor Eckler, and Pastor Smith for how they've taught me. I know God placed all of them in my life at certain times so I could get through it all. Thank you, God, for Pastor Torcello's trying to teach me how boys should treat girls, Pastor Eckler for "saving me" on that beach we met on at Camp-of-the-Woods after that second marriage's horrific, violent honeymoon, and Pastor Smith for teaching me ways to handle life with a brain injury.

I affectionately called Pastor Wes Smith "Pastor Smarty-pants" for a while because it takes a special person to be able to understand and therefore provide help to someone with "abnormal" personality quirks such as mine. He is smart because he helped me maneuver life's challenges in a real and humorous way. (One example: he compared choosing foods at a buffet to choosing to sin. I "got" his funny message.)

Because I've lived in many places, I've had the opportunity to worship in many different churches. No matter where I was, I feel that God has blessed me.

Here are some church signs that have really helped me:
- Forbidden fruit creates many jams [Pornography ruins many relationships.]
- Jesus knows me, this I love [A sign I got at the Town of Esopus United Methodist Church's Apple Festival, a deliberate reversal of the wording from the song, "Jesus Loves Me."]
- I got this – God
- Come in
  Sit
  Breathe
  Pray

Thank you, churches, for all your help!

Chapter 6

THE POWER OF PRAYER

THE LAST YEAR I was a teacher, 2006-2007, I was very sick with mysophobia – the fear of germs. Though it would be two years before I learned in 2009 that this OCD fear was caused by the undiagnosed brain tumor, when I was teaching, all I knew was that I was scared to touch anything!

A teacher in the same building with me at Rondout Valley Middle School was Mike Irwin. Though we were not friends really, just colleagues, he took me into his classroom on many different lunch periods, and prayed with me to help me feel better. Though this was a public school, we did that without anyone else being involved. He told me over and over again that someday I would feel better, thanks to God. He was right, and I will be forever grateful that he took the time to make me feel better, even if it was for only a few minutes at lunchtime.

Nowadays, I see Mike annually at the Rhinebeck, NY, Memorial Day parade. He marches every year with others who have been in the armed forces. I look to find him to give him a hug each time. I thank him in my mind whenever I remember those very difficult days.

Praying helps me calm down and focus on what is truly important. I have many signs about prayer around my condo, but my favorite says it best:

PRAY MORE. WORRY LESS.

I pray often throughout each day: I pray for my dog, Happy; for safe travels to all of my appointments; for people on my church's prayer chain; and for so much more! In fact, I have written much about prayer in other parts of this book.

Since my brain surgery, I have had a hard time closing my eyes to pray, because my head feels like it is swishing back and forth. I bow my head, but I keep my eyes open to help alleviate the swishing sensation.

Prayer makes me feel close to God. I remember that I prayed out loud as I was being wheeled into brain surgery. I told God that if I survived this, I would do what He wanted me to do with my life. So far – I'm not sure how well I'm doing with that, because I'm quite sure God wants me to behave better all the time. But for now – I'm writing this book hopefully to help others understand there are many facets of brain injury.

As a society, we often see brain injury of the type caused by car accidents or other traumatic events, but brain injury is alarmingly more widespread. It's the "invisible disability" among us, due to concussions, sports injuries, aneurysms, strokes, tumors, and so much more.

ALL brain injuries need to be taken seriously because, otherwise, behaviors are not noticed until it's too late. I've witnessed firsthand the violence that can erupt due to a trigger for what some would just see as back-and-forth conversation about something fairly routine, like politics. But, a brain-injured person can react to even one sentence impulsively, swiftly, and dangerously. As a society, we need to understand each other's vulnerabilities so we don't trigger someone unexpectedly.

Another sign in my condo reads:

TAKE TIME TO PRAY.

I KNOW there are many people who have prayed for me through the many challenges I have faced.

Thank you, "Team Janet," I could not have done it without you!

Chapter 7

What I Miss About Teaching

EACH AND EVERY single day, I miss going to my classroom to write the date on the board. At the early part of my career, that was on a chalkboard. By the end, it was either that way or on a whiteboard with the dry-erase markers. Either way, I wrote a note to my class that we read together each day. I labeled this our "A.M. Routine." It usually gave them an idea about what we'd be doing that particular day. Then – we'd read the schedule chart for that day of the week.

I also miss D.E.A.R. (Drop Everything and Read) Time. I tried to instill a love of reading in all my students. My favorite book to do this with was *Love You Forever*, written by Robert Munsch and illustrated by Sheila McGraw.

The first time I learned about this excellent book, I was attending a teachers' conference in upstate New York. When the facilitator read it, I don't think there was a dry eye in the auditorium of over 300 educators.

Ever since that day, I did read that wonderful story to my students on the first and last day of each school year. I gave them copies of it for their birthdays or graduations or even when they were in the hospital. It represents life as it comes and goes and trying to find the good as each day passes. I have hard and soft covers of *Love You Forever* at my home, and I read it to myself when I need to feel better about losing the profession I adored. I will love that book forever....

Another thing I sorely miss about being a teacher is all the field trips I planned and took with each class every year. Because of my memory problems, I can't remember all of them, but I do recall a few.

My friend Maggie mentioned in her writing about me (later in this book) the camping trips I took my Pine Plains students on. What a blast! Once, when our camping trip was canceled due to rain, we got permission to sleep in our classroom overnight, so we moved the desks to the hallway, brought in mats from the gym and held our sleepover there. I'm quite sure nowadays that would probably not be allowed to happen, but I'm glad we had so much fun doing that way back in the early 1980s!

Another trip I tried to plan annually was a trip to a nursing home to sing songs to the elderly at the holidays. We were always well-received and my students loved our rehearsals. We even practiced on the bus as our driver got us safely to our destination.

Our field trips were planned to wonderful places like restaurants, malls, movie theaters, farms, pools, museums, horseback riding stables, and oh, so much more, to teach our special needs students life skills. To this day when I drive by a place I know I once took a class to on such a trip, I try to remember all the fun things we learned there. I have so many pictures of these adventures, and when I look at them, it reminds me of what memories I gave my students and they gave to me.

Holiday parties were also tons of fun. We dressed in costumes for Halloween. I miss dancing with my students to the "Monster Mash" by Bobby "Boris" Pickett & the Crypt-Kickers, when we were all dressed up for Halloween. Some of my students could not afford costumes, so I always had a pile of things they could pick from to wear for a party. One costume that the girls loved to wear was an old dress from the Radio City Rockettes.

You see, my grandparents were friends with a janitor from the famous Radio City Music Hall MANY years ago. When some of the costumes were thrown away, this friend grabbed some and gave them to Grandma and Grandpa McColl, who had three granddaughters (my sisters and me).

After we enjoyed them as children, I "inherited" them for my first teaching job. Those glittery, long dresses were worn many times by various female students of mine over the years for Halloween, and other times too. Oh, the fun times I had way back when!

We also dressed up as Pilgrims and Native Americans for Thanksgiving and as elves and reindeer for Christmastime, and so much more, to take a break from routines on these various special days. We prepared lots of snacks and meals and invited other school staff and students to join us in the celebrations.

I also miss how we took care of needy children in other countries with Operation Christmas Child. Though this is led by a church organization, we were able to get approval to conduct it in our public schools (see letter in appendix).

I also miss the "little things" – like teaching a handicapped child how to tie his or her own shoelaces. From a craft fair, I would buy pretend wooden sneakers with colored laces, "sneakers" that they would keep in their desks. If someone had completed a task ahead of the others, he or she would take a sneaker out to practice. The look of excitement on their faces when they could finally tie it for themselves was priceless! Thank you, Karen O'Han, for making those adorable sneakers.

I also miss special things I did over the years. One unforgettable lesson was when we tapped a maple tree to make syrup. I inadvertently peeled paint off the wall of our classroom when we mistakenly boiled the sap down indoors. The pancakes we prepared with our own syrup were delicious though.

One field trip I remember like it was yesterday involved maple syrup. Since I never wanted to ruin the classroom's wall again, I took my students to the Bruderhof Woodcrest Community in Rifton, NY.

There, my students were taught how to correctly gather sap and make maple syrup. They were also treated to a delicious, free lunch when their tour was over.

For St. Patrick's Day, I excused myself from eating lunch with my students and went back to our classroom to "trash" the place. I threw the garbage on the floor, overturned desks and chairs, scattered papers all around, and sprinkled green glitter by an opened classroom window. When the kids came back from lunch, they were excited to see what a little leprechaun had done to our nice, neat classroom. Years later, a former assistant of mine named Patty called to tell me she had copied my leprechaun idea with her classroom now that she was a teacher. That memory brought tears to my eyes when I played her message over and over again on my answering machine. I felt wonderful that some other classroom was having the fun I once had with mine.

I miss teaching Summer School, which I did for quite a few years. It was a six-week program for the life-skills students whom I had taught during the school year. We continued the work we were accomplishing during the previous year, so when school resumed in the fall, those skills would not be lost.

I assigned less classwork, and thus less homework, during the summer, but we still put in quite a few hours of repetition of lessons needing their attention. I tried to make the learning as fun as possible because some of their siblings were not having to attend school in the summer and our students had to come, probably wishing they were somewhere else.

We had special days planned just with the word "fun" in mind. My personal favorite was Waterplay Day.

I don't really remember how I came up with this idea, but it sure was a good one! We played outside in our swimsuits for the entire day. The students had to earn their "invitation" to the wet festivities by completing their work for days and weeks before, as well as by being well-behaved. Some of my former students, whom I still keep in touch with, tell me how this extraordinary day is still remembered by them decades later.

We had squirt guns and sprinklers. We painted their feet, and they walked across rolls of mural paper before having their toesies sprayed down. We put beach balls and water balloons into a parachute and bounced them around. We got soaking wet for all of these games.

We also had kiddie pools and pool toys galore. We would take "breathers" by sitting them down on our beach blankets and/or their towels spread on grass instead of sand.

We had egg races with teams lined up with eggs and spoons. Then, we'd throw dozens of eggs at each other and need another "hose-down." Picking up all the eggshells left over from this event was a race also.

We enjoyed buckets of Kentucky Fried Chicken for lunch. Dessert would be a pie-eating contest. The first year we did this, I bought Freihofer's individual apple pies, which, of course, tasted yummy, but the fillings were hard to see on their faces as they hurriedly downed them with their hands behind their backs. All the remaining Waterplay Days, I bought cherry and blueberry pies so their faces were covered in colorful fruit fillings after they scrambled to win first place. Some of my best pictures of these days were taken of various students laughing uncontrollably with pie all over their faces!

I also miss an idea I used for many years called our "Compliment Pizza Party." Because many of my students had behavior issues, they didn't always act appropriately when around others in our school. So, when they "got it right," and someone complimented them for anything they were "caught" doing, we'd mark it up on a pizza slice made of paper. When all eight "slices" were filled with compliments, we ordered pizzas, and everyone enjoyed celebrating our accomplishments.

Sometimes our parties happened often and other times we had to wait for a long while. It all depended on their good behavior being observed and then mentioned by others. The kids were so excited when they saw the last slice fill up because pizza was coming soon! I've included in an appendix the invitation we sent out when our "pizza wheel" was full.

Another fun time including pizza was Pizza Hut's Book It! program. We set up a goal for how much reading a child had to accomplish in a month. If the child reached the goal, he or she won a certificate and a free personal pan pizza from the local restaurant. Since most of my students weren't taken to the restaurant, I collected their certificates and then picked up boxes and boxes of little pizzas. Then, we ate them all together. They loved this special activity, and I believed that helped them enjoy reading.

For Earth Day, we made "dirt"! We crushed Oreos, added chocolate pudding, peanuts, chocolate chips, coconut sprinkles colored with green food coloring and more to resemble dirt, rocks, and grass. It was all put in a clear cup and topped with a Gummi worm. This was after we learned about taking care of our planet. As on other special days, I wore my "teacher earrings" that were shaped like the globe and said, "Earth Day." I have a huge collection of these fun earrings, most of which were made by Art in Heaven of Altamont, NY, and I still wear them out and about years later. For example – I wear my birthday cake earrings when I attend someone's birthday celebration, my pizza earrings when I go out for pizza, and my groundhog earrings on Groundhog Day. I have over 60 pairs of these cute earrings, and I love looking at them to remind me of my school days gone by.

I used to make a big deal out of a student's birthday. I grew up in a family that did just that, so I think that's where I got that idea. My mother would make sure I got my favorite breakfast. During that mealtime, I got to open a gift before going to school. Then, when I came home, our family got to eat my favorite dinner either at home or at a restaurant of my choice. Then – there were more gifts with dessert. I still love sending cards (and receiving them) on special days. But – let's get back to teaching. So – my staff and I would plan a party at the end of the school day for our "birthday student." Their favorite goodie was served (or a cake we either purchased or prepared). There were cards and gifts. Not all, but many of my students throughout my career, didn't have a lot of money, so we spoiled them on this day.

One year, I began a birthday tradition where we squirted whipped cream from a can into the mouth of the celebrator while their head was tilted back (as well as anyone else at the party who wanted to partake). When it was my birthday, I got to be the one who sat under the nozzle. One year a student really had fun squirting it all over the place, so from then on, we wore aprons when it was our birthday. What a lot of messy fun that was!

Another thing I miss about teaching was a day I dubbed "Reading Day." We moved the desks out of the way and lay on our carpeted floor with beanbags, comfy chairs, and lots of pillows. I read to my students all day in my Mickey Mouse slippers. I wanted them to just have a day to enjoy books all day long. We ate our lunch like a picnic right there in the classroom. I miss them telling me which books they wanted to read.

Speaking of those special MM slippers, another great day we had was Mickey Mouse's birthday (November 18). I did a math lesson to teach them subtraction with the year it was and the year he debuted (1928) so we could figure out how old he was. We also played math games with dice decorated with his picture.

We dressed up in the many T-shirts and sweatshirts I collected over the years. We prepared MM pancakes for breakfast. We read many Disney books and watched a Disney movie at the end of our day. I'm sure that there was much more to it than that, but my memory right now (spring, 2016) only has that left in it.

I miss dispersing all the Disney World souvenirs I used to buy for my students. They loved the Rice Krispies treats (in the shape of Mickey's head) the most. Pencils and pens were my favorite (of course, "Teach"). I loved gathering fun things there to fly back to New York with. I'd jam my suitcases with these items, and my mother would get stuck with the job of boxing up and then mailing my clothes after I left, since there was no room for my stuff!

And back to Summer School, another special day we had was

Moon Day. On July 20, we learned about the first men who walked on the moon in 1969. We read books about the moon, space, and astronauts. We also made a "clean" mess by making moon pictures. We used Ivory soap flakes mixed with water and then plopped some onto black paper. The students, using their hands, turned them into the shape of the moon and used their fingers to poke craters into the soap mixture. After the pictures dried, we wrote on the black paper with white chalk… "Moon Day, 1997" (for example).

As usual, we had a snack related to this theme – Moon Pies come to mind.

Because most of my career was spent teaching Life Skills special education classes, we prepared food a lot. Most of the time, this lesson was planned for Friday mornings.

Many of the food selections we prepared were consumed by our students and staff that same day. But, many times we had leftovers. Some of my favorite memories were bringing those leftovers to homeless people I knew of.

One man who hid in the woods near where I lived for a while got all excited when he saw my car pull up on Fridays. He'd run to grab the container out of my hand, and then run just as quickly back into the woods with it. To this day, I wonder what ever happened to him after I moved away. He always screamed, "Thanks," as he scurried to eat our offerings. Did I ever tell my students about their leftovers going to the homeless???

I miss how I tried to make Mother's Day a special day for my students' mommies. I went to a flower shop and bought enough beautiful flowers so each student could go home with the one he or she picked out and had wrapped in wet paper towels with foil.

Even though I've never been a mother, and for many years lost touch with my foster son, Brian, I tried to do my best when I helped my students make cards to take home with those flowers. Nowadays, I just "hibernate" on that day, because it's too much of a reminder for me of what I've lost and what I've never had.

I miss those Scholastic Book Sales. I bought lots of books for my classroom at those sales. And, if my students had no money for a book they wanted, I bought those also. I never wanted any of "my kids" to go home empty-handed.

One summer in the 1990s, when I worked for Ulster County BOCES, I got permission from my supervisors to take one-on-one, after-school field trips with the students in my class, who happened to be all boys.

After the school day was complete, the student and I would head to my car, drive to the local Hudson Valley Mall, eat in the food court, go shopping at a store of his choice, and then go to the movie theater.

I saw two movies repeatedly (*Jurassic Park* and *Free Willy*) because each boy got to select which of these two movies to see.

These few hours I still remember. I only had about six young boys in my class then. We had so much fun.

I know special requests like that would not be allowed nowadays. But, once, when I bumped into one of my students from that time who was now grown up, he told me his favorite time in school was when I took just him to the mall. That made my day, hearing that!

Another vague memory is that we used to finger-paint with chocolate pudding. I can't remember how this idea got started, or for what theme it was linked to, but I sure do remember the fun of it all.

The kids would "paint" a picture with a blob of chocolate pudding. Then, of course, they would lick their hands. This project made quite a mess of the room as well as of their faces, but it was worth it!

I also miss when my own parents would send our classroom a box of Honeybell oranges from Florida each January. They are so juicy that special straws were needed to poke into them to sip them. The kids, staff, and I loved that slippery mess of orange juice running down our faces and necks as we "drank" from the oranges.

I still remember the happy faces I saw on the students who were in my class for a few years, when they walked in on some cold, January day and saw the box from Florida. They knew it was going to be a fun snack time that day!

Recently, I found the 1881 "Code of Conduct for Teachers" of the Bentley Memorial School, which put some of my experience into a new context. For example, one of the nine requirements stated, "After ten hours in school, the teachers may spend the remaining time reading the *Bible* or other good books." Wow! Things sure have changed since the 1800s! [No chocolate pudding, then.]

These fond memories I think about now. I miss all the work that went into planning things like that. The activities made my job so enjoyable. Sometimes, I wish I could just go back in time and relive all of that, knowing that one day, it would be gone forever, so enjoy every second of it!

In many instances my effort received warm recognition. For example, the former head of Ulster County BOCES, Laura R. Fliegner, wrote me a commendation concerning my teaching:

> *.... Your job is not easy. The hours and the emotions which you invest in your teaching roles cannot be measured in the normal way we calculate such things. That "extra something special" which you bring to the job is immeasurable, and may make the difference between the total success or failure of your children to improve their lives.*
>
> *Thank you, Janet, for all that you do for our (your) children.*

I thank God every day for the opportunity I had to teach and that I can remember some of these happy times, gone, but not forgotten....

Chapter 8

CLIFF, MY FIRST STUDENT

I BEGAN TEACHING special education students in 1982. One very special student was Cliff, who, as an adult, has written the following for me:

I started Seymour Smith [School] in Pine Plains, NY. My new teacher's name was Janet Johnson. It was Room 210 and then 209. She liked Room 209 because it had more space. She had cereal for all the kids in the morning. She took the class for walks to the water tower. Then she got married to Mr. Schliff. Mrs. Schliff coached all the kids in her class for the Dutchess County Special Olympics. One year I went with Mr. and Mrs. Schliff to the NYS Special Olympics in Syracuse NY. Mrs. Schliff took the class camping three times at Wilcox Park. She also took us swimming at Lake Taghkanic and to the Trevor Zoo and Four Brothers for lunch. One day she drove the small school bus to FDR then to her new apt for lunch. We both liked the same music groups. Mrs. Schliff came to my graduation in 1990. I still see her and talk to her on the phone about the old days.

When Cliff wrote what we've printed above and turned it in to me so I could share it with my editor, I asked Cliff if I could pry some more details from him, and he obliged. So – here are the notes I took while we visited each other in the winter of 2016:

- He filled me in on the computer we had way back then. He said it was a TRS-80. I have no recollection of the computer, and when I said that, his response was, "Mrs. Schliff was good on the computer." [Wow!]
- We reminisced during this visit about when I chaperoned his prom, years after he had been my student. Rod Stewart's "Forever Young" was the theme. Though now 45 years old, Cliff still seems refreshingly young to me.
- He reminded me of his favorite bulletin board in our class. It was titled "Kid of the Week." I think he was on the board at least once.
- We spent hours learning how to tell time.
- We prepared an actual Thanksgiving dinner and invited family and friends to our evening get-together. He stated that he loved being in our classroom after dark. We held this dinner a few days before the actual holiday. [And to my best recall – it was the ONLY time I've ever cooked a turkey!]
- He had to go to detention once for breaking one of our classroom rules. He still remembers this!
- He misses riding the bus and having me as his teacher.
- He reminded me about how I invited him to speak to one of the classes that I taught at Ulster County BOCES after I resigned from Pine Plains CSD.

I have always referred to Cliff as "my first student" because right after I was hired by the Pine Plains CSD, I heard rumors that some parents were nervous about sending their special needs children to a teacher who was fresh out of college. So – I set up my very first classroom way earlier than our first day of school and invited the families that were on my class list to come in and meet me, see their new classroom, and get more comfortable before the actual school year began. Cliff was the first person who walked in that day, and to this day, he has always been "my first student."

What a memory, Cliff! These stories are over 30 years old!

[I just learned that Cliff won a prestigious award (and $500) at his job for doing excellent work. I'm so proud of him!]

Chapter 9

My Foster Son, Brian

In 1989 I left the Pine Plains Central School District to work for Ulster County BOCES. I began there teaching Summer School, and I met a little eight-year-old boy named Brian [who has given me permission to use his real name here]. He was in that very first class.

The first time we had a field trip to the pool, Brian took off his shirt, and his back was filthy. The gym teacher had to take him to the restroom to help him get cleaned up, so he would be allowed into the pool for instruction.

Brian was placed into the foster care system by his mother. He had not been removed from his home, but, instead, she gave him up "temporarily" to help her get back on her feet. Brian ended up not living with his mother for many years.

I was his teacher that summer. I was married at the time and owned a house in Rhinebeck. I had told my bosses that if housing was needed, I'd be glad to take him home with me for a few months. My husband agreed, but neither of us knew what we were getting ourselves into....

We went to many special training sessions and got certified to be N.Y. State foster parents. We didn't expect Brian's stay with us to last as long as it did. Months turned into years, and the situation took a huge toll on our marriage.

Brian was labeled at the time as "emotionally disturbed." His behavior was erratic. Sometimes, both at school and then at "home," he was well-behaved, but then other times, he would misbehave. He craved attention and being in the spotlight. Sometimes this worked well for him and my husband and me, but other times it was difficult.

What truly made it hard at home was that I did my teaching job 24/7, non-stop. The homework that I assigned to my students during the day was the same homework I assisted Brian with in the evening. This, and many more such examples, negatively affected our marriage. Every couple needs to take a break from work in order to be happy. My husband and I separated while Brian was still our foster son.

But, there was good, too. We took Brian to Disney World. He exhausted my parents and us, as he literally RAN around the parks because he was so excited to be there! Although Brian is in his 30's now, he still reflects on how much fun we had there, as well as at so many other places we took him to.

Nowadays, I don't think teachers are allowed to become foster parents to their students. I agree with this change because foster parenting really alters your life. I wasn't emotionally prepared for how hard it would all be. I do commend anyone who is able to be a foster parent.

These days, though we only live about 30 minutes apart, I only see Brian every few months. I collect all the water bottles I drink from, and he recycles them for extra money. Sometimes, we have a quick lunch before I go into my trunk for the multiple bottle bags that he walks to a store. He always makes me feel better about my life, because each quick visit, he reminds me of all that I am to him.

You can read more about this time in my life from Brian himself. He wrote the next chapter.

Chapter 10

TRIBUTE FROM
FOSTER SON, BRIAN

I [BRIAN] WAS going to a special ed. program called "Ulster BOCES." There were a few constants in my life, and BOCES was one of the constants, a program that has splinter classes throughout Ulster County, where kids with Down Syndrome or Asperger's or kids who can't read or even speak English go, basically kids who need a special-needs environment to learn. One summer there was a teacher who was unlike any other teacher I had met: she made learning fun and engaging to the point where you wanted to learn something new.

I was walking into summer school and my new teacher was there. She said, "Hi, there. My name is Janet. Are you Brian?" [Back then, Ulster County BOCES students were allowed to call their teachers by their first names.]

I said, "Yes."

She had big, colorful eyes, and she was wearing bright colors, but most important, she made you very comfortable, considering she was dealing with special-needs children.

Janet didn't know it, but in her teaching career she would set the bar at a high level for my future teachers. She would pull off the impossible. The first day in summer school, she was teaching us the hula dance. Yes, I can regretfully admit I did the hula at the ripe age of seven.

One time I went to the YMCA to go swimming, but the gym teacher, Roy, could not let me in the water cause I was filthy with dirt on my back. I cried cause I could not go in the water. There were a lot of things like that in my life that I could not understand, so school was like that, and then I went into foster care when the fall came around, and Janet was still in school in the fall. You see my normal teacher, Marla, took the summer off, and Janet got her class.

I thought Janet was going to leave when the summer ended. Turns out, there she was. Janet has a way of popping up when you least expect it. She is more stealthy than a Navy SEAL.

School was the one constant in my childhood as well. Looking back, I had it good, and I took a lot for granted, as we all did. We were safe, looked after. We got a top-notch education, and we went on all the cool field trips.

Then one day, Janet told me I was going to a new foster home. Weeks went by, but I had no idea where I was going, until the day I was leaving the home I was in. I was in school all that day, having no clue about what was going to happen to me. Then Janet Schliff asked me to step into her classroom, and she said, "Brian, I am aware that you're going to a new foster home."

She asked me, "Are you nervous about your new foster home?"

I said, "Yes, I have no idea where I am going."

She said, "I can understand that. How would you feel if you were going to come live with me?"

I paused for a moment and smiled and said, "I would like that. You're really cool."

She then said, "I am glad to hear you say that, because I have some news to tell you: I am going be your new foster mother."

I jumped with relief and great joy.

Here was this woman who had become a big part of my school life, and she was a really nice and cool lady, the one teacher you looked forward to seeing every day. What kid in foster care would not want their favorite teacher to take them home? I hugged her for the first time. I went home and packed my bags with joy, then got in the van and took the long drive to Rhinebeck, NY.

Rhinebeck, NY, was a revelation. I had no idea people lived like that until I went to that town. It was the first time in my life I had mother and father figures under the same roof. It was an adjustment to get used to. I had to get used to a wealthy community where most of the kids you meet there take a lot for granted, things I simply would never take for granted. Janet and her husband made my life stable, and I was for the first time in a position where I was happy.

Janet and her husband also broadened my horizons. They taught me just how big the world really is. They gave me something that I will forever be grateful for: they gave me the courage to stand my ground and be Brian. They would always say, "Don't ever let anyone turn you into something that deep down you know you are not, because who you are on the inside is the only guarantee you have in this world, and as long as you have that, you will always find a way back to where things make sense to you."

I found myself maturing faster than the rest of my companions. Janet and her husband managed to take a kid who was a complete mess and culture him, educate him, and teach him to be polite, charming, and a completely different person. They took me to the Albany Museum for the first time as a kid. I stood there in front of the mammoth skeleton and I was in awe. Both of them constantly showed me things like that.

Then one day, Janet's parents showed up. Janet's mom could cook like no other. Her dad was a goofball and love to horseplay. One thing he loved to do was give what he lovingly called an "elephant bite," which was grabbing my thigh and shaking his hand while squeezing at the same time. It would both sting and tickle. It was not long before

I was calling them "Grandma and Grandpa." I never knew my real grandparents, so they filled the gap in a wonderful way. A few months later, Janet, her husband, and myself were sitting on an airplane heading to Florida. I had to go to the bathroom every five minutes.

Then we landed in West Palm Beach, Florida, and stayed with her parents in Boca Raton, Florida. Again, Florida was a revelation: this was me learning how another group of people lived. I was standing there on the beach, realizing *I am in a place where I normally can only read about*, which is also what ran through my mind when we went to Disney World. I was in awe at the huge globe in Epcot Center. It was an amazing feeling, but about 500 yards in front of the globe there were these huge disks launching water streams from one disk to the other, as though the water was playing hopscotch. It seemed seamless, as if it were one stream of water, so I stood there, reached my hand up, and my hand got soaked. I thought *maybe I can swallow the water with my mouth*, so I climbed up on the platform and watched the water go to one after another, and then I stood there, opened my mouth, and, not only did it not go in my mouth, it soaked me from head to foot. I jumped down covered in water and was absolutely drenched and laughing my head off.

At one point, the three of us went on the teacups ride. Now Janet's husband, when he was not working for IBM or hanging out being a foster father or weightlifting, was pretty buff and spry. We noticed that all the other teacups on the ride spun but our teacup seemed to spin round and round and round faster than all the others. I never realized how fast our teacup was really spinning.

Now Janet's husband kept bugging me to ask if we could ride in the front of the monorail, so eight-year-old little me did ask the operator, and we got to ride in the front with the driver, which was really cool, and I got to see how these really operated.

Living with Janet as a kid was really cool. She loved rock music. We went to see all the Disney movies, and I got to eat at more restaurants than I can count, so learning table manners was a must. I got used to living in polite society and I liked it. This was a stable, happy time in my childhood, considering I had to face very adult situations. I liked where I was, and Disney World was not the only place I got to see. One place Janet and her husband went to when they were dating was Niagara Falls; he wanted me to see it so badly, and I did not really understand why, but one day he and his mother took me there, and I stood at the very spot he and Janet once stood by themselves. I stood there at eight years old, and I was in awe of the size of the falls. I felt very insignificant in front of this huge, massive waterfall.

Disney World and Niagara Falls were not the end of my traveling. I got to go to Hershey Park as well. Janet and her husband planned the trip to Lake Placid, the cornerstone of the Winter Olympics. That trip was to be another unforgettable one that sticks out in my mind to this day.

Janet and her husband taught me that if you truly love a child, you will do what's best for the child even if it does not include you. That's real love, and that is how you steer a child right, by doing the hard things that help the child be a better person.

I remember the day the social worker came and loaded my stuff into the car and I had felt the pain of knowing I was leaving. It hurt so bad I cried really hard. Janet did, too, as she hugged me and held me tight. She took a picture that day of me, and I often look at that picture. My eyes from that moment on until today have one thing in common: I had pain and heartbreak behind my eyes. I felt like my entire world caved in and around me. I didn't want to leave. I had a happy life, and I could not understand why my family could not see that. The selfishness and stubbornness behind everything they did hurt, but as they loaded me into the van to take me back to my mother, I said "No! Why do I have to go? Please let me stay!"

Janet said, while crying, "I want you to stay, but it's not up to me. Brian, I love you."

I could hear the case worker as she started the van and said, "I hate this job. I really do. This is so wrong in every way."

I cried until I exhausted myself and cried some more, and that was the first time in my life that I had felt heartbreak.

Chapter 11

What I **Don't** Miss About Teaching

As you've read, I loved teaching! But, as in all professions, there are things you don't like. My list isn't long, but I do have some….

I now have Sunday nights for whatever I want to do. It used to be that all I could do those evenings was write lesson plans for the upcoming week. Some teachers do that during their work hours, but I never found the time for that. So – I missed a lot of fun things to do on many Sunday nights. The only time during the school year that I got a break from that was when we had Monday off for a special holiday. Then, Monday rather than Sunday night was spent doing the lesson-plan ritual.

Another thing that I don't miss about teaching is the day after Halloween, though it is, coincidentally, my birthday, November 1st. I hated it because the kids were experiencing "sugar hangovers" from all the trick-or-treating the night before. They'd either be so what I called "hyper-diaper" they couldn't concentrate, or they'd be so worn-out they couldn't stay awake. It was usually not a fun day on which to celebrate my birthday nor to have my students learn much.

A third thing I truly disliked was how computerized special education all became at the end of my career. Individualized Education Plans (IEPs) for special ed. students used to be uniquely personal. Then they became too cumbersome, with selecting data vs. just writing the information. They became like multiple-choice-test answers rather than expressive essays. I became terrible at computer skills. I even had an administrator, at my very last job, belittle me, regarding how I had filled out the IEP, in front of parents at a meeting about their child.

Many people had to help me work on the computer at the end of my career. I found out later from one of my many doctors that computer skills would have been affected by my brain tumor. I have never bumped into this horrible administrator since my surgery, and she's lucky for that, because I'm pretty sure I would not be able to control my tongue, as I am taught to do at church and other places. No one should ever say such rude things as that about you when there's an audience — especially when we all were unaware of the brain tumor that was behind my mistakes….

[In contrast, two teachers helped me enormously back then, and I wanted to include them in my book. For the life of me, I couldn't remember their names. Then, God helped me. I bumped into both of them within a week of each other in two separate restaurants. So — thank you, Nischa and Angela. You both took good care of me at the end of my career. You are excellent human beings. Thanks, also, to Kim, Eileen, Joe, Toni, Barbara, Pat, Janis, Sheryl, Karen, Nancy, Jill, Mike, and Lorraine, who also helped me a lot (I had to find an old directory to remember the names of some of the sweet colleagues who helped me at the very end of my career).]

Now, back to some things I don't miss about teaching….

When I began teaching, everyone had to stand to recite the Pledge of Allegiance. By the end of my teaching career, not only did they not have to recite the Pledge, they stood only if they chose to while it was being recited. I think this is a sad display of how things have gone downhill, as far as respect for our traditions and forefathers. By the end of my career, I was disappointed to have to remind my class over and over what the Pledge symbolized. To this day, I put my right hand over my heart as I say the Pledge.

Nowadays, when someone sneezes, I can say, "God bless you" again. Once, when an administrator was visiting my classroom, a student sneezed and that's what I said. I was told later on in the office that I could only say, "Bless you."

I also loved decorating a tree at Christmastime in my classrooms. When we were no longer allowed to call it a "Christmas tree" anymore, I left our artificial tree up all year long and each month decorated it to match that month's theme (for example, with hearts in February or turkeys in November...).

Yet another thing I don't miss about teaching is catching scabies. This happened twice (once when I was student-teaching and then my first year of teaching).

Scabies are those little buggies underneath your skin. You have to wash lots and lots of clothes that they may have "jumped" to, besides slathering your skin with awful meds. This was totally gross and I'm grateful I never caught them after that.

The family I caught scabies from was very poor. I vaguely remember the teacher I student-taught with bought them laundry detergent and the medicine for the brother and sister to use. The second time I had scabies, my doctors were pretty sure I didn't catch them from students this time, but from clothes in my closet that the tiny buggers got into the year before but hadn't been worn due to the change in seasons.

Lucky for me, I never caught lice, though students in my class had lice practically every year that I taught. I know of teachers who did catch lice from their pupils, so I was saved the aggravation of that hairy mess!

Another thing I really don't miss about teaching is my trips to the ER because of something that took place with the children while I worked. I know I was bitten more than once, breaking the skin at least one time. I was punched in the nose in a pool and there was so much blood, the public pool had to be drained. And – I got "in the way" of a piñata stick and had a broken finger.

The students who bit me I've never seen as adults, but the "pool puncher" apologized to me when I ran into him unexpectedly once. He was an adult by then, explaining how afraid he was of the water when I tried to help him with a swimming lesson when he was a very young boy. I thought it was sweet of him to remember that many years later.

The accident from the piñata stick was also apologized for when I met up with this young man for dinner to talk about days gone by. He was so polite and friendly and we laughed (and even teared up a bit) at some of the stories that took place when he was in my class. He was another one of my favorites.... Here's one story about him: on one of the Reading Days towards the end of my career, as I slipped my feet into my MM slippers, I discovered a large, sharp knife in one of them. Luckily, my foot wasn't cut. We found out pretty quickly which student put it there, and why.

He was being teased by other students in our school because he was in a special ed. classroom. He brought the knife to school to threaten those other students at lunchtime. He hid it in my slipper under my rocking chair, not realizing that I would take off my shoes this particular day. Of course, I had to take him to the principal's office. The police were called and he was taken to a local hospital's psych. ward for evaluation. As soon as school was over that day, I immediately went to the hospital, showed my badge and ID for my job, and they let me in to visit him.

Because I was an adult woman, and he was a youth, I was not allowed to be left alone with him in his "room," so someone who worked there found us a mat to sit on in the hallway, where he cried in my arms, telling me how sorry he was.

I just held him and kept telling him how much I loved him, no matter what mistakes he made. I had brought my favorite classroom book, *Love You Forever* (mentioned in the other chapter about teaching), and

I read it to him as he cuddled in my arms with hospital staff scurrying by caring for other patients there.

After our visit time was over, I left and tried to drive home. At this time in my career, I lived in Dutchess County, NY, so it was a long drive home, over 30 miles, from where this took place in Ulster County. I guess my driving was erratic due to how hard I was crying. I was pulled over by a state trooper.

When I told him what had happened that day, he was very comforting and didn't give me a ticket, and told me to be more careful (I guess I was speeding and swerving). As he assured me he would, he followed me for quite a while, which I really appreciated. I think he might have learned how much teachers can care for the welfare of their students by stopping me that day.

Since my brain surgery, I went to a wake for a family member of this student. When I knew him as a youngster, he was in a foster-care home. At this wake, I met his mother for the first time.

When he introduced us, he said, "Mom – this is the teacher I always talked about."

She thanked me for the job I had done for him many years before. I left that funeral home feeling slightly better that, even though I can't teach anymore, there are signs that I did well when I could.

Another dangerous thing that took place in several classrooms I taught in over the years was the "flying furniture" episodes. Chairs, desks, tables, and more were thrown by various students who became agitated with their work, our staff, and/or themselves. Luckily, I can't remember any trips to the ER for these occasions, so I guess I dodged these airborne "gifts" well.

I also don't miss that very-hurried lunch break. By the time you stood in line to get a school lunch, headed to the teachers' room to gobble it down, headed to the restroom, if needed, and then back to class, there was always a rush! When I finished scarfing lunch down, I used the students' playground time to write to parents about their child's behavior and work completion that day. I did this for every child, every day. I began that practice when I started teaching at Ulster County BOCES because I was told the teachers there had daily communication with the parents.

Instead of writing in individual notebooks like some of the BOCES teachers did, I copied someone's idea of a Daily Report sheet. It was the quickest way I could relay important information. It was also the way families could let me know what was up at home. I don't remember whose idea it was, but I changed the layout of it a little bit. I have an example of this idea in one of my appendices.

I need to mention another thing I disliked about teaching. It was those stupid standardized testing days! Too many are a waste of valuable educational time!

Another thing I don't miss about teaching is fire drills. Those bells and alarms that ring are so loud and frightening for us all IF we weren't told ahead of time we'd be having a drill. Some of my students screamed and jumped up while others were able to calmly line up to exit the room and then leave our school.

Something I have to admit here, though, is that I caused at least three fire evacuations over the years due to my trying to do too many things at the same time. One time a fire I started came from our classroom's cooking, but I can't remember much more than that. The other two fires, I remember like they happened yesterday.

The first memorable fire was the smaller of the two I remember. We were popping popcorn in the microwave in the teachers' room. We accidentally pushed too many minutes on the buttons, because a student ran away and we were focused on catching her. Before we knew it, there were sparks and LOTS and LOTS of smoke pouring out of the microwave. The alarm sounded, and the whole school had to go outside.

Nothing makes for other staff's being annoyed with you more than disruption of their teaching to go stand in the cold until the fire department arrives. But, that's what happened, so, of course, I got comments and looks from colleagues who were less than thrilled with that afternoon.

The next fire that my classroom had was due to my rushing and telling my staff to do something that in hindsight, was just plain stupid.

We were about to celebrate our monthly Book It! Program. I had gone to Pizza Hut (which is the company that developed this reading program) the night before and picked up all of the free pizzas that my students had earned from reading that month. I had worked out a deal with this restaurant, because usually the families were supposed to bring their child in for the meal, but since most of the families I worked with could not do that, I went instead. I did pay for pizzas for my staff and me to eat with our class so we could all enjoy this reading celebration together.

When it was time to take the pizzas out of our classroom fridge (a small fridge I still had from my days in college), I told my staff to put the pizzas into our classroom's little oven, still in their boxes, because we were late for something and we had no time to empty all the personal pan pizza boxes. Well – we sure wasted lots of time with that decision of mine!

As I was at the front of the classroom teaching some math problem on the chalkboard, a student, J., from the back of the room, who could see the oven better than I could, shouted out, "Ms. Schliff!"

I told him to stop calling out. A few seconds later, he shouted out even louder, "Ms. Schliff!!" Again, I told him to get back to work on his math sheet.

Then, he screamed my name, and when I asked him to please be quiet, he yelled out, "Fine – I won't tell you your classroom's on fire!" At that, I ran to the back of the room and flames were shooting out of our little oven. I unplugged it, pulled the pizza box that was on fire and threw it into the sink and poured water on it.

The entire classroom was filled with smoke, and because this happened on a winter day, the whole school was sent to the gym after we got out safely, so the firemen could inspect the entire building. This ended up being a three-hour event that actually was mentioned when

I was thrown a going-away party from Ulster County BOCES several years later.

After all of us were safely back in our classrooms, I was called to our office to speak on the phone to my boss, Mr. Howard Korn, who called me to make sure we were all okay. I said we were, but lots of staff in the building were pretty upset with me (for obvious reasons – cardboard in an oven!).

But – what ended up being a happy ending is that as the firemen were getting ready to leave our school's premises, a house went on fire across the street. I was told the next day that the house was saved probably because the fire trucks were so close.

When I was roasted at that going-away party, someone gave me a fire extinguisher as a present. Very funny!

That's it, my list of dislikes. Given that I taught for 25 years, this is a short list, because I can hardly remember much I disliked about this wonderful job.

Chapter 12

My Mickey Mouse® Obsession

As I stated in the very first chapter of this book, I am quite the Mickey Mouse collector. Often, I'm asked when this began. To the best of my memory, which is sometimes sketchy because of the brain tumor, it started in the mid-to-late 1980s. Back then, my family went to Disney World a lot because my parents and sisters had moved from upstate New York to Florida. I visited as often as I could, which usually was about three times a year.

Because they lived within a couple of hours' drive time from the parks, we usually just enjoyed day trips there. My favorite was always the Magic Kingdom and specifically Main Street, USA. When they say Disney World is the "happiest place on earth," I can truly say that it is for me! When I stroll down that street and peek into all of the shops, I am beside myself with excitement.

I left shopping while on Main Street until the end of the day so I wouldn't have to carry my new purchases throughout the park. I know that many other tourists do the same thing, because there are way more people in these shops later on in the day than in the morning.

I just love how clean everything is there. I visited more than once when I had mysophobia, and it was one of the only places I went into the restroom without freaking out.

The staff at Disney World is so incredibly friendly. No matter how I was feeling when I arrived, I always felt much better when I left.

My condo has tons of Mickey Mouse memorabilia from those fun visits, and it has been dubbed a "Mickey Museum." One of the ways I got this book started was because of these items, as described as follows:

A former reporter from our local newspaper, the *Daily Freeman*, attends the same church I do. She wrote excellent articles about collections people have.

One Sunday, I saw her in church, and I said, "Paula, great article about that man's baseball card collection. I wish my collection took up less space and was that easy to dust."

Paula Mitchell responded by asking what I collected, and I filled her in.

The next thing you know, she's setting up a visit by both her and a photographer, Tania Barricklo, from the paper. When Paula was quizzing me about The Mouse, she asked what I did for a living. I burst into tears, and she shut the recorder off.

I told Paula I had been a teacher for 25 years, but now I'm on disability because the brain tumor has caused permanent brain damage. I told her I missed teaching, every day. The article ended up being front-page news and was about the life I lost as well as my Mickey Mouse obsession.

When I spoke of this at one of my support groups, Dr. Lois Tannenbaum, our facilitator and the writer of my memoir's Foreword, told me about Douglas Cooper, an editor. She said he could help me put my story on paper so others can learn what happened to me and what I've learned from it all. I contacted Dr. Cooper, and so this book began.

In the chapter I wrote about the things I miss about teaching, I listed a bunch of things we used to do over the years that included MM.

These days, I visit Disney stores in malls and in Times Square. I only go to New York City once or twice a year, but when I visited the Disney store there recently, a few people walked in before me, and the greeter at the door said, "Welcome" to each of them. When she saw me, she said, "Welcome BACK," so I guess I'm memorable! I'm dressed from head to toe in clothing with Mickey Mouse all over me.

As Walt Disney famously said, "I only hope we never lose sight of one thing – that it was all started by a mouse."

This book got started because of that newspaper article about that mouse....

Chapter 13

"Steal Away"

A VERY SHORT time before I knew I had a brain tumor, my boyfriend, Aiden, and I went to the Bearsville Theater – near Woodstock, NY – and heard the singer Robbie Dupree. I've loved his music since I was a young woman.

One of my favorite songs of his – and one that he performed that night – was "Steal Away." When I woke up after the seven-hour surgery done to remove my brain tumor, the neurosurgeon told me to sing songs so he could check my memory. The first song I sang was that one.

Right after that, I sang "Amazing Grace" and then the Mickey Mouse Mouseketeers' song ("M.I.C.K.E.Y. M.O.U.S.E…"). I got many of the words to all three songs correct. The brain surgeon told me to listen to music all the time and work on remembering the words.

I did just that as soon as I was driven home from NYU. I sat in Aiden's car's backseat as he and a friend of his drove me home. I looked out of my window and cried while I tried to remember the words to "New York, New York," as we drove home from the hospital in NYC.

Aiden and his friend talked throughout my happy tears as I sang away. The radio wasn't even on but the car was full of music. I cried those happy tears because I was alive.

A few years later, I was at a coffee shop getting my favorite cup. As I self-served, the song "Still the One" by Orleans was playing. I'll talk to anyone – including strangers – and so I just casually asked the guy next to me if the bandmates who wrote that song were still with their original partners. I just talk and talk and talk. Little did I know I was asking someone who would actually know the answer.

That guy said they all were still with their partners, the ones still alive. I asked him how he knew that, and he said it is because he works with a lot of the bands that play at the Bearsville Theater. I told him I had just been there to see Robbie Dupree again. Then **I told the stranger a story he had already heard, but little did I know that. This is what I told him:**

> *I went to hear Robbie Dupree's songs again after my surgery. I bumped into Robbie near the restrooms before he performed. I told him the story about what had taken place at NYU when I first woke up after my tumor was removed.*

> *Robbie said it was "cool."*

> *During his performance a few minutes later, Robbie sang "Steal Away." I figured he would announce to the audience that he had just met a woman who sang all the words to his song when she awoke after brain surgery. But – he said nothing to the crowd, and so I just assumed that the story was no big deal to him.*

The stranger at the coffee shop who worked with Robbie told me that he's been on the road with the band ever since the night I told him my story. The stranger told me that **Robbie has announced my "cool story" to every audience since.**

I asked why he had not done that the night I told him all about it. The man said, "Mr. Dupree did not want to embarrass you."

I smiled and paid for my coffee. That news felt wonderful.

Well – fast-forward more time, and I bumped into Robbie again at Price Chopper food store in Saugerties, NY. He recognized me, gave me a hug, and asked how I was feeling.

I told him I was okay but had some brain damage. Then I told him I heard that he was telling my story when he performed. He said he does this because musicians love to learn how their music affects others.

I started singing "Steal Away" as he paid for his pretzels.

The young people at the register said they were thrilled to meet someone their mothers loved to listen to.

To this day, every time "Steal Away" plays on the radio, I think of that hospital recovery room bed and the staff filming my singing and hugging the brain surgeon. "Why don't we steal away...?"

Robbie Dupree isn't the only famous person I've met. Somewhere in my book, I mention my telling the Village People how people usually form the letter "M" at wedding receptions, when their song "YMCA" is played. But, another famous person whose music I love and whom I served, was James Taylor. I was a teacher for the Pine Plains School District by day, and a waitress in Hyde Park, NY (at a restaurant once called "The Springwood Inn") by night. This excellent musician had just performed in Poughkeepsie and came over to the restaurant with the owner (Renée). He ordered something to drink, and as I poured it, he asked if he could use the house phone. I peeked into the kitchen and asked Renée if it was okay (because this was in the 1980s – pre-cell-phone times). Of course, she said he could, so I rudely eavesdropped on him calling his ex, Carly Simon, about their son. He was a very sweet and gentle customer. As the song states so well, "shower the people you love with love."

Just a short time after my brain surgery, I met Judy Collins. She sang "Over the Rainbow" on a CD for a book about that beautiful song. She came to a church in Rhinebeck, NY, and performed for a small group of us who came to listen to her beautiful voice and also to have her sign our books. I started to cry as she signed mine and another one I bought for my mother since my mom is a huge fan of hers. Judy Collins touched my hand as she signed her autograph and asked why I cried. I told her I had just survived brain surgery and I was happy to be here. She wrote me a very sweet note in my book:

"To Janet,
May you sing the song of life!
Judy Collins"

So – if I've met other famous folks, I can't remember them anymore. You can see from all of these examples how much music has played a part in my life. Rest in peace, John Denver, Whitney Houston, Michael Jackson, Karen Carpenter, Donna Summer, Glenn Frey, Jim Croce, Sonny Bono, Bob Marley, The Gibbs Brothers, Barry White, Dan Fogelberg, Davy Jones, George Michael, Glen Campbell, David Cassidy, and so many more whose music I love and who are gone too soon....

Chapter 14

SUPPORT GROUPS

I ATTEND THREE very worthwhile support groups about brain injuries. I have learned SO much from all three in different ways....

The first group I joined is held at the RCAL building in Kingston, NY. "RCAL" stands for "Resource Center for Accessible Living, Inc." Our group's facilitator is Josephine Tordaro, and she's very helpful! She has taught me so much about how to handle life now.

This group has been meeting the second Monday of each month, from 3:30 to 5:00 p.m. We all have different stories to tell, and even though the group's title is "TBI" (Traumatic Brain Injury), I am fully included in all discussions. As a matter of fact, it was facilitator Josephine who was the first person who correctly told me my actual label, "ABI," for "Acquired Brain Injury." I had been to several doctor appointments but had never heard that before. I scribble notes wherever I go, so when I heard that one, I wrote it down and brought it to my very next neurologist appointment. Luckily, I see this doctor every 3-4 months, so I didn't have to wait too long to hear if Josephine was correct. She was. This group is where I learned that brain injuries are the "silent, hidden epidemic."

According to the May Institute (mayinstitute.org), "Acquired brain injury refers to a traumatic or non-traumatic brain injury that occurs after birth. Traumatic brain injury (TBI) is caused by an external force. Non-traumatic brain injury occurs as a result of disease or illness."

At Josephine's group I've heard a great many stories about how others handle their brain injuries. What was so shocking to me when I first attended was how smart, capable, and knowledgeable these people have been. The jobs they held were impressive!

Without sharing private information here, suffice it to say that these people have HUGE adjustments to make from the lives they once had to the lives they have been given now. I am NOT the only person who struggles with this adjustment. It's like: once someone worked for NASA and now must work on personal behavior.

One of the many things I learned was about 3D glasses and brain injury. At one of Josephine's meetings I attended when I first joined, she asked us to go around and say what we had done as far as celebrating the recent Fourth of July holiday. The usual things were listed, such as parades, barbecues and fireworks.

But, when I told the group that I had bought these new 3D glasses to watch the fireworks along with Aiden, Josephine interrupted me and asked the group what I just said that I shouldn't have. As usual, I assumed I had inadvertently been rude to someone. Turns out – the group knew something I didn't: 3D glasses can cause a seizure with someone who has had a brain injury. I hadn't heard that before. As always, I checked with my neurologist, and I found that it is true. Luckily, I was fine that fun fireworks night at Cantine Field in Saugerties, NY. But, I gave those 3D glasses away so that I wouldn't risk a problem in the future, because I also learned that it could happen years down the road after the injury.

And – I shared all this info with "my" movie theater – the Lyceum in Red Hook, NY. You can never be too careful! I have to say that I do miss going to 3D movies now.

I also learned from Josephine that summer heat can be dangerous for the brain-injured. She always reminds us to say indoors, with AC if possible, and to drink lots of water to stay hydrated.

There are many other things I learned from this group and from the other groups I'm going to discuss next. In the next chapter, I will give a long list of things I have learned about how to deal with others who have had brain injuries.

Another group I attend is held at the Albany Medical Center in Albany, NY. This group is for people who either now have or once had a brain tumor. This group has been meeting the first Monday of the month from 5:30-7:00 p.m. Of these three groups, this one is the one I attend the least often, only because I belong to the Dutchess County Scottish Society [DCSS], which happens to meet at the same time. So – each month I alternate between going north from my home to the brain tumor group or going south to the DCSS meeting.

The group in Albany has changed quite a bit since the time I first joined them. Our facilitator then had quite a large turn-out of people who met there. I really enjoyed attending these meetings back then, not only for the delicious snacks we all brought, but because it was very interesting to learn from stories told by others about brain tumors that were removed but then grew back.

Having my tumor grow back is one of my biggest fears. I was told there is an 80% chance it will not grow back, but, of course, as I can be too negative, I focus on the 20% chance that it will….

This group has changed since it now has a new group leader. The attendance has decreased for various reasons. Once, Aiden and I attended and we were the only people there! Dana, our new leader, writes very helpful emails about things to think about, ponder, absorb. I am sad about the members who have since passed away due to the returning of their tumors. Rest in peace, Mark and the others.

One thing that upsets me sometimes when I attend the Albany Med. brain tumor support group meetings is survivor guilt. There are so many people whose brain tumors grow back, and so they don't live to tell their tale….

I feel guilty when I sit there and complain about how different my life is now. But, I still have a life, so who am I to gripe? Widows, widowers, and others attend, and I'm pretty sure they wish their loved ones were still around to moan and groan about how their lives have changed. Instead, these folks are polite and don't tell me to stop. But when I hear one more story of someone's tumor growing again, or worse yet, someone from our group has passed away, I feel so guilty that I survived.

I guess this is just one more example of how we all should enjoy each day, because we have no idea what's just around the corner. When I look at pictures from my life from long ago, I marvel at how much I took for granted, how much time I thought I had to teach, how much I thought I'd do. If I had known then what I know now, I would've enjoyed it all so much more.

I've included at the end of my book a Brain Tumor Vigil that is used every May at these meetings, since May is Brain Tumor Awareness Month.

Another group that I attended regularly is the Brain Injury Support Group at the Poughkeepsie, NY, Galleria Mall. These meetings were held the fourth Saturday of each month, in the Conference Room, near the food court, from 12:30-3:00 p.m. The facilitator's name was Dr. Lois Tannenbaum, and she's another group leader that I have so much respect for. I look up to her so much, I asked her to write the Foreword for this book. [Unfortunately, Lois had to retire early due to her own health issues. I hope this group continues, with the new facilitator, Catie, as well as it did when Lois was running it.]

Lois's style of running a meeting was very similar to how I did it when I was in charge of a committee. She was full of hand-outs and black-and-white examples of how to handle the huge changes in your life.

I listened to many stories from others who attended, and it was mind-boggling to hear them tell of their enormous losses. Some of the people who attended are very upbeat. Some had a difficult time expressing themselves. And, there are some, like me, who were quite agitated by this new life. One person there called herself a "Mess in Motion." That's true for me too.

When I left these meetings each month, I prayed that I could become happier, as a few of the attendees were. I talked to God, while Aiden and I walked to the car. Aiden drove me to most meetings and doctor appointments that were not close by, because I get agitated when I become lost, confused, or late. Doctors still want me to drive one hour or less when I'm by myself.

On the rides home from this meeting, I usually kept quiet – very unusual for me – so I can absorb all that I heard and learned. Lois always had interesting topics and speakers who helped explain things.

One time we group members took a "test" about our negativity. I failed the test miserably, worse than any of the other group members. I thought long and hard about working on how negative I am. I've made some small improvements with that, but I am still working on it....

In the spring of 2015, I met actor Gary Busey at a conference in Albany, NY, about brain injury. He was the keynote speaker of the Brain Injury Association of New York State's annual conference because of his helmet-less 1988 motorcycle accident and, thus, head injury.

As he was speaking, the lunch staff was serving our meals. The clanking of the metal covers to our plates was very loud. Many of us sitting there with our individual brain injuries were struggling to hear him on the microphone.

In true G. B. fashion, Gary let the staff know how annoying it was. Many of us laughed because he had the guts to say what we were thinking. I love that guy! He makes an intense subject (an altered brain) into something humorous!

Gary speaks his mind. Sometimes, it's TMI (Too Much Information), but that's par for the course for brain injury.

He also has enjoyable "Busey-isms." Here are some of my favorites:

Never
Underestimate
The
Spirit

and

Finally
Understanding
Nothing

What's so much FUN to tell you here is that when he was done speaking, he asked if we had any questions. Of course, my hand shot right up and a microphone was handed to me, because we were in a huge room. I told him that I take notes for everything and I couldn't remember what he said FUN stood for.

Before I could finish my question, he interrupted me and asked, "Has anyone ever told you that you talk too fast?" Of course, everyone around me laughed hysterically because they all know me.

He went on to say, "You know, brain-injured people can't process language that fast." This I knew, so I slowed my question down.

Later, we could have our pictures taken with him. I love that picture with him, Dr. Lois Tannenbaum, and me (see my photo section). Right after that, I lost my balance and stepped on his foot. So, he ended our time together with one more funny comment: "Boy, you talk fast and you step on others. I bet you're a piece of work to be around."

He couldn't have said it any better! I love you, man – thanks for helping me enjoy my injured brain!

[And, to prove that there is life after a brain injury, I just read in the paper that Mr. Busey is about to star in an off-Broadway play. I hope I get to attend! Also, comedian Tracy Morgan is back on track with his life after his traumatic brain injury caused by a highway accident. Way to go, guys!]

One of the things that I get out of these support groups is that each of the attendees once had a life that is permanently gone now. We have to pick up the pieces and carry on. That is true for everyone, brain injury or not. None of us gets a life we once expected and/or actually had for a time. That was then; this is now. Dealing with that reality can be very difficult at times. Enjoying the moment is truly necessary in order to have a satisfying life. "Woulda," "coulda," "shoulda" are a waste of time and energy. Get the most out of the here and now. As Amy, a participant in a group, who gave me permission to use her name, said, "Find your pockets of peace." [Easier said than done for some of us with brain injuries.]

Once, I met a woman who told me that after her husband's recent stroke, his behavior toward her changed dramatically. Before the stroke, he was always warm and loving. Since the stroke, she says that he sometimes "throws daggers at my heart" with the mean things he says. I told her she's a beautiful person for staying "in there" with his form of brain injury. I'm not positive, but I think I made her feel just a slight bit better when I said this is a common-type behavioral-change story for someone with an acquired brain injury, because she told me, "thank you" with tears in her eyes after I "filled her in." [Unfortunately, the man I thought was my caregiver was not able to hang in there for me.]

So, to those of you who are also getting those "daggers" from someone you love who is brain-injured, hang in there and try to remember what you love about that person. Remember – the brain injury isn't ALL of that person. [Sadly, this was not the case for my boyfriend. He couldn't "take it" anymore.]

One activity I learned about at Dr. Lois Tannenbaum's support

group was Vision Boards. She gave us construction paper and magazines to cut out sayings and/or pictures to make a Vision Board of what
could help us through our daily struggles.

I cut out words, not pictures, and some of them I list here:
- Remember the moment. Forget the rest.
- Time it right.
- Wake up right.
- I am....

Activities such as this helped me to enjoy our group, but also to
recognize how far I've come in my own behaviors. Lois has also taught
me so many vocabulary words that helped explain why I do the things
I do. One example is the term "emotional dysregulation." It means
that some of us with brain injuries have a difficult time regulating our
emotions.

Lois's example for this was her "illustration" of a pressure cooker.
Handlers have to be careful so the pot doesn't explode. Our caregivers
need to be aware of this.

So, I need to make myself a priority so I can understand what
triggers me, so I can "see" that pressure cooker getting ready to blow.
Hopefully, this will happen more often so that I don't "blow."

Another term that I learned from Lois Tannenbaum's brain injury
support group is "the amygdala hijack."

What she taught us is that once someone who is brain-injured experiences this hijack, the amygdala (the emotional part of the brain)
takes over the neocortex (which is where the thinking takes place), and
therefore intelligence and reasoning "go out the window." Working
memory is lost and adrenaline is pumping. All of this can take 3 to 4
hours to clear up.

This is what happens to me way too often! I become so triggered
by others' insensitive remarks, questions, and/or comments. So, I try
to do what Lois taught us, which is to "freeze." Instead of "fight or

flight," which can cause trouble or safety issues, "freeze" means just to be quiet, stand or sit still, breathe and bring yourself back to a healthier state of mind.

Since she taught our group that, I've used this technique several times: I didn't answer a snotty email to me until I "froze" and could write back without an attitude; I ignored rude customers in the store who were incorrect in what they were saying to each other about another person in line with us all; I just didn't respond at all to someone who said something sexually inappropriate to me when I was out walking my dog; I decided not to take it so personally when a usually-friendly store employee wasn't as pleasant as usual (probably because he was overwhelmed by the owner's changes there). Each time possible, if my feelings have been hurt, I lie down on my Yogibo. [A Yogibo is a fabulous beanbag-like piece of furniture that comes in all shapes, colors, and sizes. It's been my "resting place" many a time!]

I'm sure they'll be tons more "freeze examples" as I compile this book, but I need to finish it up….

So, to wrap up this chapter, I'll list some more things that I learned from Lois:
- March is Brain Injury Awareness Month
- RED (Reactive Emotional Disorder). [I "see red" many times each day as I react to others' actions.]
- Anger meltdowns are hurting my: arteries, digestive system, immune system, and causing headaches and more.
- Seizures can BEGIN 10 years (or more) after a brain injury. [I've heard actual stories like this from others, but it needed to be heard again.]
- Depression can happen with a brain injury. [Luckily, I'm not sad that much. Anger is my "forte."]
- Excessive laughter can take place after a brain injury. [Again, this doesn't usually apply to me, but I've witnessed more than

one caregiver need to remove a brain-injured person from a social setting due to this behavior.]

I've added a section at the end of my book with helpful handouts I received at support groups.

I so appreciate the work Lois Tannenbaum did for those of us who learn best by reading it, not just by listening to it being presented. I re-read many of these handouts to remember something I need to improve at.

I highly recommend you join a good support group near you if brain injury is part of your life. These groups not only help make sense of it all, but you get to be around others with similar experiences.

A hand-out I once received at one of these groups was written by another survivor of brain injury. Her name is Barbara Webster. She's from Massachusetts, and she's written for Brainline.org as well as her own book about her story. Many quotes from this article were helpful. I'm sure her book (*Lost and Found: A Survivor's Guide for Reconstructing Life after a Brain Injury*) will be a valuable read for me when I'm done here.

That excellent website is to help you understand brain injury better. My favorite entry, by another author, was this one, titled "9 Things NOT to Say to Someone with a Brain Injury," but I've listed only the 6 of the 9 that apply to me:
- "You seem fine to me."
- "You're such a grump!"
- "How many times do I have to tell you?"
- "Do you have any idea how much I do for you?"
- "Try to think positively." [Easier said than done with a brain injury that causes rumination (repetitive negative thinking).]
- "You're lucky to be alive."

So – I try each day to be "Teflon" versus "Velcro," as I've heard at these various meetings. Some days are "stickier" than others....

Chapter 15

"How Come You Have a Notebook?" (A Brain Injury List)

Brain injury can lead to many changes in your life. Some of my changes sometimes went unnoticed by others (like my increased sense of smell, sound, and taste). Others were noticed (and commented upon) ....

As a student long ago, I took lots and lots of notes. Back then, it was noticed as a positive thing, because if a fellow student had a question about something taught, I was the one to ask. As a teacher, I took plenty of notes at meetings and other events. If something was said at a meeting, a fellow teacher could, and many times did, later on ask me who said what, when the subject was discussed again.

But now, I'm asked this having-a-notebook question by several people in various locations and situations. Since I'm no longer a student or a teacher, I guess it seems odd to others that I still take fast and furious notes.

I have a notebook for every event I attend. That means notebooks go to doctor appointments with me, to church, to special celebrations and events, etc., etc. I even have scribble pads in my car, so when something pops into my head, I jot it down at the next stop before I forget.

This is one of my many coping mechanisms for my brain injury. That's the way I function better and get things accomplished. I spend lots of money on Post-it notes, small pads, journals, and notebooks. This system works for me.

But, as in anything you do that others don't do, it is questioned. At Christmastime 2014, I was at a beautiful church gathering to hear a wonderful woman sing and talk about her life. The group was sponsored by our church's WOW– Women of the Word. It was a Christmas celebration, and the church was decorated beautifully. Women from all age brackets attended, including little girls and teenagers, too.

This would be the kind of event that most people would just sit back and listen to. Not me – I took out my "church notebook" and began to scribble the date (Saturday, December 6, 2014). This woman next to me, Barbara, a pleasant person whom I've known for many years in various settings, asked me the question that I have titled this chapter with, "How come you have a notebook?"

That got me thinking: *that will be the name of the chapter in which I list all the things that I have learned about brain injury, since my injury.* The population at large needs to be more sensitive to those of us with this "invisible disability," as it is referred to at the support groups I attend with others who have also experienced changes in their lives due to some brain trauma. More than one of us have been asked something like, "Why don't you work? You look fine."

Barbara's notebook question actually helped me, because it pointed out clearly how others want to understand my behavior but somehow, sometimes, don't know how to ask. She was wise enough to see my reaction and said something in addition to reduce my obvious agitation at having my "unusual" behavior pointed out. She has heard my testimony at church and probably has read my entries in our church's prayer chain, but still – clarity for behaviors that stand out as different is needed, so here we go....

If you're reading this book because someone you know has had a brain injury, then you probably already know that each brain-injured person is different. Someone once described it as being like snowflakes – no two brain injuries are the same. As Dr. Lois Tannenbaum states, "If you have seen one brain injury, you have seen one brain injury."

That's why this list of things that have gone on with me since my tumor was removed and since I learned that I have permanent brain damage is just that: things that have gone on with ME. Some of this list will pertain to other brain-injured people. Some will not.

The point is: please be sensitive to anyone whose life has been altered this way. It's hard enough for the person to accept the changes. It's even harder when loved ones, friends, and others don't get it....

Some people with brain injuries may look normal, with excellent vocabularies, but you don't know what is bubbling right under the surface.

I face challenges from other people every day because I look like them and I talk like them, but what is not noticeable until you "push my buttons" is what's brewing right beneath the surface in my brain. I rarely get to turn off my brain's hyperactivity and get to rest, so I'm thinking, thinking, thinking all the time. Sometimes this is helpful, but many times, it is not!

I've had too many meltdowns to count! These displays of bad behavior have taken place in lots of settings – restaurants, doctor appointments, vet appointments, church. Yes – even in church. There are some folks in these places who trigger me.

What's truly upsetting is that, though I have a letter from my neurologist, Dr. Tamai, which I show to tons of people, I still am not understood. Sometimes I'm so triggered by others who rush me, I forget to show them the letter.

My doctor-written medical description about my tumor-caused injury is stated as "non-traumatic," but believe me, there is plenty of trauma involved with a life that's changed forever due to anything that's taken place in your brain.

The "non-traumatic" wording is the medical definition of what has happened to me. The BIANYS (Brain Injury Association of New York State), when I attended a conference they held the spring of 2014, reminded me that "A" stands for "Acquired." Though these conferences had been held for many years before my first attending, I only learned of them after my brain surgery. What's ironic about that sentence is that I was a special education teacher and actually had students with TBI, but I didn't know much about brain injury back then.

And that's why I decided to write this book. It became quite clear to me that much is not known by the public about this condition. I'm quite sure that some of the things I outline here about brain injury will have some family member somewhere say, "That's why Uncle So-and-so behaved like that. Remember all the hits to his head he took? He probably had a brain injury, but we never knew that back then."

That's what I'm hoping for with all of this work – that one family/workplace/church/etc. learns something here that helps that group forgive someone whose behavior may have disrupted the wellness for other group members.

My mother has said to me more than once that maybe my brain tumor was there for much of my teaching career so I could spend the second half of my life teaching others about something it caused. I know that the behavior modification techniques that I used in the various schools I taught in, I now use on myself each day. I know for a fact that I taught MANY students who were better behaved than I have been post-surgery. I may look "normal," and I have an excellent vocabulary, but that is only the "surface."

So – the following long list is the things I've compiled that are attributed to my brain injury. Many of the items on this list are experienced by others with whom I attend support groups for the brain-injured. I had many folks there read my lists and check off whether they had experienced the same things I had. Of course, this is not a comprehensive list. This is MY list with feedback from others. As was stated already, no two brain injuries are identical. But – this is what I know so far about this "invisible disability".... [I've added some words about certain ones here from the checklists I wrote that other brain-injured people reviewed. I wish I could list all the things others added to my lists, but this book is so big already!]

- **Impulsivity:** It leads to problems later on sometimes. I ought to "think it through" first. I've made many bad decisions impulsively. I do not think things through clearly enough before I speak and/or take action. One unsafe, impulsive decision I've made too many times is to cross my nearby train tracks when the red lights begin to flash. This is a STUPID decision, and I NEVER did that before my brain was injured. I had much more common sense pre-brain-damage. When I was honest, and I told Aiden what I'd done, I got scolded once more. The only time I do this is when I'm alone in the car, I'm completely safe when I'm driving with my dog or other people. [Many people in the support groups I participate in said that impulsivity was a problem for them, too.]
- **Stress:** It happens WAY more often now. All of this increased stress has led to ulcers in my esophagus and stomach, according to my gastroenterologist. [Again, a majority in the support groups agreed stress was a problem.]
- **Overwhelmed:** When slight pressure is on, it feels much heavier. I ought to do less. I constantly agree to do something without thinking it through. I easily become overwhelmed by multiple things that are taking place at the same time. For example – if I run the sink water to wash some dishes, and at the same time a clock is letting me know by its song that it's the new hour, and the phone rings, I answer the phone and forget that the sink is filling up. I have flooded my kitchen by being overwhelmed like that! That same "overwhelmed" happened a few times at my stove. I started three minor fires, and when I told that to my doctors, they suggested I stop cooking until I

can do better. I live in a condo, and, therefore, if I started a fire, I would hurt others also.

- **Irritability:** I am so much grouchier since my brain injury occurred. I'm not saying that I wasn't ever grouchy before, but nowadays I'm WAY too easily triggered by others' insensitive comments, sarcasm, rudeness, selfishness, inability to let me vent, *etc.* For example – one of the problems I have with MANY people is that when I am venting about something I'm upset about, they automatically give me the other side's opinion before I even calm down. I call my venting "verbal vomit," and if they would just let me get it out, I'd feel better. Instead, they offer other viewpoints immediately. If they just waited, I would be able to discuss it better. When someone is actually puking, do you let them get it out, or do you offer them food??? I think you get the idea….

- **Memory:** I forget repeatedly every single day. I forget things that shouldn't ever be easily forgotten at my age such as: Did I brush my teeth? Did I lock the car? Did I pay that bill? And so on. I have piles galore of dates and things to remember. This forgetfulness is very dangerous in the kitchen preparing food – so, as I stated already, I don't cook. Some people comment how well I remember dates. It's because of how many places I jot them down so I won't forget them. Also – I forget names of people ALL the time. I really hate that! I have forgotten my purse many places. I do remember things if I have lots of lists. Unfortunately, there are chunks of my life I have forgotten. People have to fill me in about some parts of it. I have HUGE deficits in my memory nowadays. Many people compare themselves to me with sentences like, "I forget all the time." But, what they don't realize is how it literally brings me to tears when I can't remember something simple like a computer password that I've used for several years. (And I only have two passwords to memorize.) I used to remember SO much more than I can now. To go from an excellent memory to forgetting many simple things every single day is very upsetting. I also forget the names of family members, friends, pets, *etc.* [In one support group, 9 out of 9 people identified this as a problem. In the second group I polled, 14 out of 14 did, too.]

- **Repeats:** When I have to do something that I tend to forget, I say a phrase repeatedly in my head so I get it right. Recently, I was at a brunch and the tea I ordered came not in a tea bag, but loose, and had to be strained. The last time I was at this restaurant, I repeatedly forgot to use the strainer with each teacup I refilled, so I had loose tea floating in my cup repeatedly. When I went back and tried stating to myself, "Janet, use the strainer," I got it correct in three out of four attempts. To the naked eye, I'm enjoying a sip of tea. What's really "brewing" is my angry thoughts that I'm way too young to have so many memory problems! I also play the "repeat game" when someone wants me to remember his or her name. The other day, I was at a *Bible* study, and a woman asked me if I remembered her name. I didn't, so she told me it, and then I said it over and over more than 100 times in my head so the next time I saw her (a few days later), I was able to call her by name. I'm proud not to have become offended by her question and to have found a method to remember names. But, as I write this, I can't remember her name!

- **Sensory overload:** I can't have loud sounds anywhere around me when I'm doing anything. Loud drums, someone whistling, snapping gum, or clicking a pen is so painful. Also – flashing lights, certain perfumes or candle smells, spicy foods (and so much more) hurt my head. I can only be in a bowling alley for a couple of minutes due to how loud it is. Once, I had to leave the gas station because their pumps had a TV broadcast playing the news, and I couldn't hear myself think as I tried to pump gas. I have to look away (if I'm not the driver) when

I see cops put on their lights to pull a car over. The lights are excruciating. I have to wear sunglasses in certain places due to lighting. I've also had to wear sunglasses indoors because I cried so hard that I've lost all of my mascara. I've been teased about my indoor sunglasses, which makes it more embarrassing. A couple of questions I find particularly annoying are, "Do you think you're a superstar?" and/or "Why do you think you need sunglasses inside?" I don't know if these questions irritate others with brain injury who need to wear shades indoors, but they sure do aggravate me! Do I ask you, "Why are you covered in tattoos?" or "Why do you dress like that?" (Which could be said to the two people who recently asked me these sunglasses questions.) Leave others alone unless you have a meaningful question. These types of questions, in my opinion, are sarcastic, immature, and just plain rude. I've had to leave restaurants because of the loud clinking of silverware, plates, instruments being played, etc. As I heard on the National Geographic Channel's show *Brain Games*, New York City's Times Square is "sensory overload on steroids!" That is 100% accurate for the brain-injured! Any time I visit there, I have to go somewhere quiet, such as a restroom, so I can decompress. Times Square is a great place to be, but only in small segments of time. These are just some examples. I could list tons more! I strongly recommend to the brain-injured, that after a very busy day (such as my trips to NYC's NYU Langone Medical Center), take the next day off. Plan nothing and rest, because the brain needs at least a day to recuperate from the over-stimulation. [Again, agreed to by majorities in these groups.]

- **Sensitivity:** This means that I'm overly sensitive of words and actions as well as lighting, noise, smell and on and on and on. I use earplugs for loud church services with drums and in noisy stores. I have to leave certain restaurants which have strong food smells – for example, St. Patrick's Day servings of corned beef and cabbage. (The only reason I went was because Aiden enjoyed that menu choice.) This sensitivity list could go on for pages! Just know that I once had to put my head down and block my nose, eyes, and ears at a concert with four drum sets being played simultaneously while strobe lights were blinking and incense filled the air. I was crying because it was a warm-up band for the artist I was really there to hear perform. My seat was so close to the stage, it would have been very difficult to exit politely. In the old days, I would have enjoyed the warm-up group. Instead, I was practically curled up in a fetal position on the floor in front of my seat so I could later listen to the music I came for. Looking like that in front of others was embarrassing to me and not understood by the folks who stared and giggled. Also, I tear up at the simplest of experiences, like: little animals scurrying across the road so they don't get hit, TV commercials, a baby smiling at me, certain songs in church or on the radio, someone teasing me, abruptness from someone's tone of voice, Mother's Day since I'm not a mommy or a grandma (or when I'm in a group of women and all they talk about is their children). Speaking of grandmas – once I teared up at a brunch that served sausage that tasted just like Grandma McColl's did. It was something I had only tasted when she cooked. I wept and wept over missing all of my grandparents. I was supposed to be enjoying a brunch. The tears there, and many other places, lead to lots of mascara purchases. This is another list that could go on and on…. [Again, a majority of those in the groups surveyed agreed.]

- **Smells:** Smells are overly powerful to me. Once, when I was almost at the completion of this chapter, my landlord came over to paint my screen door. The fumes were so powerful, I had immediate, very painful headaches two days in a row after he was done each day. This never used to happen before my brain injury. It's just one more example of how life is permanently different in ways that others wouldn't even notice. I had to take several Extra-Strength Tylenols to feel better, and leave my own place to write this, all for a neighborhood improvement.

- **3-D:** I learned at a brain-injury support group (and then checked with my neurologist for confirmation) that I shouldn't ever use 3-D glasses. They can cause seizures for the brain-injured even years later. I shared that information with my favorite movie theater (the Lyceum in Red Hook, NY). Learning this information first from a support group rather than from a doctor's office is another reason why I decided to write this book. I thought maybe my experiences could help other families.

- **Money skills:** I really struggle with counting out money, over-spending when unnecessary, and anything that relates to being money-wise. I've been teased about this by some adults who should know better, which hurts my feelings. On the other hand, at a local nail salon in my mall, two former students of mine that I bumped into had to help me pay for my appointment because I gave the cash register girl the wrong amount. My students and I laughed when one of them said, "Aren't you the one who taught us money skills?" Yes, A., I was! I have a difficult time with my checking account. Sometimes, I will write a check for $38.00, but record it as $18.00, so I am off by $20.00. I have to check and re-check every check I write. I was never great with managing my money. But, before I was on disability, I didn't have to be so careful. I made a teacher's salary, and since I had no children of my own to support, I wasn't as financially tested as I am nowadays. Back then, I could spend what I wanted on trips to Disney World, dinners out, students' birthday parties celebrated in school, *etc*. But now I have to be way more careful, and I'm really not too good at that. I had been building a savings account from my very first jobs back in high school (the Greig Farm in Red Hook, NY, and Four Brothers Pizza in Rhinebeck, NY). Most of that life savings is gone now.

Not all of it was spent on help for my behavior after the brain surgery, but the majority of it was. I'll explain more about that in the chapter about help I've received. Over-spending on others and on my version of retail therapy, "stress shopping," is another part of my story.... What also is a large problem for me is counting out change. I count quarters, dimes, nickels, and pennies very slowly when I'm at a cash register. Most of the clerks are patient with me. Unfortunately, lots of people in the lines behind me in various stores are not so patient. Once I was in line at Adams Fairacre Farms in Kingston, NY. I could not get the change counted quickly enough for the woman waiting to have her groceries rung up right after me. She said something really snotty and then bragged about being a teacher. I certainly hope she treats her students with better correcting skills. Her rudeness made me thank the clerk, Amanda Quick, because she was kind and patiently helped me.

- **Balance:** Walking down stairs frequently requires holding onto the rail. If there is none, I hold on to someone's arm. At church, if I sing on a set of movable stairs, I stand by the railing and ask nice women to help me step down when our song is over. (Thanks, Anne, Rita, Christy, Nancy, Sandy, and Marian!) I have fallen many times in various places. Once, I fell down a flight of stairs at Aiden's house when I was sent there from one of his hospital stays to gather his stuff. I trip over things practically daily. I can't ride a bike anymore. I have to sit to get dressed each day, since I fell too many times putting pants on while standing, like I used to be able to do. Going up a flight of stairs is fine, but I have to remember to stop climbing on benches or chairs to hang stuff. I've lost my balance too many times doing this. I need a "spotter" when there's a job like that to be done. A subscription I read regularly, *Neurology Now: Your Trusted Source for Brain Health,* had an article by Amy Paturel, MS, MPH, with an excellent quote: "Balance and coordination rely on high-level thinking,…, memory, and response time. As that declines…because of a neurologic condition, balance becomes even more compromised." [About half of the groups' members had a problem with balance.]

- **Overly-observational:** I notice so much more than I ever did. Usually, this is unnecessary (such as people's mistakes), and it annoys others if I comment. I point out clothing tags sticking out of a woman's collar. Some women are appreciative of this, so they're not advertising their size. Another way this habit was helpful once was the day I followed a school bus that had a left brake light not working. I pulled up beside the driver, and she warmly thanked me for noticing the defective light.

- **Comprehension:** When others speak too quickly at a drive-thru or on my answering machine or over the phone, I have to ask them to slow down their rapid-fire speech so I can understand them. This is ironic, considering how fast I talk. But, speaking and listening are very different. The medical term for the condition I have is "receptive aphasia." This fast-talking, slow-listening condition of certain people with brain injury annoys people who do not understand it. When I attend meetings or visit certain doctors' offices, the quick speech of others makes me confused much of the time. I talk fast but I process slow. I speak at a very fast pace, but I comprehend much, much slower! I have to take notes for everything to be able to absorb it and remember it later. Back before my tumor was growing, I was such a fast talker that one of my favorite high school teachers, Mr. Fish, nicknamed me "Rapid." I talk that way again now, but when that tumor was very large and undiagnosed, I slurred my speech and spoke very slowly. Nowadays, I wish others would speak slower to me so I could understand their words better. I also wish people who leave messages on my answering machine would speak slower, because when they don't, I have to replay them over and over to get what I'm being told.

Also, I really wish people would be friendlier to me when they are telling me that I talk fast. And, there are some concepts that I am slow to understand. For example, Aiden had to explain to me five years in a row, as we travelled there, why Red Hook's Apple Blossom Day was in the spring and not in the fall. I kept thinking apples are picked in the fall, so why is this celebration in the spring? Finally, I understood the "blossoms" part of his explanation.

- **Sequencing:** I have to do the same thing over and over the same way, or I get completely mixed up. I do not react well to "curveballs," which is common for everyday life experiences. Everything must be in ABC/123 order, or I become easily up-set and/or confused. I'm a creature-of-habit: each day, I have to do the same thing to begin my day. First, I drive out to get my coffee and newspapers before I can do anything else. Any time this pattern is changed (like a snow day when roads are treacherous), I'm "off" for the rest of the day! I sit in the same place in church each time. Change is very difficult for the brain-injured.

- **Calendar skills:** I carry around a thick calendar where I paper-clip in important things I have to do. This is the way I remember important information. It's also the way I've been teased and/or questioned by so many others. If it works for me, why does it matter to you? I have calendars all around my condo. I've donated a few to my church each year also.

- **Literalness:** I have a very difficult time understanding analogies, jokes, newspaper political cartoons, pronouns, and any other conversation that isn't exactly point-blank specific. I literally take everything literally! I minored in English for my bachelor's degree. I used to be excellent at understanding, and also teaching, analogies. Nowadays, though, I scramble for meaning when anyone uses an analogy, in either written or spoken form, although written is easier for me, because I can go over it again and again until I "get it".... When someone says an analogy quickly, I usually just scribble it down and try to figure it out later when it is quieter. One time a written analogy escaped me when I was shopping in a lovely store in Woodstock, NY, called Lotus. It's owned by Jamie, the daughter of my friend Suzi. Jamie had to help me understand a sign in her store. It read, "A closed mouth gathers no feet." I stood there reading it over and over and over and could not get what it meant. I finally asked her to explain it, and in a soft, gentle way (just like her mother's), she did. I bought the sign because it is so true; *i.e.*, open mouth, insert foot.... I added it to the over 200 other signs I have around my home that help me learn, think, smile, giggle, pray, laugh, and hang on. And, those signs are joined by magnets, pillows, frames, calendars and so on that also have words on them to help me get better. I read them often, even when I'm dusting them. I have chapters here about these furnishings.

- **Schedules:** I am ruled by timing. Any change in a routine is very difficult and nerve-wracking for me. I always was organized, before I was sick, but now I border on obsessive. For example, if a dinner date is changed to lunchtime, I become all flustered, because I have to be there way earlier. I'm driven by the clock. If I go to a place to meet regularly and there's no clock in the room, I go shopping and install my own clock so I can feel more comfortable there in the future. Because of this, I've dubbed myself "the clock police." I am constantly checking the clock wherever I am to keep on schedule. In my condo, I have 12 clocks! One of them is a waterproof Mickey Mouse clock for the shower. I've donated seven clocks to my church for rooms I'm in for *Bible* studies, volunteering, etc. All of these clocks make for "some fun" in the spring and fall when it's time to spring forward or fall back one hour. On a typical Sunday, I get to church 30 minutes before the service begins so I can get "settled in" and read the bulletin, put money in an envelope, donate baked-by-someone-else goodies, etc. On those clock-setting days, I arrive 40 to 45 minutes early because I have lots to do with those extra clocks. I'm not quite sure what this is all about. I just know I wasn't like that before my brain was damaged. I've actually dubbed myself a "clock freak." One of my clocks plays "Amazing Grace" every daylight hour. This helps keep me calm. I sure do spend a lot on batteries! [I have to add a thank-you to Chris, whom I had just met, who tried to fix this broken clock for me, and when he could not, he bought me a new one!] This is a very difficult way to live, because changes in schedule happen all the time. I need to learn to "go with the flow," as my cousin Lauren wrote on her emails, but this is truly a difficulty for me. I get teased by some people for being early to functions, which I like to be to get comfortable before the activity begins. Teasing doesn't go over well with me. [Scheduling difficulties were reported by a majority of the members of the groups.]

- **Easily lost:** When I drive myself to a place I've never been to before, I get lost so easily. I'm constantly making dangerous U-turns to get back to the place I missed. This happened the day I met my editor for our very first appointment. Aiden was supposed to take me to the Orange County Chamber of Commerce building (where the appointment was scheduled for), but he had been in the ER until 4 a.m. the night before. So – even though I only had two hours of sleep myself, I ventured out. I got lost more than five times. Joggers, dog-walkers, teenagers with cell phones, a police department, and a doctor's office had to help me arrive on time. I made it, but what an experience! I told most of those helpers that I would thank them one day. So – here it is – to the folks in Orange County in the fall of 2014 who led me to my editor, thank you! [GPS annoys me – if you were wondering why I don't use that.]

- **Driving:** It's still quite amazing to me that I drove MANY years with an undiagnosed brain tumor. Think about how many accidents I **could** have caused but didn't! I drove my "Mickey Mobile" (a yellow Saturn purchased because of its color, to match Mickey Mouse's feet) when the tumor was growing larger and larger. I became so attached to this car that I drove it until it literally died in a busy intersection on a bustling Friday afternoon. I cried when the mechanic said he wouldn't take my money to fix it one more time. The tears were because I knew my Mickey Mobile "took care of me," when I now realize that I should not have been driving! The only accidents I ever had was when I backed up three different times and I tore the right mirror off the car. One boyfriend (Jim) fixed it the first time, and then the next boyfriend (Aiden) fixed it the second and the third. Describing the time spent in my car reminds me that I bought the car in 2000 (before I even met Jim). I had that Saturn for 15 years, longer than all of my romantic relationships! I owned a Saturn long after that company folded. I know that I'm still lousy with directions, but when I drove the Mickey Mobile while I had the tumor, I was SO confused that people had to lead me out of new locations so I could get to a main road. That gradually helped me navigate many small trips I took for birthday parties, housewarmings, baby showers, *etc.* Because the Mickey Mobile was so recognizable, being bright yellow, I ruined a couple of surprise parties because as soon as the special guest arrived at his or her party, he or she knew something was up once seeing my unusual car in the parking lot. (Nowadays, there are more yellow cars on the road than there were back then.) After those ruined surprises happened a couple of times, I began to park it in the back of establishments and walked through back entrances so no more party planners could be upset with me for ruining their hard work at providing the surprise. So, R.I.P., my Mickey (218,000 miles)

Mobile. Thank you for keeping me safe all of those years when I drove, though some days I had no idea where I was, due to the tumor. I know God was in the passenger seat all along.…

- **Dropsies:** I drop things repeatedly. Sometimes, this can be really messy! Once, before I knew this would become an everyday occurrence, I dropped a full cup of soda in a computer store. The staff was pretty upset. When I had just picked up my new-for-me (i.e., used) Subaru, I spilled a container of milk in it. Ugh! Drinks and so much more get dropped by me daily. As I wrote this, I stopped counting at 10 dropped items for just today.

- **Catastrophizing:** I make most things bigger than they actually are. I create a "bigger picture" of something than is actually taking place. I learned this word at one of my brain-injury support group meetings.

- **No filter:** I don't "watch" what I'm saying in certain situations. Once, at a church's clothing giveaway, I was talking about my boobs. I embarrassed some of the church ladies around me. Some things are better left unsaid. Many people have told me, "You've lost your filter!"

- **Naps/rest:** I need to "turn off my brain" at least once each day. At the beginning (meaning right after my surgery), I needed two-to-three-hour naps daily. Now, 30-60 minutes is enough to recharge. On a very busy day, when I skip this, I "pay for it" later with bad behavior noticed by others. My absolute best "thinking time" is early in the morning. Before my brain tumor, I used to take naps every once in a while. Nowadays, they are absolutely necessary in order for me to decompress. I'm an early-riser (5:30-6:00 a.m.) and get most of my "thinking activities," such as banking, calls, chores, *etc.*, done in the morning. By afternoon, my brain needs recharging. These naps are the ticket to being able to do anything in the evening. On the days I miss one, I'm in bed by 8-8:30 p.m. Even on the days I have a nap, I'm still turning off the lights and heading to bed around 9-9:30 p.m. This seems very early to others who like to make late evening phone calls. But, for me, it's necessary so I can accomplish anything the next day, especially since I often get up for an hour or two in the middle of the night, due to restlessness, stress, and over-thinking. [Naps and/or rests are needed by a majority in the groups.]

- **Dizziness:** If I close my eyes for too long (like at a prayer time in church), I feel wibbly-wobbly. I have to remember to pray with my eyes open or I feel like I'm being moved. Washing my hair in the shower has led to many falls into the wall since I have to shut my eyes. I can also feel dizzy in an over-stimulated environment like a crowded mall.

- **Misplacements:** I continually put items away in incorrect places. I've found my hairbrush in my toothbrush holder (and then vice versa). This makes me miss my Grandma Johnson, because I remember a story my dad used to tell us about how his mother accidentally put a loaf of bread under his bed, so he thought about this and went and found his sneakers in the breadbox. I've often found things I thought were long gone.

- **Write incorrectly:** When I'm scribbling down directions to something, I write what pops into my head sometimes instead of what I was told. So – if a doctor's practice is at more than one location, I've gone to the wrong one and then have had to get back in my car to drive to the right spot. This is unnerving if it makes me late. I've written down someone's address incorrectly numerous times also.

- **Sign-checker:** I'm constantly reading signs as I drive or as I'm driven places. Once, when our church sign announcing our start time of 9:30 a.m. was changed to 9:25, I was obsessed with finding out why. The secretary, Julie, told me no one else had mentioned it. I wondered if anyone else even noticed it. But of course, I did, and then I talked about it with lots of folks, including the man who changed it. I've noticed misspellings on LOTS of signs. (For example, "meader" for "meter," "Veterns" for "Veterans" – on a school sign! Happy "Valentin's" Day for "Valentine's," "Wensday" for "Wednesday," and, oh, so much more!)

- **Flooded:** There are times when my brain becomes so overloaded with information, I literally have to sit down in a quiet place and "shut down." I've done this at church in a nursery room with a calming rocking chair (when the room is empty). I learned at a support group for brain injury that this is called being "flooded."

- **Heightened awareness:** Things no one else notices (like someone spelling their own first name incorrectly on an email), I notice. I'm super-aware of way too much unimportant information.

- **Food sensations:** Certain foods really hurt my head when I eat them. I have to chew popcorn on the right side of my mouth, because chewing it on the left side (where the tumor was) is so loud, it hurts! The same is true with potato chips or any really crunchy food. Hot tea or an ice-cold soda sends a sharp wave of pain up the left side of my face, and it actually stings. I literally can feel it for seconds.

- **Aphasia:** A loss or impairment of language, affecting speech, reading, and/or writing, resulting from brain damage. I often say the wrong word with the same first letter. When I was in the early stages of recovery, I didn't notice the mistakes I made. Others had to say, "What does that mean?" when I said the wrong word. But, now, I do notice and once in a while – it's funny. One day as I volunteered at my church with a small group of four-year-olds, a little girl came up to show me a cut on her finger. I incorrectly said to her, "Do you need a Band-Aid for that BOOBIE?" (I meant to say, "BOO-BOO.") Her retort was priceless! "I'm only four years old. I don't have boobies yet." I laughed and went to tell the pastor my mistake. Her mother thought the whole thing was cute. Another humorous example is: once, when I was volunteering to park cars at a stadium while there was a DRUM and bugle corps competition going on, two police officers pulled into the parking lot. I leaned into their police car's window and asked, "Are you here for the DRUGS and bugles?" Both officers chuckled as I explained that I meant to say "DRUMS." One of the officers asked, "Are there drugs here today?" I smiled, and I have told that story a million times since. There are other times since then that my incorrect words are very embarrassing. Once, I called a restaurant "Two Butts" instead of "Two Boots," when I spoke about it to a group of people. Another time, when I was explaining to a group of friends what I didn't like about someone, I said, "despise" instead of "dislike." They all were upset with me before I could explain that I had used the wrong word. Cut me some slack, girls, please! Since my brain injury, I'm not always able to think of the correct word when I am speaking. People love to "fill-in-the-blank" for me, which can really be annoying, since what they state may or may not be what I'm trying to express. This causes lots of confusion in social settings! Please, folks, let us with brain injuries speak for ourselves, even if that means you have to be more patient with us as we struggle to say just the right word. And I'm not the only one with aphasia. My friend Jeanne, who is not brain-injured and is mentioned here in other places, was in charge of a women's church fundraiser. When she was auctioning off "Santa's Lucky Tin," she said, "Satan's." Everyone cracked up, including me, because I knew I'd be adding it here. It's reassuring when others who do not have a brain injury say the wrong words, too! [Many in the support groups reported this as a problem.]

- **Overly-talkative:** As my mother has told me many times, I "came out talking," but now, I talk even more in almost every situation. This gets really annoying for most people involved in my life. They don't understand that my brain injury makes it hard for me to control this. Also, I've witnessed first-hand the over-talking done by others with brain injuries. [But, a funny story is this one: recently, I was VERY nervous about volunteering to teach preschoolers for the first time at my church. As I began to teach a lesson about how God loves us and sent His Son, four-year-old Jack blurted out, "You use too many words. Talk less!" I cracked up laughing and knew that this was a present from God, to reduce my nervousness. There are MANY people that wish they had the courage Jack had to tell me that. "Out of the mouths of babes…."]

- **Violent:** This is an extremely difficult one to not only admit to, but also have to write about. The reason I chose to include it (vs. covering it up by not listing it here), is because I really do want to help other families who are dealing with their own personal brain-injury stories. So – here goes: I've thrown and broken many items including: cell phones, a computer, glasses with liquids in them, TV remotes, and on and on. I don't handle what others email or text very well sometimes. My anger level gets so hot over the least little thing and/or the big things that take place in life. I've smashed a window, grabbed keys out of a moving car, and caused other dangerous escapades. Luckily, I've never hurt myself or anyone else in my path, but that behavior is still so wrong. As I've stated here already, many of my former students didn't behave this uncontrollably. And, I'm very proud to state that these violent outbursts have ceased. I pray to God each night at bedtime to thank Him for none that day, and for no more tomorrow. I've never been aggressive with children around. They keep me calm all the time. Only adults "push my buttons." [I was reluctant to ask about this in the support groups, but suffice it to say, I witnessed it on more than one occasion at the various meetings I attended.]

- **Overly-generous:** This may seem like a good thing (giving to others less fortunate), but as I stated here about my difficulties with managing money, this is one of the reasons why, for a long time after my surgery, I handed $20 bills to numerous "homeless" people I saw. Turns out, some of them weren't actually homeless. I've purchased expensive presents for someone when spending a lot was unnecessary. I used to pay for a $6 lunch voluntary-donation meal with a $20 bill and donated all the rest. I could list more and more examples of this, but it's very hard to write about because it's one of the reasons I have very little savings anymore. I even had to see someone to help me learn how to be better with money. Though I've curbed this one a lot, I still need to improve. We'll see....

- **Dentist appointments:** I never really liked these trips to have teeth work done (does anyone?), but now they are extremely frightening. I have become so scared and uncomfortable there, I've pushed that metal tray and knocked things over. Again, this childlike behavior is difficult to understand, but I do know that when anyone works on the left side of my mouth (the side where the tumor was and where anesthesia left part of my upper lip numb permanently), I am in a lot of mouth pain, and the noise in my head is excruciating. If the staff is "warm and fuzzy" with me, I do better. When anyone there is gruff, I'm gruffer. I used to take anti-anxiety meds before I went so there were no more dental tools flying. Aiden used to drive me to and from all dentist appointments. Now, I drive myself, so no meds can be taken.

- **Coping mechanisms:** Due to all of the things I've listed here, I have a very difficult time coping with my life as it is now. I have an extremely hard time laughing things off or dismissing things so they don't fester too long in my head. Things that I used to be good at, I struggle with daily, and that makes the journey of life pretty hard most of the time. I've aged cognitively prematurely and lost many of my former abilities.

- **Teasing:** I do not enjoy anyone teasing me anymore. I used to be able to decipher someone's words better, before my brain injury. Nowadays, I'm never really sure what someone is "getting at," since I am very literal. Someone might say something that's meant in jest, but I take it personally and then go over and over it my head silently hours later. I also don't care for it when people state, "I'm just kidding you," when really they are teasing but trying to make it sound "better." Once, when I was in a group setting, a professional who should have known better told others not to sit near me because "Janet's trouble." I can't express enough how teasing does not make the other person feel good. I cried when I went home, even though it was probably meant to be funny. [And, this is bothersome to the majority I polled in my support groups.]

- **Arrivals/Departures:** It seems like in this too-fast world we now live in, practically everyone wants something done immediately. This is very difficult sometimes if you've experienced a brain injury. I need time to get "settled in" in a setting outside of my own home. I don't need to hear things like "she's here – everyone sit at the table for soup," when I arrive for a holiday meal EARLY and haven't even put my purse or bag down – or even taken off my coat! This actually did happen and that triggered me to be rude to that hostess when I spoke to her nephew about her, which was inappropriate on my part, but it was because I felt she had rudely dealt with me, as so many people do when they don't have the patience to wait. All of this applies to departures as well. I need to gather my belongings in silence so I don't forget anything. When someone wanted to talk to me when it was convenient for them only, I've often left my jacket, purse, etc., behind and then have had to travel back to the setting to, hopefully, find what I forgot. Luckily, nothing has ever been taken/stolen from me. I need the quiet space to pack up.

- **Clutter:** I always used to have piles of things, both at home and in my classrooms. But, since my brain injury, I clutter more now. Part of that is because of this book: there's references, books, scribbled chapters, and oh, so much more all over the place. But, some of the clutter is not related at all to the book. As I heard at one of my support groups, we, the brain-injured, hold onto more since we've lost so much. Hearing that helped me because I felt relief that it's not just me. Many of the items in the clutter are there to remind me of something I don't want to forget.

- **Numbers:** I hit the wrong phone numbers and push the wrong buttons on my calculator. This had led to calls to the wrong people and incorrect banking.

- **Note-taking:** So, I'm going to end this chapter where it began. I have so many notebooks in so many shapes and sizes, I'm lucky I remember where I keep them all. But, this habit has helped me so many times since my brain injury, because they "represent" my memory. I can "look something up" when I need to remember important information. I record daily to-do lists, and this is one of the ways that I arrive at the places I do on the correct dates. It's also the way I get everyday chores completed. Something as simple as remembering to brush my dog's teeth each day (to help with tartar buildup), has to be written down; otherwise, I forget to do it. I put hours and hours into prepping for each day. The only thing I always remember to do, without a reminder, is to pray to God.

So – I have to learn new skills to deal with my damaged brain, as do all the other brain-injured folks. Others in our lives have to learn how to tolerate our various behavioral changes.

This list was MY list. I'm quite sure each person who has experienced a brain injury has some things to add or delete from it. I know that we all need way more patience from the people in our lives that care for us. Remember – it's hard for us to navigate the changes. It is harder if we're not met with loving kindness from our loved ones.

A quote I borrowed from one of my favorite TV shows, NBC's *Chicago Med*, stated, "Why is it brain injuries are never like you read in the textbooks?" How true! That's why this book was needed to be written by someone who's experienced it, not by someone who's only come in contact with it.

As also stated on that TV show, and confirmed by my doctors, the frontal lobe controls behavior and judgment. Since my damage is there, that's the reason for some things listed here. I know that sometimes I am overbearing to be around. But, I do have a warm heart that truly wants to get better and behave more appropriately. I just pray that happens sooner than later. Writing this book has helped me somewhat with that because I've seen how far I've actually come.

[I need it noted here that I diligently wrote this section of this chapter with a gash in my head after I bumped into an electric meter. I was in pain, but still did my "homework" for my editor.]

Also – some of the items on this list took place before my brain injury, but now they are exacerbated. Though the brain tumor caused the obsessive-compulsive disorder behavior of mysophobia, and the surgery to remove the tumor also took away my unusual fear of germs, what has lasted is some OCD behaviors, as I'm sure you could figure out from this list. But, as always, I'll be eternally grateful to God that I'm here to tell the story....

Chapter 16

CONCUSSIONS AND MORE...

I'M NOT GOING to write a lot about concussions, because this book has become way longer than I expected it would be at the beginning of this "project," but suffice it to say, that there's plenty of information out there about how concussions can lead to dangerous consequences.

I've seen newspaper and magazine articles, movies, and news reports about this form of brain injury. Please don't "brush it off" as minor, because the effects could be major later on. Also, I've just read about the brain disease CTE (chronic traumatic encephalopathy) caused by playing football. I believe that topic was covered in a movie, *Concussion*. I have that listed in my movie chapter.

As one high schooler, Randy Ayala, was quoted as saying: "I just realized the damage that can happen to your brain with a big blow like that, and I didn't want it to happen again." He has decided to quit playing football. It must be very hard to say "enough" to something you enjoy doing. But, safety first.

Headaches, imbalance, speech, vision, and hearing issues happened to him after a concussion caused by playing football.

I read about him in one of the magazines I listed in my Recommended Books and Literature chapter, in a magazine named *Hudson Valley Healthy Lifestyles.*

So, I KNOW this is a very controversial subject, and all I will write is that once your brain is injured, your life is different forever. That may not seem apparent immediately, but it might. Do your "homework" if this has happened in your life.

Chapter 17

A TRIBUTE FROM
MY FRIEND MAGGIE

IN THE FALL of 1985, I was a new music teacher at Seymour Smith Elementary School in Pine Plains, NY. It was there where I first met Janet Schliff. Janet struck me as a "seasoned vet", and I was very impressed with her right away. She was a special ed. teacher for intermediate elementary school students in a self-contained classroom. I didn't have a lot of training in this field and had little experience with this population. Her students were "mainstreamed" into my music classroom, and Janet proved to be an invaluable resource to me.

My first impression of Janet was, WOW! She talked very fast, had a tremendous amount of energy, was incredibly smart, and was filled with great ideas. Her passion for education and her students was clear right from the start. She helped show me the ropes of the public school system and started brainstorming ways we could use music with her students. She was very charismatic and incredibly funny! We quickly became friends; a friendship that has lasted over 30 years.

Janet worked very long hours; all for the betterment of her students. She individualized her instruction for each child in her class. Janet had not only a professional interest in them, but a personal interest as well. This reached beyond her students and into their family units. Many of the children in her class came from homes that were also in need of services. Janet was a tireless advocate who was held in very high regard by the faculty and administration.

One of the many things that set Janet apart from others who I worked with was all of the extra projects she would do with her students. When she realized that most of her students had never been camping, she arranged for an overnight camping trip at a local park! She had me come so that we could have a sing-along complete with guitar around the campfire as they enjoyed eating s'mores for the very first time.

Not only did Janet encourage the children in her class to be in chorus, but she approached me to have a separate vocal ensemble for them. We did this for two concerts and gained much school-wide acclaim! Through music, she was able to draw attention to the fact that even though people have differences, there is common ground that makes them the same.

She taught people to value diversity in a time where that just was not done. Janet set the bar high, and then surpassed it! She taught her students to a higher academic level than thought possible while giving them real life skills.

Even though we wound up doing different things in different places, Janet and I always remained friends. We saw each other through the dissolve of her two marriages, the births of my two children, and deaths of family members for both of us. We would see each other when we could, and kept in touch on the phone.

As the years passed, I became very concerned about Janet. In our phone conversations, she would describe to me the struggles she was having especially in regard to developing a phobia of germs. It manifested in what/how she was able to eat and by the inability to touch things such as cell phones, money, and even the chalk in her own classroom. It got to the point where Janet was not able to do basic things such as go shopping for clothes. These things led to Janet not being able to work as a teacher anymore which was a tremendous loss for her students and their families.

My biggest concern for Janet, at that point, was her markedly slowed speech. It got to the point where her speech pattern was almost unrecognizable from the quick pace and witty banter I was used to from her. The day she called and told me she had been diagnosed with a brain tumor, I was shocked at first, but then it all made sense of the symptoms she had been suffering.

Immediately after her recovery from surgery, I received a phone call from Janet. What a difference! It was astonishing! It was like the clock had been turned back to the Janet from the old days. She was speaking rapidly and effervescently again. She proudly told me how she was calling from her boyfriend [Aiden's] cell phone without any concern about germs!

In the following months, it became evident that even though the tumor had been removed, it left its mark on Janet. She had problems with one of her eyes and her emotional temperament was difficult for her to control.

Janet has left no stone unturned in trying to regain whatever her brain tumor stole from her. Life has never been easy for Janet because of difficult relationships especially with her family. Despite these difficulties, she remains one of the most positive people I know.* She was a remarkable teacher and is the most loyal of friends. She has a passion for seeing that all people are treated fairly. In a world too filled with people who are only concerned with themselves, Janet stands out as someone who cares about others. She has an extremely strong sense of right and wrong and always wants to help others. I am proud to know her and look forward to another 30 years of friendship!

Sincerely,
Maggie Rothwell

*[I must come across to Maggie as much more positive than I feel.]

Chapter 18

HAPPY AND ANGEL

I HAVE A dog that I named "Happy." She's a 50-pound Puggle, a Pug-Beagle mix that I rescued via the Dutchess County, NY, SPCA, which called her a "designer dog," as she is larger than your average Puggle. Happy had had other names from owners before me, but I re-named her "Happy" because I needed to get back to being happy myself. I figured that if I said that word over and over again, maybe I would begin to feel happy.

As I heard recently on a rescued-dog TV show, I saved her life, but she saved mine, too. I get so much comfort and love from her when I am upset. Happy is incredibly in tune with me. She picks up on my tone of voice and jumps on my lap when she hears me talking to someone on the phone who is upsetting me. My 50-pound "lap dog" won't leave my lap until I calm down. Even when I am sitting silently, she can sense if I'm having an upsetting thought, and she climbs up on my lap to console me.

I have had dogs my entire life, but this dog is truly a blessing. I have a very difficult time when I'm away from her. When I go out of town, each day I call the kennels I leave her at every day that I am away, just to make sure she's doing okay. I need to hear that she's well. I really don't know what I'd do without her. She was a present from God when I needed her most.

As I have written here somewhere, the latter half of 2009 and the early part of 2010, which was the first year after my brain surgery, I was "high on life." I wanted to adopt a dog then, but my doctors told me I wasn't ready for that responsibility quite yet. I still had a lot to learn about how to navigate my life with the brain damage the tumor and the changes due to the operation had caused.

So, I was told in both 2010 and then again in 2011, that I wasn't prepared to care for an animal yet. I was very disappointed, but I followed both of my doctors' advice. But, in 2012, I was told I could start the process of adopting a dog.

One Sunday morning, as I sat in church and wept quietly over one more thing that had offended me (yes, that's how some brain-injured react to offensive remarks), Aiden whispered to me that he would take me to the Dutchess County SPCA right after church. I stopped crying and then paid attention to the service.

So – off for the ride we went. Though I don't live near that place anymore, I'm attached to it, due to my first dog adoption there, years before. As I walked around the outside of the building, where some dogs were in cages, I looked at this one dog staring at me. Almost as soon as I saw her, a male volunteer came up to us and asked if we wanted to hear this dog's story. We agreed, and here it is.…

This female dog had lived with a married couple. The husband, when he became intoxicated, would hit his wife. This dog watched it more than once. But, one time when this drunk man came home and smacked his wife, "This dog bit him in the balls."

As soon as I heard that, I said, "Let's get the paperwork started. I want her!"

Originally, I had intended to adopt a smaller dog, but this particular story struck a chord with me. I knew I HAD to have this medium-sized dog.

I knew this was the pooch for me because she had protected that woman. Because hard times fell on this woman as she divorced that terrible man, she gave this doggie up for adoption. After that, this same dog was supposed to be adopted by some man who got transferred by his job to a faraway place, so he couldn't keep her. And so, that's when I came into the picture.

This adorable dog had heartworm, so she had to be cleared of that first. I had to fill out pages and pages of paperwork to get approved. I can't believe how much the system has changed over the years, because it was easier long ago to adopt a pet. But – now it's a safer process for these little animals, and I didn't mind.

It was official on November 13, 2012, and so 11/13 has been celebrated as her "birthday" each year ever since. When I met her, they thought she was three years old, so now she's approximately seven years old.

When we celebrated her first year with me in 2013, I went with Happy to have our picture taken. Please see how adorable my "Happy-girl" is in the picture on the back cover of this book. I love her so much, and she's most of the reason my bad behaviors have not led to worse predicaments. She has calmed me down too many times to count.

Happy — I saved your life and you have saved mine!

The dog I had before Happy was also rescued by me via the same organization. His name there was Prince Charming, but I changed it to Angel because I knew it would be a little weird if he ran away and my neighbors heard me outside calling, "Prince Charming, Prince Charming, where are you?"

Angel was a Collie mix, and I had him for many years. To this day, I still miss him very much, and I have a hard time dealing with the guilt I feel about giving him away at the end of his life because I could no longer help him.

Angel developed kidney problems at the same time I developed the mysophobia from my latent brain tumor. Cleaning my carpets was excruciating for me because I was petrified about the germs left on my hands. I scrubbed over and over but never could get anything that was soiled to become clean enough for me. The mysophobia got so intense, I couldn't even pet Angel anymore.

My former boyfriend Jim helped me find someone who could take better care of my dog than I could. That person cared for Angel until the end.

When the veterinarian suggested Angel be put to sleep because he was so ill, Jim took me to the house where Angel had been staying. I was literally shaking when I bent over to say good-bye for the last time to my Angel. I told him how sorry I was that I had no longer been able to be there for him. Little did I know that it was a brain tumor that had caused this fear of touching my dog.

I have pictures of Angel around my home, and I try each day to get over the guilt. I do that by loving Happy with lots of hugs and belly rubs!

JANUARY 27, 2016

As I write this, my beloved dog, Happy, is undergoing surgery at the local animal hospital. I am beside myself with fear. Though, as I write this, I am heavily medicated by my prescribed controlled substance. I'm trying to remain calm. I'm not all that calm.

When I adopted her in November 2012 from the Dutchess County, NY, SPCA, she had a mole growing on her right side. I was told then that it wasn't cancer. The vet said he could remove it before it grew bigger.

At the appointment before the surgery, the vet discovered another growth underneath the one that is visible. This is what has caused the most fear in me. I just pray that both growths are not cancer and can be removed as easily as possible. He referred to them as "fatty tumors."

Every morning I begin my day with books to read that help me make sense of my world now. My condo resembles a mini-Barnes & Noble, with books stacked everywhere. A list of the books that have helped me (and some that I have referenced or quoted throughout my book) are listed in my book recommendations.

The chapter I opened up this morning in the book *Shades of Light: A Spiritual Memoir: A Mother and Daughter's Pathway to God,* by Phyllis Cochran, is entitled, "Fighting Fear." What a perfect way to help me read how another person made it through something too scary.

This is a heartfelt book about a little girl named Susan who had a large brain tumor. Though I haven't completed the book as of today, I can't express enough how this author's choice of words has helped me each morning since my friend Ilse tried to find this book for me and then my editor finally did. [Because I couldn't locate it after I had heard of it.]

The author quotes the *Bible* throughout her book. This particular chapter quotes *Psalm 91*:5, "You will not fear the terror of night, nor the arrow that flies by day." I'm so afraid that my doggie will not make it through surgery. That's why my doctors told me to take my medicine (with supervision by Aiden) so I could stay as calm as possible. I took it, but I also prayed, read the *Bible*, read Phyllis Cochran's book and others that help me to get by.

So, luckily, I just heard that Happy survived her surgery. I will be eternally grateful to God for that. Unfortunately, there were a few problems attached to the post-surgery period....

I had told the vet's staff ahead of time that I would be medicated when I came at 4 p.m. (their assigned time) to pick her up. Aiden has to chauffeur me under these circumstances (since I'm so medicated, I have trouble processing anything, never mind driving). I obey the law diligently about not driving while medicated.

When I got there, the staff spoke so quickly, I couldn't comprehend them. There were multiple directions to follow ("use a warm compress for this," "give this med once a day but this one twice," etc.). I practically exploded because none of it was written down (and my SHE dog kept being referred to as "he").

I know all too well how it is when you take a person home from a procedure: there can be pages of printed directions. Here, there were none, and I was so out-of-it (remember – I told them ahead of time that I would be), I was very bothered. Picking up a pet after surgery should be treated similarly to picking up a human being. I left there very upset and scared to death that I would make a mistake, even though they hurriedly produced a full page of handwritten directions.

[As a sidebar here – when I went to back to this vet to have Happy examined five days after her surgery, I calmly told the vet my suggestion – to have printed out the various responsibilities when you take your beloved animal home with you after any surgery. The vet responded with, "We'll work on that."}

I assumed that once Happy was back home, the hard part was over. Actually – it was WAY harder than I expected! Trying to get her to keep that cone around her neck so she wouldn't lick her draining tubes or bite at the 19 staples on her right side was very difficult.

Aiden sat with her when I had to go to other appointments. This craziness lasted for two weeks, because that's how long the staples were in her. I canceled many plans I had (even not going to a play) so I could be near Happy as much as possible because I was so worried about her. She looked at me with the saddest eyes every time I had to put that cone on her neck or wrap the sweater around her for a walk outside. Though I've never had children of my own, I turned into "mommy" for all of this.

We went back to the vet to have the staples removed two weeks later. I thought Happy would throw a party for herself, if she could, the day that cone didn't have to go around her neck at bedtime or car rides (since I can't keep an eye on her). I know I sighed with relief when my doggie was back to her old self.

As I have stated here, I have a ton of signs around my condo. The day I move out, I will be spending quite a bit of time plastering up the walls. But, for now, I enjoy reading and rereading these carefully selected signs. Here are some of my favorites that are related to pet ownership [and my opinions added on]:

- My therapist has a wet nose
- I want to be the person my dog thinks I am
- My dog doesn't think I'm crazy [Though some people do.]
- This house is maintained entirely for the comfort and convenience of the dog
- Poop happens! Just pick it up and move on [It's very difficult to move on sometimes.]
- I woof you
- Dogs welcome – people tolerated
- Dog friendly – beware of owner
- Dogs laugh with their tails
- You had me at woof
- I love dogs – it's humans that annoy me
- Count your blessings in dog years
- Life is better when shared with a dog [How true!]
- The dog and his housekeeping staff live here
- All you need is love… and a dog
- The best things in life are rescued
- The head of the house is the one with the tail
- Love is… being owned by a dog
- Who saved who? Home of a loyal and very special rescued dog
- Rescued is my favorite breed
- Beware of dog kisses
- Dogs leave paw prints on your heart…and on your floor
- If you slow down, you can catch your tail
- Happiness is me and my dog
- My best friend has four legs

- Heaven is where you meet all the dogs you ever loved
- Talk to the paw!
- Home is where your dog is
- Must love dogs
- Wipe your paws
- A house is not a home without a dog
- The welcome home doggie dance performed here
- All pets go to heaven
- The more I get to know some people, the more I love my dog [Amen!]
- Poop happens. Remain pawsitive
- Mixed breeds have pure hearts
- The day God made dogs, He just sat down and smiled!
- It's all fun and games...until someone ends up in a cone.
- Keep calm and woof on
- "My old life is over. My new life is beginning." [Not a sign, but a quote from *Lucky Dog,* CBS-TV, 5/28/16.]
- You have left my life, but you will never leave my heart. [This is a frame holding a picture of my Angel.]

June 22, 2016

Once again (like months earlier this year), I'm writing as my dog Happy is under anesthesia at the same vet's office. This time, she's there for shots, tartar removal, and some kind of tooth repair.

The staff told me at 7:30 a.m., when I dropped her off, that I would get a call from them when it was over and after that, I was supposed to call them at noon. I didn't hear from them all morning.

I was not able to take my meds to calm down because I have a chiropractic appointment today. I'm still in the back brace, and so I have to be able to drive, since Aiden was expecting help with construction at his house and thus couldn't drive me.

I am literally shaking as I scribble this down because when I called at noon, the vet's staff said Happy was still having surgery. They gave me no other information, and I forgot to ask for more.

Sadly, I don't live by the motto, "no news is good news." I'm WAY too negative for that! I'm assuming the worst every minute the clock ticks because no one has called to tell me anything.

So, I called again less than an hour later because I couldn't wait one more second. The woman in the office said that Happy is okay, but still with the vet. He had to remove two teeth, and that's why this is taking so much longer than expected.

So, Aiden was able to come over to try to calm me down when he ended up having time. He hates when I take my meds for calmness, so he just stayed with me and drove me to my chiropractic appointment.

Right in the middle of my session with the wonderful Judith Dougan working her hands on my very-stressed-out back, they called me to tell me how Happy had fared. Judy is such an excellent chiropractor because she just patiently waited as the vet went over everything with me (which meant I was on my cell for at least three minutes of Judy's time). Happy's time at the vet's went much longer than expected because two teeth had to be removed. I was so relieved to hear she was okay. After I hung up, some of the stress in my back went away....

I went with Aiden to pick up my very-medicated "Happy-girl." I thanked the vet, the staff, Aiden, and God for the healthy return of my best friend.

I've been told that I worry too much about my dog. This sentence infuriates me. I know there are folks who don't have pets, but if you do, you know how attached pet owners can become.

Once, I heard someone negatively comment about animals and pets right after I had overheard her describing her enjoyment of ironing sheets and towels. Boy, did I bite my tongue that day. Ironing "trumps" pets. Wow! She and I have been only acquaintances, and after hearing that, I definitely realized how different we all can be. So, she went home to iron (oh, so much fun), and I went home to cuddle with my Happy. I'll always be of the opinion that I had more fun than she did.

A friend from my church sent me a card once with important advice from a dog: unleash your talents. Thanks, Jeanne!

When Isabella Shaw, a little girl from my church, was ten years old, she was petting a therapy dog that attends our church regularly with its owners. Isabella and I struck up a conversation before our service began one Sunday as we both played with the dog. I could tell she loves doggies as much as I do, so I asked her to write something for my book. Here it is (way to go, girl!):

They give you: company, happiness, love. You get to play with the dog, love on the dog.

To take care of the dog, you need to play with it, walk or exercise it, give it food and water, toys to play with.

Services they do for you: seeing-eye dogs, police dogs, therapy dogs, herding dogs, hunting dogs, bomb-detecting dogs.

So – I want to end this chapter telling all the dogs I've had in my entire life to rest in peace: Tuffy, Sandy, Tara, and Angel – you are all sorely missed. I think of you nowadays since I have my Happy still alive and well. Dogs are like family members. I'm sure all of them are having a good ole time up there in doggie heaven….

Chapter 19

FRIENDS

WHEN I THOUGHT of this chapter, I had to include some people who "get me" and have been there for me, no matter what. And then there are others who helped me when I was sick with the latent brain tumor, but I have lost a connection with them gradually since its removal. The disconnect is partly due to my behavior and, in a couple of cases, partly because of theirs. But they still did help me. The friends listed below deserve my eternal thanks and love:

- **Maggie Rothwell** – As you can read in her contribution here, Maggie and I have known each other for more than three decades now. She has this incredible ability to see me for who I was and who I now am. She's so gifted in pointing out my accomplishments when all I can do sometimes is find my flaws. She's the sweetest friend. I admire her musical talents and how they have provided me with calmness. I love her more than words can say! She's an excellent listener and never passes judgment. I truly listen to her advice and suggestions. She is a gift from God. At the time of this writing, I went to listen to her play guitar and sing at one of her many gigs. The floor got wet since rain was tracked in by other restaurant patrons. As I stood up to go to the restroom, Maggie, mid-song and on the microphone, said, "Be careful – don't slip," to me because she knows that I lose my balance. I cried on the walk to the restroom. Those were happy tears for having such a dear friend.

- **Ilse Fenwick** – I know Ilse from my church. She, like Maggie, is such a wonderful listener. She helps me refocus on God when I stray from Him during my difficult times. I listen to her when she offers a different perspective on lots of topics. She has brought me closer to God in her loveable mannerisms. She sends me cards when I need uplifting. She researches books for me to read when I can't find them in bookstores. She actually pays for them until I can pay her back. Is that a friend, or what? I've been to her beautiful home for her helpful counseling. It was there that she told me that I feel worse than it appears I do to others, but I'm further along than I think I am. At one of the many *Bible* studies I've attended with her, I heard many stories from other women about how great a helper she is. That's my Ilse! She's another gift from God. And, she's such a sweetheart, she's invited me over on Thanksgivings and Christmases so I wouldn't be alone. I took her up on it Christmas night of 2016. That was the only fun I had on that very dismal day, described elsewhere here, even though Christmas is supposed to be a happy time.

- **Marian Palmadessa** – She took such great care of me when I had the mysophobia. She invited me into her home to feed me because I was so scared of germs I could hardly put a fork to my mouth. She would wash the silverware right in front of me, lay paper towels over her table and chairs, etc. and etc. I was wasting away to an unsafe weight, so she fed me when I could not do it. She and I had lots of other fun times together. She's a sweet person to whom I will forever be grateful for her assistance and love when I was sick. I love when we get to spend some time together. I also love the cards she sends me, especially for Mother's Day, a "thinking of you" card (because she knows how sad I am on this day). And, she gives me leftovers sometimes, because she knows I can't cook anymore.

To give you an idea about what a good friend Marian has been, I'm adding here the recommendation she filled out for me for when I was applying for a Youth Ministry position at my church in 2009. The questions are in italics, her responses in normal type.

1. *How long have you known this applicant?* 4 years in December '09

2. *In what capacity or under what circumstances have you known the applicant? Have you ever observed that applicant working with children? How would you describe those interactions?* Janet Schliff is my neighbor. She lives 3 units away from me. We met in December 2005, picking up our mail. She introduced herself and we exchanged phone numbers. I told her any questions regarding our rules etc. in the W*** Townhomes, not to hesitate to call me.

   As time passed, we became close friends and she was invited to our home for dinner quite often.

   Janet is so proud of her teaching career. She taught Special Ed. children for 25 years. In 1992 she received an Excellence in Teaching award. She also taught reading classes to other teachers....

3. *Has the applicant, to your knowledge, been involved in any incident or activity which might disqualify them from working with*

children? If so, please describe the incident or behavior. Absolutely not!

4. *Would you recommend the applicant be allowed to work with children or teens? Would you allow the applicant to be responsible for your children?* Yes to both questions. As far as I am concerned, Janet Schliff is a Modern Day Miracle from God! The night before her surgery, she called me saying how frightened she was and would I please pray for her. I told her she was a good woman and that God would take care of her. The following day, she called me again, and I went into shock that so soon after her surgery, she could call me, speak so clearly and tell me the mysophobia was gone, along with the tumor the size of an orange!

The majority of her past students…so loved her most of them have been in touch with her in one way or another to tell her how happy they are for her.

*   **Sandy Evans** – We met at church, and I will always be grateful to her, for helping me when I could hardly help myself. When I was germ-phobic, I heard a DJ on the radio say that movie theaters and church pews were dirty. So – I stood at the back of our church because I was afraid to sit down. Sandy placed jackets down after I told her what was wrong. She sat with me during services. She listens to me rant and rave about various topics. We both have a lot of medical issues, and so it's hard to be there for one another, but I know she helps me when she can. I believe God placed her in that church to help me and others. And to this day, she sits near me at meetings to help me keep calm and help me express things I'm scared to bring up.

And here are some more:

- **Suzi** – I referenced Suzi in the chapter I wrote about helpful businesses because of her daughter Jaime's lovely behavior towards her store customers. Suzi is also someone I met at church. I've been to her lovely home for various *Bible* studies. I attended a group she taught at church about grieving, after my dad passed away. She has a warm heart and a gracious spirit. She helped lead my then-boyfriend Aiden and me to a wonderful counselor when our relationship was in jeopardy. She has sent me helpful emails. Suzi just knows when to do or say the right thing right when it's needed the most. Another gift from God.

- **Jim** – He was the man I dated before I met Aiden. He was so patient with me when I was the sickest I've ever been. That tumor was huge at this point in my life, but we didn't know it then. What I did know is that Jim helped me with the household chores I could not do for myself – like taking out the garbage, since touching cans and bags was impossible for me when I was petrified of germs. He helped me complete paperwork and make out my checks because my memory was terrible due to the brain damage caused by the tumor. I appreciate how he led me in the right direction often and helped me make many decisions. I'm sure there's much more that he did for me than I actually can remember, so I will be forever grateful to him for his kindness. To this day I feel guilty about not "being there" for him as he was for me….

And, I also have a bunch of friends who have helped me with various things through the story of my life. Here's to some of them:

- **Ellen** – a friend I've kept in contact with since we roomed together in a dorm at SUNY Plattsburgh almost 40 years ago. She has the sweetest family, and I love traveling out of town to their celebrations for graduations, weddings, anniversaries, etc.

I also love talking with her over the phone because she always asks me how I am doing. Her parents did an excellent job raising her to be a loving person!

- **Marla** – As you can read from her contribution here, Marla and I were colleagues over 25 years ago at Ulster County BOCES. Our friendship began then and has remained. She's very good at inviting me to retirement and end-of-the-year parties. I also get together with her and our mutual friend, Beverly, whom we used to work with. Catching up on our lives is always a pleasure.

- **Debbie One** – I have four Debbies as friends. The first one I met about two decades ago when she worked in one of my classrooms. She's a sweetheart and was very patient with being a one-on-one aide for a special needs child. I love bumping into her about once a month at her current job.

- **Debbie Two** – The second Debbie I met just a few years ago at church. She's been a wonderful listener. She has sent me texts and cards with God's word, and they are very helpful. She gave me permission for me to use her name and phone number on a card in my wallet to explain my condition to, for example, a police officer. She is now my emergency contact. I've called her numerous times in total distress, and she ALWAYS calms me down. Her family is very sweet to be around. [And – she makes the BEST mac and cheese I've ever had…and she'll even fry me some bacon as well!]

- **Debbie Three** – Another Debbie I met at my church. She too listens very well to me and drives me to doctor appointments when I can't. Visits to her house are delicious!

- **Debbie Four** – This is the Debbie I wrote about in another chapter. She's gone from being not only my reflexologist, but also to being my friend.

- **Joey** – She is an excellent cook, and she prepares food for me. I love seeing her at my church.

- **Linda, Joyce, Allison, Margo, Henry, Janet, Donna, Juanita, Bea, Lenny, Otto, and Louise** – I used to know some of them when I was very young. We now meet up at a fundraiser luncheon. All of us meet there monthly when we can, and I enjoy their friendliness. [Since these luncheons are held in a parish hall of a church, I really should "duct tape" my mouth sometimes! My lack of a "filter" causes embarrassing conversations from time to time.]

- **Barbara and Kim** – I've met these two women through sad circumstances, but we have formed a bond. Barbara's sister, Sue, had a brain injury, and thus Barbara attended a support group with me. Kim's husband, Terry, suffered a brain injury, and I met Kim through Barbara. Kim, Barbara, and I, at the time of this writing, travel to meetings with "mucky-mucks" (my word for politicians in the New York State capital, Albany) to discuss the needs of others for legislation for the brain-injured. Our personalities are very different from one another but we get the job done. Kim has a calming effect on me. She reads my body language very well. Barbara has spent a lot of time going through her sister Sue's belongings after Sue died from that brain injury. Kim is now grieving the sudden death of her husband. (Rest in peace, Sue and Terry.) On a more upbeat note, Barbara's digging through her sister's stuff has helped her discover various Mickey Mouse items and she gives them to me, which I appreciate. Barbara and her husband even made me a T-shirt and a sweatshirt with wording to help me calm down when others asked me why this book wasn't finished by 2016 (as my first business card said it would be). The shirts said:

  My Book?

  Believe me,
  when it's finished…
  you'll know!

AND

My Book?

Rivers know this:
There is no hurry
We shall get there some day

Winnie the Pooh

[And one piece of advice I'd give anyone who's writing a book for the first time: don't talk about it right away. I did talk too soon, and non-writers were frequently stressing me out about my timing. Begin to discuss your book a bit later on in your writing process....]

- **Jan** – This Jan is "Jan Nails" (because I have another friend named Jan). I met her so many years ago. When she lived in Dutchess County, NY, I went to her house for manicures. Since she's moved to the Carolinas, we speak every once in a while and send cards to each other. When we speak, it's like we've never had time or distance between us!
- **"The girls" – Cathy, Caroline, Barb, Webby, Doris, Monica, Jan, Shirley, Sally, and Lil** – Our get-togethers over the years for birthdays, holidays and other things have been a nice break from my busy schedule. We also have supported each other with our various hospital stays. (Rest in peace, Lil.)

And, like most people, I have many other friends whom I speak to once in a while, send and/or receive Christmas and birthday cards to/from and whom I appreciate knowing. Also, I've made some new friends when I travel to Hyde Park, NY, for their many fun activities there, such as: the Fourth of July Parade, Cranberry's bistro and bake shop's delicious scones that I eat at the Vanderbilt Mansion with my dog Happy, Fireside Chats and Mother's Day Teas that are held at the St. James Church and visits to the nearby Mills Mansion in Staatsburg.

FRIENDS MAKE LIFE MORE BEARABLE.
I'M LUCKY TO HAVE THE FRIENDS I HAVE....

[Once, in September 2016, when I attended a retired teachers' breakfast to celebrate that we had that first day of school off, I was rudely spoken to by a former colleague and, boy, did I let her have it! We had both recently been to another colleague's funeral, and I was politely telling her why I had to leave that funeral early (because I was too upset). Instead of responding with warmth, she coldly said, "You shouldn't have left – it was a beautiful service."

Do you live in my head? I was taking care of myself by leaving that funeral. So, I rudely responded, "I don't think wouldas, couldas, shouldas are appropriate. Since I have a brain injury, I leave when I'm about to lose it."

My tone of voice was really snotty, and once again my friend Marla (who was sitting right next to me), "pulled me back" with her warmth.

Later, at the same breakfast, I heard some stories about my behavior when I had the tumor. I was glad I was done eating and left with only saying goodbye to a couple of friends. On my way out the door, my friend Karen asked me if I was okay. Though I said I was, I really wasn't. She had picked up on my upset.

Friends are so loving and they can detect when you're not "right." Thank God for my friends who "get me." Thank you to all of my friends who have shown me love and warmth.

I just wish people would be more careful how they judge others. At least I know I have to work on that. I'm not sure that some others know they need to also.]

Chapter 20

"Aiden"

[This chapter remained in here though this relationship has ended. My ex-boyfriend, "Aiden," heard this chapter (and the various other stories I've also told about him elsewhere in my book), and he's approved of it all verbally. Sadly, before Aiden was an ex, my editor said I should get it in writing that he approved of it all. Since our break-up was very abrupt, that never took place, so his name has been changed, and some stories have been deleted.]

This is one more difficult chapter to write. I really don't even know where to begin. I do know that I met him, and fell in love with him, when I was very ill – though we didn't know the exact illness until two years into our relationship.

I met Aiden on a Thursday night in September 2007 at a karaoke night at our local Holiday Inn. Late that afternoon, my boyfriend-at-the-time, Jim, had taken me for a nature walk at the Ashokan Reservoir. But, as usual, I had to leave earlier than we expected in case I needed to use a restroom. See, in those days, I had wetting accidents often. Again, that was blamed on the meds I was on for the mysophobia, when actually, I found out later, the brain tumor caused those large messes. I know urinary incontinence is a problem when we age, but this example was when I was only 46.

To digress from that nature walk for a bit, those wetting mishaps even took place at the last school I taught in. I had a bag next to my desk with a second outfit (right down to socks and underwear), just in case I needed to change at work. I did have to change clothes a few times because of these accidents, and some co-workers noticed the different clothes on the same day.

But let's get back to that nature walk. As Jim was driving me home, I had the sudden urge to tinkle. Jim was a very sweet man, and he layered his passenger seat with towels during this phase of our lives. These towels were because I had occasionally wet his car seat accidentally. He never got upset or mad about that. He took care of me very well. So, as we were about to pass the Holiday Inn, I told him, "Hurry! I have to go to the bathroom right now." Jim sped down the ramp to the parking lot, and I went running to the restroom.

And then, when I emerged happily relieved that I made it in the nick of time, he told me about the karaoke that was going on in the bar. We went in together. I enjoyed taking this all in, but knew that I would probably never touch that hand-held microphone to sing anything (too many dirty hands touched it, and I was grossed out by "germies").

As I was listening to others try their best to read and sing the words that Larry the DJ put on the screen, I noticed Aiden for the first time, over at the bar area with what looked like friends of his. I found out in later weeks that they were just that – his friends.

Of course, I was there with Jim, so I just sat and took it all in. A few visits later to that establishment, I introduced myself to Aiden and his buddies.

At first, Aiden, Jim, and I were all part of a friendly little group. Soon, I found myself even more attracted to Aiden than to Jim. After quite a while trying to decide whom I wanted to date, I broke up with Jim and started a relationship with Aiden. Of all the relationships I've had in my life, this one with Aiden was the biggest roller-coaster, because we were polar opposites. Because of that, we had seen three relationship counselors. The last one told us that in her 30 years of couples counseling, she had never had a more dissimilar pair.

We both did love one another, but our 14-year age difference is just one difference on a very long list of differences. However, we tried to stick by one another through ten tumultuous years, though we were not good together for at least half of them. But, let me focus on the positive right now....

Aiden was a great cook. He did his fair share of cooking when he was on his job. After he retired, he prepared a large portion of whatever he was into, and I got containers of his leftovers after we were done eating some of it together. Because of my memory problems, I don't use my stove or oven. I live in a condo and my starting a fire would affect other families too.

Let me digress one more time. After my brain surgery, I flooded my kitchen once when I turned the kitchen sink on to wash some dishes. Because I forget what I'm doing sometimes, I left the room, went to use my bathroom, listened to my messages on my answering machine in my bedroom. When I remembered, I ran back to the kitchen and water was everywhere...all over the counters, the floor, etc. I had a lot of cleanup work to do!

I started three small fires in that same kitchen before I made the decision (with help from my doctors) to only eat p. b. and j. sandwiches, microwavable foods, leftovers from Aiden or from dining out. This is safer for all involved! So, Aiden's extras were a big help. I have friends that bake for me, too. The Voughts bake an apple pie that I purchase frozen from them for a fundraiser they participate in. Yummy!

Another way Aiden was helpful was with my dog, Happy. I was extremely busy with writing this book, attending meetings with politicians in Albany about brain injury, joining support groups to help me cope with my new life, and so much more. If I couldn't make it home in time to walk my doggie, Aiden did it for me. Sometimes he was even Happy's sitter. I drove the 15 minutes to deliver Happy to Aiden's home, and they shared some quality time together over there. That always made me feel less guilty about not being around all the time, for the dog.

Aiden called me a few times most days to "check-in" and see how I was doing. If I needed anything, he was usually eager to assist. I called him "Mr. Fix-it," because he repaired the things I accidentally dropped and broke. [I counted how many times I dropped something the day I wrote this chapter. I stopped at 10. This is one more "life difference" since my brain surgery. Luckily, my friend Sandy has turned into "Ms. Fix-it" for me.]

Aiden was also my chauffeur. My doctors have stated that I should only drive myself to destinations one hour or less. So, that means for my appointments with my editor, Dr. Cooper, Aiden drove me some weeks. On the days that he was unable to, I left an hour early so I would have extra time if I got lost. All those GPS voices get on my nerves, so I don't use it. Aiden drove me to too many places to list. I am grateful for all of those trips.

I do believe that God brought us together, so that is why we had worked so hard to stay together, despite our very different personalities. Sometimes, I wished I was more laid back, as he is. But, I also wished at the same time that he was more scheduled, as I am. He thought nothing of it if we traveled to some far-away appointment he had made and when we arrived, got told he was not supposed to be there until the next day. I fumed over the wasted time. He saw it as an adventure to do something else while we were there. Of course, I found a restaurant or store I'd like to visit instead of fuming too long. These kinds of mistakes he laughed about at himself. I wish I could be so jovial.

Aiden had two cars. Only one car was used for trips with my dog, Happy, and so it got covered with dog hair. The other car was "reserved" for just us, or if Aiden was driving someone somewhere.

The "Happy-Mobile" was also used when either my car or his nice car was in the shop for repairs. His having this extra car had helped me time and time again (especially when my yellow Mickey Mobile was dying).

In the spring, summer, and fall, we took Happy on scenic rides. Actually – the two of them took me for a ride. For some strange reason that I can't fully explain, a calmness came over me, as we drove quiet, back roads. God's beautiful nature is very soothing (and the milkshakes we used to stop for were also helpful).

We went on roads that didn't have a lot of traffic on them, and Aiden pointed out favorite spots of his or places he once installed satellite dishes. I still can't believe how much Aiden used to do before he retired.

So, I just enjoyed the scenery while he drove, and once in a while, Happy loved to bark at a cow or squirrel we passed. I missed those relaxing trips when the weather was dangerous in the winter. As soon as the snow melted, I started asking if we could take a ride. Aiden also sometimes cleaned my car, which I appreciated.

Another way Aiden was helpful to me was how he sometimes helped me stay calm when I became easily agitated. He would tell me to breathe, "Change the channel," (an expression not meant literally as if we were watching television but instead to think about something else that is not upsetting). Aiden would sometimes change the subject entirely if he observed my stress level rising.

He did not want me taking my prescribed medicine (a controlled substance) because he knew how addicting that can become. He witnessed firsthand how I overdo that and how I'd been lucky nothing dangerous had taken place. My impulsivity causes me to want to "shut down" when someone has hurt me or triggered me. But – taking pills only makes the problem worse. So – I have to work on calming down by talking to God first and foremost. Sarah, a lovely mother of two children I help with at my church told me, "Let children be your medicine." How sweet a thought, because whenever I volunteer with kiddies, I am not ever triggered. Children bring me much comfort.

A perfect example of Aiden's ability to help me calm down (when someone other than he triggered me), happened as I was preparing part of this chapter.

I almost had a meltdown at a publicity function I had been invited to participate in. I got dressed up (an unusual occurrence for me), rearranged many other plans that day to arrive early (since it was far from home and Aiden and I had never been there before), and I was excited to be included.

However, the person in charge forgot that she had asked me a few days prior to be part of the picture-taking event, and so, when others were called up by name for the photo-shoot, I just stood there. I waited for her to signal me to come up. Instead, she told others to join in. So – I just stood there, hurt and feeling that way we did as children when we weren't picked for a team in gym class. Remember that?

I started to shake, and here's where Aiden came to my rescue. He put his arm around me and said, "Everything is going to be okay." He knew I was upset. I wondered whether I was left out on purpose or inadvertently. Having been triggered, I decided to leave rather than do something embarrassing. I left in tears and didn't even join in the festivities. (You know I'm upset when I walk away from free food!) So – Aiden drove me to a nearby Cracker Barrel restaurant, because he knew that after we order, I'd go outside and rock and rock and rock in the rocking chairs. This movement brings me to a calmer place (and their gift shop and delicious food help also).

As I was wrapping up this book, I attended a Judy Collins concert in Bearsville, NY. Two men came in wearing funny reindeer antlers (since it was the holidays).

When they sat down, one of them took his antlers off for the show so the couple behind them could see the stage. The other guy left them on until his partner overheard the people behind them discussing it. The guy who knew to remove his antlers had to take them off the other guy's head. Really? You don't think enough of other people that it's okay with you that someone's view is blocked so you can wear a silly costume?

I wanted to "butt my nose" into this, since I was sitting near all four of these people. Aiden rubbed my arm and said, "Janet, this is none of your business. Just enjoy the show." That was helpful because I did just that!

I know Aiden had rescued me many times. When a car I was driving died on some road, he was the one who dropped what he was doing and came to my aid. Silly but true – one time I locked myself INSIDE my own new-for-me car. Over the phone, he had to slowly, very slowly, tell me which buttons to push so I could get out. (I guess this is a contraption in newer cars so kiddies cannot get out by accident?) Since my brain injury, I get very flustered with tasks that appear simple to others.

Once, my mother came to help celebrate my 55th birthday. As I wrote here when I penned my family chapter, my mother and I had "lost touch" for quite a while. She initiated the conversation about coming to New York from her home in Florida so we could celebrate my birthday together.

When she first contacted me, I was nervous about her coming north, because I couldn't have one more disagreement with her. I'm way too fragile emotionally to take that anymore. But, I prayed about it, and God spoke to me and helped me arrange for a visit. She stayed at a local Hampton Inn because that was less pressure for me. My condo is just not "user-friendly" right now, as it looks so messy due to all my piles of research for book-writing. The dog and I are okay with it, but my mother's Parkinson's means she could fall easily. I wanted for her to be safe and for me to stay as calm as possible.

When she arrived, she needed a trip to a hair salon while she was here. I had practically every minute she was here pre-planned, so I had no time to take her, since I still needed time to write and do my everyday chores. See – another effect of brain injury is that I don't do well with schedule changes. So – Aiden volunteered, and off to the mall they went. I thought that was very sweet of him.

I know a lot of partners wouldn't be as accommodating as he was sometimes with my peculiar behaviors. He pretty much "goes with the flow" and didn't get upset when I was asking for help. [Until the end, when he got VERY upset.]

Another way he tried to help me is with my impulsivity. If I was stopping at a store with him to pick up something I needed, he reminded me just to get those items, because too many times I filled the cart with gifts and cards for others or supplies for church functions or other things. I needed help remembering that I'm on a limited income now and I have to watch my finances more carefully. He was good at that, and I appreciated his gentle reminders not to overspend on others.

While I was preparing part of the chapter, I had one more "curveball day" where too many changes took place and I couldn't handle it. I ended up taking my medicine, which then meant Aiden had to drive me to our church's choir rehearsal. Of course, we were in different sections in the choir, so I just sang and tried very hard not to chit-chat, because others would hear my medically-caused slurred speech.

The sad part is that all that had happened to cause my meltdown was that a doorknob broke in my condo and so I couldn't get into a room to put some supplies away, at the same time that my landlord was calling me about changing the water hose for my washing machine. I broke down in tears over these two small events as if they were big. Brain injury!

I know many people get flustered when the routine or schedule is changed, but I get so upset it can lead to a meltdown. After the meds kick in, I calm down and things go smoother than they would have if I hadn't taken them, but hours later, I feel horrible because I had been snotty to others while I waited to feel relief.

Aiden had witnessed some of my meltdowns. Sometimes he was good with that, and other times he'd had enough. I can't blame him for getting bothered by my childlike episodes, but I do wish he could have helped me get over it more often.

He had also helped me in the middle of the night. An alarm battery went dead very late one evening. I had never replaced this type of battery in my carbon monoxide detector before. The beeping sound it was making was scaring both my dog Happy and me. I called Aiden. He drove over to help me replace the battery and then get me to a calmer, quieter place so I could rest. He easily could have just stayed home and given me directions over the phone, but, instead, he came to my rescue one more time.

Once, I needed a late-night trip to the ER for one more bladder infection that was not getting better with my usual meds. He took me as soon as I called him. I truly wish I could have remembered these loving gestures of his when I got all riled up about something he did that I didn't like.

That feeling of being upset instead of content happened way too often. Because we had opposite personalities, we didn't see eye-to-eye on the majority of topics that arose. So – we plugged along trying to understand each other better.

He was not familiar with the kind of situation that my particular brain injury presented. As many experts say, "if you've seen one brain injury, you've seen one brain injury." There are no two exactly alike. The only thing that they all have in common is that they rob the injured person of the life that person once knew. Family members are left to "clean up the mess," and this can sometimes tear a family apart.

Some people with brain injury are forever bedridden. Others need wheelchairs or walkers. Others are more mobile, but have cognitive and/or behavior issues. That behavior category is where I fit in. I look normal, have an excellent vocabulary, but I have numerous issues relating to interacting with other people. Let's not pass judgment on degrees of brain injury. Let's realize that it is a forever life change for all involved, but especially for the person who is dealing with it the most – the person who had the tumor, the aneurism, the stroke, the accident, and on and on and on....

One strong suggestion I would make for any brain injured person or the caregiver: do NOT make large life decisions for at least one year after the incident, surgery, or event. Engagement or marriage, memberships, etc. should be postponed until improved wellness takes place. Give yourself at least a year.

And that's where we'll get back to Aiden in this, the Aiden chapter. He proposed to me in a very romantic way at that Holiday Inn where I told you we had met. He did this seven months after my brain surgery. At that point (February 2010), I was still high on life after surviving what I had survived.

Aiden had asked both of my parents (when we visited their home in Florida for Christmas of 2009) if he could marry me. They were thrilled at that point because Aiden had stuck with me through this horrible brain surgery ordeal. Two months later, he got down on one knee as the band that played that evening at the Holiday Inn announced that something special was about to take place. I eagerly said yes and we went out to the lobby to call my parents.

We didn't rush into making wedding plans. We had our engagement picture taken, but that was about it. I was still in early recovery stages, so my thinking skills were slower then. We discussed various ideas, such as a honeymoon in Australia, but nothing was finalized.

Why nothing got organized right away was because of what I've written about here in the chapter about my beginning of meltdowns.

Only three months after Aiden's proposal, I began to unravel. As you'll read in the next chapter, Mother's Day weekend of 2010 was the beginning of a long journey that I'm not completely finished with yet.

Then, after I began to "fall apart," things got even worse. Without going into too much of Aiden's private information here, let me just say that he had to get a handle on some of his own issues. A pastor at our church and then another pastor at a different church helped him, and thus us, with that. Because of Aiden's issues, I canceled our engagement. I had been divorced once and had my second marriage annulled, so I was being very cautious.

I pretty much knew a wedding would not take place for us. I do know that when he was father-like with me and helped me calm down after one of my immature temper-tantrums, I was drawn closer to him.

But, many other times, I knew he made things worse for both of us by joining in, with his narcissistic behaviors.

I struggled with our differences. I'm a pretty good listener, yet he hardly talks. He didn't listen very well, and I talked too much. I'm way too sensitive for his insensitiveness. His just "forgetting" (to get me a card for a holiday) got me way too upset. We are opposites who tried to find common ground.

One of the mean things Aiden called me was "oddball." Though he's actually accurate that some of the things I did and/or said are "out there," it still hurts to be named-called. On the other hand, one helpful thing he said often to me was, "Analyze, analyze, paralyze," because he witnessed how often I over-analyzed situations with everyone, not just with him.

I'm the first to admit that sometimes my behavior is a little "off," but I do know that I bit my tongue A LOT around him and others who agitate me with their carelessness in word choices. Though he attended many meetings with me to learn more about brain injury, he didn't always apply it. I've learned to keep quiet more often when others irritate me. That's way easier said than done!

Aiden said it best about himself, "I know I'm an odd fellow."

Aiden and I had a very different upbringing. I grew up in affluent Rhinebeck, NY. I went on a family vacation cross-country to California, another to the United Kingdom, and more. Most summers were spent either in the Hamptons or the Adirondacks. I also owned a house with my former husband in beautiful Rhinebeck.

Aiden told me many times that his birth family was so poor. Once, he had to miss a school field trip for ice cream because they couldn't afford a ten-cent ice cream cone.

That may be one reason why we saw the world so differently.

The part of this relationship that was excruciatingly hard for me was how sensitive I was to his insensitive comments. I know I don't always do the right thing, but he had the hardest armor against the world that I've ever known. Nothing I, or anyone else, said to him seemed to get "under his skin." He was able to pass it off.

I'm not able to, so therefore, when angry sentences like the examples here were said by him to me, I crumbled:

- "Your ass is fat." [True, but mean.]
- "That's Janet being Janet." [Intended to be derogatory.]
- "What's wrong with you?" [Said harshly.]
- "Why are you so literal?" [Brain damage, ever hear of it?]
- "My kids despise you." [More than obvious, but still hard to hear.]
- "I hate your dog."
- "You act like a nut!"

[And one thing I have to add here is that I used to say something very mean to Aiden which I should not have said: "Remember – I fell in love with you when I had a brain tumor." That was accurate but mean.]

I know we all say things in the heat of an argument that we wish we could "take back" later, but what happens in my brain is the overplaying of these cruel words. So, I knew that all of this was in God's hands. Aiden and I didn't get together by accident. He helped me (as I've shown here), and I helped him (by restoring his faith in God).

But, our differences were too great. Though it reads here that he did so much for me, he also destroyed my self-esteem for a very long time, with examples I've deleted from this chapter.

Now that I'm free of this relationship, God is healing me.

Chapter 21

"Current" Events

TODAY MARKS THE seventh "anniversary" of my brain tumor surgery. At the time of this writing (11 a.m.), I was "under the knife" at NYU seven years ago. This day always has significance for me because I survived. Sadly, it happens to be the day I could have died.

I know that no one in my life remembers this date anymore, except for me, which is okay. Last week, when I was scheduling this week's plans, I said to Aiden, "July 7th is coming up soon, are we celebrating?"

As usual, he had no clue what I was referring to, so I gave him some hints:

1. "You made a lot of calls to people." (Nothing.)

2. "My sisters Joyce and Jayne came." (Nope.)

3. "2009 – I survived." (Oh – now he remembered.)

I end up usually spending that anniversary day alone, quietly re-flecting on what could have happened. I talk to God and thank Him. I'm not upset that I'm the only one who remembers it, because I don't remember big days for other people unless I have notes galore around to remind me. (One area of my kitchen actually looks like a miniature post office, with cards, stamps, stickers, etc., to help me with that.)

I'm glad God helped me survive that long surgery, even though that nasty tumor caused permanent changes in my life. He had more for me to do, and I'm doing it.

Chapter 22

THE ADIRONDACKS

WHEN I WAS a young girl, my family and I went north in New York State to go camping in the Adirondacks. The scenery there is the prettiest of any place I've ever seen. It is so quiet and still. If you have never been there, you need to go!

When I was at one of my many doctor appointments for skin cancer in 2010, after my euphoria from living through a brain tumor and surgery, I was "losing it" as the nice doctor, Dr. Jaiani, was telling me my latest diagnosis. I got so worked up, he went out to the waiting room and asked my boyfriend, Aiden, to come back to my exam room. The doctor was crystal clear with us. He asked me where I could go away for a few days to relax and calm down. Immediately, and without hesitation, I blurted out, "the Adirondacks." I instantly remembered – in my very agitated state – that the Adirondacks had a calming effect on me and always had.

I spent many summers camping at Camp-of-the-Woods in Speculator, New York. My grandparents took my father and his brother, Uncle Bobby, there many summers. My uncle worked there as a teenager. Another aunt and an uncle had vacationed there over the years. It's a Christian camp, and it's so special. It's where I learned to water ski.

My sisters and I had gone to Tapawingo – an island camp that you leave Camp-of-the-Woods by boat to get to. It's there that I learned the camp songs I taught my students many years later when I took them camping. When my dad was on his deathbed in 2012, he asked that some of his ashes be sprinkled at Camp-of-the-Woods.

Back to that meltdown in the dermatologist's office: I had begun to unravel bit-by-bit around Mother's Day 2010. This was right before my appointment with Dr. Jaiani. It had hit me, while I was at my cousin Lauren's baby shower that Mother's Day weekend, that I would never be a mommy or grandma like so many women who attended her wonderful party. I was about to turn 50, and I had never had a baby. The year before, I had been told by my doctors that there was a 20% chance that the brain tumor could grow back. As I sat at this party and looked around at what I would never experience, I cried.

When I got back home, I prepared for one more doctor appointment. When that skin doctor could see that I was having what I now refer to as the first meltdown of MANY meltdowns to come, he knew enough about the state of mind of his patient to help me with more than the skin cancer. His question about where I could go has led to a trip back to the Adirondacks each year so that I can unwind. I am so calm there, no matter what is going on with my life back home.

The tranquility of sitting on a bench at Loon Lake, drinking a delicious chocolate malted from Chestertown's Main Street Ice Cream Parlor and Restaurant is incredibly helpful to me. I watch the birds fly around in the beautiful Adirondack trees as I listen for the quietness. Sometimes, the only sound I hear is my slurping from the bottom of the cup!

I love sitting on that lake's bench in the early morning or sunset because there is hardly anyone else there. I've been there in the spring, summer, and fall. My favorite time is the fall, because of the colorful leaves surrounding the calm water.

The way I "discovered" Chestertown was interesting: as soon as Dr. Jaiani said to plan something, Aiden and I immediately drove to our local Barnes & Noble store. I asked the desk clerk to help me find a book about the Adirondacks' bed and breakfast locations. She did, and I opened it and randomly pointed to Landon Hill B & B in that town. I called the friendly owners, Judy and Carl, and got the ball rolling for our first trip northward. (Sadly, it has subsequently closed.)

Driving on the Northway in New York State is so lovely! I still remember driving on it to go to college at SUNY Plattsburgh. The sights and sounds are spectacular.

When Aiden and I made our first trip to Chestertown, I "found" restaurants and gift shops to explore. Every year when we went back, we visited our favorite spots and then added some new ones to our list. Everyone who lives and works at these establishments is so gentle. That's exactly why I have to go there.

Another B & B we discovered in a nearby town called "Adirondack" is the Adirondack Pines B & B. I think it is so endearing that the title includes the town's name, "Adirondack," and it's in Adirondack, NY, in the Adirondacks. Nancy and Dan are also friendly B & B owners. I would lie in their front lawn's hammock all day if I could!

Aiden and I also loved renting a canoe or boat to be out on one of the lakes. What a view! There are so many wonderful activities to do there.

Aiden and I drove around many lakes and towns when we visited their B & Bs. I love to eat the seafood crepes at Friends Lake Inn. I truly feel sorry for the poor waitress or waiter who has to tell me they're no longer on their menu (or they are out of stock).

I enjoy walking the many steps down to the lakefront benches on Schroon Lake. Taking in the sights as we drove to North Creek was so refreshing. I wish I could do all of this more often, because it is a natural way to "chill out."

Another great restaurant Aiden and I discovered near where we visited up there is called "Sticks and Stones." It's in the area of Schroon Lake, and boy, is its food delicious! They even have s'mores for dessert indoors. What fun!

As I've said, a trip to the 'dacks (as they are affectionately called by some) is well worth it! The people there are friendlier than anywhere else I've ever been. Every time I'm there, I'm grateful that my parents brought me there so long ago.

After three to four days of rest and relaxation, we headed back home. But, that's not without a stop on the Northway at Bolton Landing. Here, too, there are wonderful gift shops and unique places to visit. We began that stop at a furniture store (Bolton Garden Center and Country Store) that sells way more than just that! We sat outside and enjoyed the lemonade in the warmer months and their hot chocolate in the cooler ones. We then walked around town browsing and purchasing some unique Adirondacks things.

At home, and under stress from everyday life, I've taken various prescriptions over the last few years to do what the Adirondacks do for me naturally. The meds bring the same sense of stillness that I feel every time I travel northward. God created beautiful landscapes in those mountains! A sign in my condo that reminds me about it all says: "The Mountains Are My Happy Place."

My favorite T-shirt purchase on a recent Adirondack trip said it best, "Adirondack.calm."

A sign I purchased for my fireplace at home reads, "Love is in the Adirondacks."

A sign above my front door proclaims, "Rest and Relaxation – you've gotta get away if you're gonna get a life!"

So true!

I can't wait until I have the time to bring my dog Happy to this wonderful environment.

Chapter 23

THINGS PEOPLE GET RIGHT

I KNOW THAT my personality now notices negatives way more often than I notice the positives. This was always true about me but my brain injury has heightened it enormously.

I HAD to take time to mention here the "acts of kindness" I've noticed that truly help me cope better with my life as it is now. I know the following list is not in chronological order and not all I've seen – it's the ones I remember the most....

I love going to craft fairs. I schedule them frequently. I enjoy the unique, artistic gifts that many people have. I also enjoy the delicious bake sales that are at most of the craft fairs I attend. One particular bake sale that fits right into this chapter is the Miller School Craft Fair held each October near where I live. As I was writing this book, I went to the craft fair early one Saturday morning. The day before, I had lost my pocketbook and luckily had it returned with nothing missing. My memory loss causes me to forget things too often. At the fair was a school fundraising activity selling pies. I bought a delicious-looking one from this eighth-grader named Grace Arcadipane. I told her I might drop the pie as I walk around because I have "the dropsies," so she offered to hold it at their table. Then I told her I have memory problems, and I might forget it when I leave. Very sweetly, she said, "Give me your name and cell number. If you don't pick it up in a couple of hours, I'll call you to remind you." [Just writing this now, I'm getting goosebumps!] I teared up, went to see the crafts, and decided her kindness had to be recognized.

And, a year later, her cousin, Emma Arcadipane, and her friend, Lauren MacIsaac, offered to do the same thing for me, unbeknownst to them that Grace was in my book already, for being so sweet. These kids sure were raised right!

More adults should take care of one another as Grace and others took care of a stranger those fall mornings. A small gesture like this could make someone's day. I told this story to my editor, who called Grace "a sweet pea," and here it is – the first entry in this chapter about getting it right. Thank you, girls! Amazing!

Another person who did what could seem to be a small gesture, but it deserves mentioning, is a woman named Jane Sileo. (I hope I spelled her name correctly.) We ended up chatting for a while about our similarities in the field of special education, after I told her that her "cart kindness" was going to be noted in my book:

I had just had another "mini-meltdown" in a grocery store because the couple in front of me put 21 [as counted by my injured brain's hyper-vigilance] items on the conveyor belt under the sign that read "14 items or less." Instead of just biting my tongue and letting them off the hook, I mouthed off to everyone within earshot. As I left the store, embarrassed one more time about my inability to THINK IT but NOT SAY IT, a sweet woman, Jane, in the parking lot just offered to take both of our carts to the return area. I knew this was God's way of showing me a random act of kindness, seconds after I had done just the opposite.

She and I talked about SUNY New Paltz, special education, and brain injury. It's amazing to me how God puts certain people in your path just at the exact moment you need them there. Because a stranger was kind to me, I bit my tongue the rest of that day when other annoying experiences took place. Time and time again, I'm learning how to behave better just by watching certain other people....

Another example, from a bake sale I attended for the Christmas season of 2015, happened at a church near where I live that lets you select a pound of your favorite home-baked cookies, have them weighed in, and then leave with them to enjoy later on.

As I stood in the long line of other anxious-to-get-started patrons, my very heavy purse, filled with meds and things I carry everywhere so I don't forget them, kept falling off my shoulder and hitting the table where the scrumptious desserts were displayed. As I tried to balance it all and not drop anything, a sweet woman who volunteered there offered to hide my purse under a table so I could select cookies without the purse bothering me. I gave the purse to her, knowing it was in good hands. (I have pretty good radar for good people.)

Again, this small gesture of kindness by this stranger, Shamien Jansen, may seem trivial, but I have to point out when people go out of their way to be nice, because so many times kindness is not extended and, instead, people treat others badly. It has to get noticed when someone gets it right.

I know I've complained about people who think only of themselves in lines. Let me make a quick mention of a nice person. Her name is Michelle, and I met her in a line at a grocery store. She let me cut in front of her when she saw that I had only a couple of items. She said she likes to pay it forward. This July 2016 brief encounter needs to be listed here because some other people do not do this ever. Thanks, Michelle!

Another example of a kindness towards me by a stranger happened as I was compiling this chapter. Though I was too emotional to get her name, a woman in a local QuickChek convenience store hugged me when I began to cry as I got my coffee. It was Christmastime.

You see – this woman, whom I didn't know, was excitedly using the

ATM there to get money, as her young daughter was asking her over and over what time their train left. Though I didn't know, I suspected where they were headed. I just boldly and bluntly stated, "You are going to Radio City's Christmas Spectacular, aren't you?"

The mother gushed, "Yes, we are!"

And that's when I started to cry – because it reminded me of long ago when my family and I would go to that show when I myself was a little girl.

That mommy's excitement reminded me of my own mother's joy in our family's doing that same trip. So, I cried, and this woman just instinctively hugged me. It only lasted seconds, as they had to hurry to the train station, but it lasted in my mind all day. One hug can make a difference.

Another act of kindness that I noticed after my editor asked me to try to point out positives (instead of all the negatives I'm too focused on), was from a woman named Elizabeth O'Rourke. She and I coincidently were at the same nail salon in July 2015. I'm not really a "nail girl," but I do like my toenails polished for the summer sandal season. So, anyway – as we both sat in the big, comfy chairs having our pedicures, my "big ears" overheard her discussing the annual tradition she has, which is baking Scottish shortbread for her family and friends.

That brought me back to my childhood when Grandma McColl did just that. As I got older, my mother took on that tradition. They both did a delicious job of preparing that dessert each year to remember the country, Scotland, where they were born and raised. As Elizabeth talked, I listened, and then I had the nerve to tell her that my mom and I weren't communicating at the moment and that I would love to pre-order from Elizabeth some of her shortbread because I probably wouldn't get any shortbread from my mom. In a heartbeat, she scribbled down her name and number. Months later, as I was writing this chapter, I contacted her and she baked me a tin of her lovely recipe. Eating it made me think of Christmases long ago.

This stranger could have just told me no when I asked her to please bake me some. Instead – she was thoughtful, and that's why it deserves mentioning here. Thank you, Elizabeth. [As a side note – I actually did receive a package of shortbread from my mom, which made the holidays taste even sweeter.]

As I've narrated in this chapter plenty of times, I will seek, and thus find, a church's bake sale. One church near where I live that has an excellent "Cookie Caper" each Christmas season is the St. James United Methodist Church in Kingston, NY.

I have sometimes been the "line-leader" (i.e., the first one in to pick my pound of delicious treats). Some years I have held that honorable position and other years I'm a bit late and have to wait for others to select their favorite cookies before me.

As I was working on this chapter of trying to notice what others do that helps me, I had to include an invitation I was given as I paid for my soon-to-be-gobbled-up treats. The woman who is at the register each year taking the money for my selections, Linda Primiano, showed me a printed invitation to a Christmas pageant their church was having the following night.

So, Aiden and I went to see this group of performers, both young and old, teach the lessons of Christmas with an interesting flair. For part of the show, they wore Santa hats and glowing light necklaces, but still got the true meaning of Christmas across to their audience.

As I sat there and cried somewhat, Aiden leaned over and told me, "This is where you need to be," because he knew how much I struggled with certain places I go where I don't fit in and I'm not "fed." This beautiful, old church with gorgeous stained-glass windows and an old-fashioned organ right next to performers who dress like I do helped me immensely that night. I believe we all need to feel like we're accepted even when we dress differently from others for special occasions (like singing Christmas music, for example).

This church's inviting me in was exactly what I needed at the end of that weekend when I had felt left out from some other function. So – here's my suggestion – invite a stranger to the next thing you're helping plan and hopefully that person will feel included just when they need to feel warmth. That's how it felt for me.... Thank you, Linda.

As Meredith Vieira stated on her former talk show, as I wrote this part of the chapter (December 2015), "It doesn't take a lot to make a huge difference." She's so right – small gestures can have a big impact on someone you barely know. That sweet invitation to a pageant made all the difference that holiday. Those performers made me happy each time I remembered their message. The play was *The Best Present Ever*, and it lived up to its title.

Another example of someone doing something right is about the cheeriest drive-thru worker I've ever encountered. Tyler Kuhn takes my order at MY Dunkin' Donuts. When I jokingly asked if he could sell me some of his "happy pills" (since he's glowing each time I'm there), he pointed to the cross around his neck and said, "No drugs, no alcohol, just God." What a testimony! I look forward to waiting in line in my car each time I'm thirsty and need an unsweetened iced tea with lemon. I get so much more than that thirst quenched by this young man!

In the summer of 2016, I needed another trip to decompress, so, of course, Aiden and I headed up north (like I wrote about in my Adirondacks chapter). As we were walking around the beautiful town of Bolton Landing up there, I was becoming upset because that's our last stop on our trip homeward. I never want to get back to the pressure of everyday life back home!

So, I was trying to do what one of my doctors and my editor counsel me to do, which is to find something positive in every negative. As I walked past Town Hall, I decided to go in and tell them that their town will be in my book. All I planned on doing was dropping off my business card, but as I was doing this, a friendly woman, who I found out later was named Shannon, scurried in to ask me if the keys she just found on the sidewalk were mine. They weren't, so she spoke with the two women working at the counter.

As soon as I observed all of this, I exclaimed, "This is going in my book because my editor wants me to focus on things that people get right."

Shannon could have just left the keys lying out there, and get back to her job (Reflections Hair Salon). But, instead, she did the thoughtful thing and helped someone else out. I hope whoever lost those keys was really grateful when they and their keys were reunited.

So, I found the positive of leaving the Adirondacks – people like Shannon who take care of others. It's just one more reminder of how we all should pay it forward…. That kind of stuff really helps us all.

One day in the fall of 2016, as I was barely keeping it together emotionally due to: my facial skin cancer surgery's infection; my dog Happy's blood work testing to find out if she had thyroid problems; my mom's crying on the phone the day before because she missed going to her church again (due to no driver available) and thus being put on her church's shut-in list; and on top of all that, making schedule changes with my editor and others so I could be with Aiden when he went to an important doctor appointment up at Albany Med. to find out if he had pancreatic cancer, two beautiful things took place that I had to write about here.

The first one begins gory, but hang in there, it gets beautiful. It took place in the vet's office as I was paying my bill for Happy's visit moments before. This man hurriedly came in carrying a petrified and shaking little cat and said he had just witnessed someone run over the cat on a nearby road, but then that driver just drove away. Blood was on the man's hands, and he and the vet took the cat right in to the back room. I thought this was incredibly kind of the total stranger to bring a hurting animal to the closest vet. Whoever hit the cat and just left the scene, you're an example of what's wrong in our society. The man who rescued it, you're an example of what is good and right.

The second beautiful example is from two people I know well from my church. I mentioned the mother, Debbie Two, in my Friends chapter because of all the helpful texts of *Bible* passages that she sends me. She also is a great listener on the phone and puts entries on the computer for me for our church's prayer chain when I'm unable to do it myself.

The day before this example took place, I was in a very dark place psychologically. Three very upsetting sentences were said to me by someone at our church. I left the room there and cried. Also, I was worried about other stuff too. I tried to pull myself together in the afternoon by going to a movie to get my mind out of the "dark place." But, I couldn't even keep it together there during a silly animated film, so I threw my popcorn and soda away and went to my car and sobbed. [And believe me, when I toss movie popcorn, I'm in BAD shape!]

Right then, I received a text from Debbie, and it said this:

> "Fear not, for I am with you;
> Be not dismayed, for I am your God.
> I will strengthen you,
> Yes, I will help you,
> I will uphold you with My righteous right hand."
> *Isaiah 41*:10 [NKJV]

Could these exact words have been any better right that very minute? I was afraid about my dog and Aiden and my mom and me. Because of the words Debbie sent me, I was able to breathe, then drive safely on the bridge over the Hudson River I had to cross to get home. I know God had Debbie send that very helpful message when she did because I was truly hurting.

The very next day, she and her son Gordon brought me flowers and chocolate muffins. Man – did that cheer me up even more! Poked into the chocolate muffins that they brought over to me that day were these little decorations that had pictures of Mickey Mouse, saying some helpful words to me:

"You can do it!!"

"You are dearly loved!!"

"Don't worry, be happy!!!"

"Janet is awesome!"

I've saved these tiny decorations and re-read them to cheer me up when I'm worrying about Happy, my mother, me, this book....

Another story is when I met a fifth-grader named Rachel Kahn, who was featured in my local newspaper, the *Daily Freeman.*

This "Mad Hatter for St. Jude's" initiated a campaign to benefit St. Jude's Children's Research Hospital. She collects hats to give to the children who have lost their hair due to cancer treatments.

She baked delicious cupcakes and sold them at a street fair. The day I met her, to donate a new, crocheted Mickey Mouse hat, I met her parents as well. I told them they did a wonderful job raising her. Good job, Rachel, Rosie, and Scott!

After that, I was writing more of my book again and able to concentrate on the positive, versus the ugly stuff of life. Isn't it truly amazing how seemingly small gestures of kindness can do a world of good when someone is in rough shape? I can't wait for the day that I'm the one who needs less help and is able to give more reassurance to someone who is struggling.

One story moved me so much, my editor allowed me to squeeze in one more add-in at the very end of my work on this book. It, of course, was about a child.

One of the shows I love to watch to help cheer me up is *America's Funniest Home Videos* on ABC Sunday nights. Other than the videos of heads getting hit, I laugh and laugh at the silly things caught on tape.

This child's name is Luke Finlan, and he was filmed crying as he sang with a chorus of other fourth graders who were graduating from a school he obviously loved. It was so endearing to see him show his emotion at the end of this school year.

I wasn't the only one moved by it, because his video won first place and the $10,000 on that episode. But, the story gets even better!

AFV did something they don't normally do. A few weeks later, they showed a follow-up to how Luke spent his winnings.

This young man donated much of the money (many thousands of dollars) he won to various charities and people in need in the area where he lives (Latham — near Albany, NY). Luke was raised right! Great job, Kathy and Jon!

I've written about Adams Fairacre Farms' employees elsewhere. One more employee needs mention, even though, when I turn these words in to the editor, he's going to say, "No more additions!"

This food preparer, Paul, (a manager maybe?) was filling the food selections one day in the Kingston, NY, store. I was standing near him. I was shaking like a leaf because my dog Happy was very sick with diarrhea, and the vet had just told me she had to eat white rice and boiled chicken.

I can't cook safely anymore, due to my memory problems, so my friend Marian, who used to help me in her kitchen before she stopped cooking, too, due to her aging, told me to go to Adams.

I explained to Paul that a bag of someone's garbage had been placed inside my car by someone one day when I was in a super rush to pack my car. My dog Happy found the garbage, full of little opened bottles of vanilla shakes, and since she's lactose-intolerant, she got very sick. [Ironically – I HATE vanilla – those bottles weren't MY garbage.]

Paul had already prepared white rice, so he directed me to fill a container up with that while he ran into the back of the store and boiled chicken just for me (us).

I cried the whole way home thinking about how sweet this man was to me even though we'd never met before this frightening day. He didn't have to go out of his way for this upset customer. But, he did. In a couple of days, Happy was feeling better, thanks to Paul.

Another amazing story that gave me goosebumps as I wrote it, just as it did when it actually took place, is about a couple named Dale and Deena Carnell from Salisbury, NC. I'll get to them in a minute....

You see, Aiden and I left my condo very early on the morning of Sunday, July 31, 2016. We were driving to Florida to make a surprise visit to my mom. The reason I needed to see her was because she was having a lot of health issues one more time.

Before we decided to go, the doctor wanted to give her another MRI to make sure her brain tumor wasn't causing the new symptoms. Her tumor was discovered in 2010, after mine was, and it was not removed for various reasons.

When she was headed to her MRI appointment, the taxi driver took her walker away to put it in the trunk. My mother's Parkinson's means she needs help with movement. As a result of nothing to hold on to, she fell.

When I heard this horrible story, I drove over to Aiden's house and asked him if he could drive me to Florida, because I had to see my mommy. I was crying uncontrollably.

This all happened the same week that I was volunteering at my church for Vacation Bible School. I finished that up, and then I took the next few days to rearrange my seven upcoming appointments because we were going to Florida. The one reason we didn't leave right away was because Aiden's 50th high school reunion was approaching, and I couldn't ask him to miss that to help me.

I decided not to tell my mom, so she could have a happy surprise on her doorstep (me, my dog Happy, and Aiden). With the help from Grace at the Hampton Inn in Kingston, NY, we found a H.I. in North Carolina that accepts dogs – Salisbury's Hampton Inn.

Aiden and I have done this trip many times (since at that time I was not medically able to fly) so we knew the route. Usually, we went straight there with only stops for food and restrooms. But, we both knew we had to rest some this time. I knew I had to take my doggie, because she is so wonderful with my over-the-top peculiarities.

So, when Aiden drove the 12 hours that first day, we arrived safely at our stopping point. He was extremely pooped, so I walked Happy and then went to Longhorn's Steakhouse to get us our take-out dinner.

It was after 8 p.m. and I was exhausted, grouchy, and worried about my mom, as well as about the second day of travel the next day. They took my order, and that's when I met the couple who are going to be the last story in this chapter of positive stories.

Dale and Deena were super-friendly and listened to me. I told them that we left NYS at 7 a.m. and were trying to cheer up my mom the next day in Florida. We swapped stories about family stuff and more. I was so worn-out, but I knew these two people were good people, because they talked to a total, grumpy stranger as they sat at the counter eating their dinners.

When my $55 bill was brought over, Dale immediately told the waiter to put it on their tab.

I said, "It's two dinners and an appetizer – it's not just for me alone."

Dale responded with words that I will always remember. "You're taking care of your mama, and that deserves a free meal. My wife and I are blessed and so we're happy to do it."

I began to choke up. When I have nothing to say, you know I'm moved. I finally got out a "Thank you very much." They wished us a safe trip, picked up their doggie bag of leftovers, and hugged me good-bye. I sat alone just looking up at the ceiling while telling God this is a God-sighting. When a total stranger does a complete random act of kindness, it is incredibly moving.

I gave them my card, so hopefully one day they'll see their names here. I'll try to send them a copy of this book.

So, I know when I put the pen down for this chapter, more positive examples will take place, but I have to end it here to get to other incomplete portions. I think this last example is the perfect way to end this chapter because it shows how much one act of generosity and sweetness can help someone.

Dale and Deena blessed Aiden and me with a delicious dinner. Now it's my turn to pay it forward.... I wish there were more people in the world like these two. The world would be a better place if there were.

The people I've written about here have care and concern in their hearts in many different ways, but it's all good. Thank you for getting it right! I pray more of us get it right like these folks do!

Chapter 24

THE LADY AT THE BEACH

IN ADDITION TO the Adirondacks, another place I've been to that has helped me relax is Murrells Inlet in South Carolina. My then-boyfriend Aiden had some friends who own a house there. Aiden is thinking about relocating there, so he wanted me to visit to see what I think. [Since we've broken up, it doesn't matter.]

Well – this is what I think anyway – it's great there! I visited South Carolina's beautiful Huntington Beach with him in the summer of 2015. I have a humorous tale to tell….

I packed our beach bags, a beach umbrella, and Happy, my dog. She had almost never been to a beach before (other than a quick stop at the beach in Daytona Beach, Florida). What a fun time she had on the beach in South Carolina, rolling around in the ocean after the waves hit the shore. Aiden and I tied her up to a hook we put in the sand and attached her leash to. Of course – sand is not such a great surface to secure her. And, when a little crab crawled out of a sand dune nearby, Happy took off in full pursuit!

I was chasing her to grab her leash. Aiden was chasing the beach umbrella that flew into the air as Happy took off and pulled it out of the sand. Other beachgoers had a good chuckle at all of this chaos. When Happy reached the crab, she backed off, so I think she knew not to pounce on it, or it would be trouble. I grabbed her leash, walked her back to our spot on the beach, as Aiden set up the umbrella all over again. We talked about Happy's crab chase on and off for the rest of our vacation. I bought a sign while there that says, "What happens at the beach, stays at the beach!" But, I'm sharing Happy's story anyway.

The reason I titled this chapter "The Lady at the Beach" is because, though there's more later in this chapter about the other great things about South Carolina, I have to tell the story that brought happy tears to my face right after Happy's crab chase.

Some woman, whose name I forgot to ask though I told her and her husband I'd be writing about it, saw Happy loose. Instead of just sitting idly by, I think she quickly figured out we were "newbies" to the beach with our dog. The lady got up from her spot, quite a distance from ours, to inform us that sharks were on the edge of the ocean and to hold on to our dog tightly. We looked up and sure enough, seagulls and beachgoers alike were watching sharks swim very close to the shore. How sweet that a stranger would help us navigate safety for my pet! I teared up when she walked away, because I rarely notice when people are just plain, old nice.

Besides the beaches in South Carolina, we also enjoyed excellent food. One specialty that I had never heard of before was She Crab Soup. Why it's called that I have no idea, but I call it delicious. One of our waitresses at a wonderful establishment, Saltwater Creek, told us many local restaurants have that soup. I want to go back to South Carolina just to have some more….

Another food I over-ate there was Fried Oreos at Poppy's. I've eaten that fun selection at various fairs, but Poppy's was even more fabulous! I even took some to go on our last stop there, and thus they sat in a cooler for the 16-hour drive back to my place in New York State! What a treat they were as I ate them immediately after Happy and I emerged from Aiden's car. I'm salivating now for them, as I write this.

Another fun activity we did while vacationing in South Carolina was a dolphin watch. We went out on an inflatable boat that felt very safe and secure. Some of the other "dolphin watchers" sat right on the rim of the boat. Aiden and I sat on a bench in the back, but we still had an excellent view!

Dolphins came very close to our boat. They are such beautiful creatures. Seeing one so close has been on my "bucket list" for years. I started to cry happy tears every time one jumped out of the water. What also made me extremely pleased on this boat trip was the behavior of the woman who sat next to us. Every time I stood up to take a picture, Aiden held onto my arm because he knows I lose my balance easily. I can "teeter-totter" on an even surface, so a moving, small boat makes it even scarier.

This woman, to whom I hadn't explained anything yet, saw Aiden helping me, and instinctively, she moved out of our way so I could snap pictures. I know that many people would just sit there and not try to be so accommodating. Later on, I told her about some of the side effects of my brain injury and my balance issues: going down stairs, walking on uneven surfaces, or standing on a wobbly boat are all part of my life story now. I also told her about this book. I hope she gets to read about her kindness someday. Taking care of others is really something I don't witness often enough….

And finally, what I want to end this chapter about South Carolina with is both a positive and a negative:

The only negative thing I could say it is that, as of this writing, motorcyclists in this state are not required to wear helmets. I find this appalling, considering my knowledge of brain injuries. Each time I saw a motorcyclist while I was down there, I said just that to them. Hey, folks, safety first! An accident that causes a brain injury affects everyone in their life forever! [And helmets are needed everywhere for biking, snowmobiling, skateboarding, ATVs, *etc.* I've heard horror story after horror story of families permanently changed when this does not take place.]

And now – back to the positive: South Carolina is the cleanest state I can remember. There is NO trash by the side of the road as we see almost everywhere in New York State. There are signs about littering everywhere in South Carolina, and there is a hefty $1000 fine announced on those signs (much larger than the NY State fines for littering).

Another sign I read in South Carolina said, "Litter trashes everyone." How true! I really wish New Yorkers could learn from the folks down south because there is so much trash thrown out of cars throughout our state.

Our church, like so many other groups, actually has to plan a couple of Saturday mornings each year to gather together for a highway clean-up to pick up garbage others have thrown out of their vehicles. I think it is great that people volunteer for this disgusting job, but I also feel it's so sad that it has to be done in the first place.

I helped my church with this a few times after my brain surgery cured me of my fear of germs. I found wallet contents, an engagement ring, [GROSS-OUT ALERT] dirty diapers, used tampons, condoms, and so much more. Of course, I was thrilled about God's ability to cure me of my mysophobia (and by our having rubber gloves on), but I was grossed out by the selfishness of others.

The people of South Carolina get it right. They obviously care about their state and that is noticeable. Because they are so clean, friendly, and such great cooks, Happy and I will be back someday....

Chapter 25

MISFIT TOYS

I SOMETIMES FEEL like I'm one of the misfit toys in the *Rudolph* TV movie. I could cite example after example of this, but here are some:

There's a funeral home that I've unfortunately had to visit for wakes too many times. Inside the building, there's a staircase leading to a private area upstairs. On the staircase is a sign about "monsters" being there.

I find a sign like that pretty rude for people passing by it to a room where a dead body or ashes are set out. After witnessing it many times, I finally spoke to a worker there about it.

I told him how I thought it was inappropriate for a sign worded like that in a solemn place such as a funeral home. I also told him I'm the type of person who notices a lot more than the average person and didn't mind speaking my mind.

He just laughed me off. Does that sign bother others, too?

Another example is that it is so hard to be in so many social settings and/or watching TV shows or movies, and to not be a mommy. My heart actually hurts that I never had any children. It's just one more example of how I'm a "misfit toy."

Add to that, all the women who have favorite recipes and/or hobbies like gardening, knitting, sewing, or crocheting. I don't do any of those either. I really am very different from the majority of women. Sometimes, that feels okay. Sometimes, it doesn't.

Another example of how I don't "fit in" is one behavior that I do that I bet many don't.

When I'm driving behind an erratic driver, I call 9-1-1. I've called about someone doing 20 mph in a 45-mph zone. I'm worried they're sick or something.

I've called many times about speeders and/or swervers, perhaps due to texting, drugs, or alcohol. Once, I even called about a dog on the back of an open pick-up truck with the driver speeding over 60 mph in a 55-mph zone. Isn't having a dog on the open back of a moving vehicle against the law? If not, it should be!

I know most people wouldn't even notice as much as I do, much less go to the trouble of pulling over to make a call about it. But, I worry about others on the road, mistreated dogs, and so much more.

That's why I call myself a "misfit" – because I don't mind my own business as much as others do.

Another example is that I miss handwritten thank-yous when I buy something for someone. In this modern age of technology, I dislike that the only form of communication with most people is through a device, not voice or the written word.

I also use outdated equipment, such as alarm clocks, watches, cell phones, *etc.* I get teased by certain people about my "ancient cell phone," but I couldn't care less about having the newest device or gadget. I'm clueless to hashtags, apps, Twitter, *etc.* I affectionately dub myself "TC" (Technology Challenged).

So, please, those of you who "fit the mold" better than some of us do, show us some love. We deserve it, too!

This is another chapter that could go on and on....

Chapter 26

TRIGGERS

THERE ARE SO many things that take place each day that trigger me. This could actually be the largest chapter in this book. But – to save time (and to keep the chapters as brief as possible since that's how I now read best, another symptom of brain injury), I'll share only some of my "favorites." The following list is what has upset me the most when others have dealt with me post-brain injury.

Some folks I write about here are total strangers, but the sadder part is that many of these examples are by people who should know better, since they know I have permanent brain damage.

The first example I'm presenting happened Christmastime 2015. The person who triggers me practically every time he speaks to me will remain nameless, but my editor's name for him is "Trigger." Suffice it to say, that in his position, he should know better. I think he actually thinks he's being funny when he teases me. But what I think is that he should respond more appropriately because of being informed by a letter from my doctor about how to handle me best.

He thinks it's funny to tell me to go write something down in my notebook, though it's been explained that my notetaking is the way I process information. Others who overhear him teasing me tell me it is the devil who's playing with my brain (*i.e.*, letting this person "get" to me). Whether it is the devil or not, any person in a leadership position should never purposefully make someone feel awkward. I will take notes forever so I can remember the day's events. It's not a joking matter.

In the book *Where is the Mango Princess? A Journey Back from Brain Injury*, by Cathy Crimmins, such note-taking is titled a "compensatory strategy" which, for her husband after his brain injury, was an appointment book and "to do" lists. All of these I use diligently to make sense of my life. [I've listed MANY helpful quotes from this book in my recommended readings chapter at the end of my book; please check them out; her book is excellent.]

Another trigger for me is when Trigger teases me about other things. Once when he was trying to line up a table in the middle of a large room, instead of just asking me to help him, he said "Oh – you're the perfect person for this job because you like everything perfectly even!" Now – some people would be able to react on an even keel to that sentence. I, on the other hand, am way-too-sensitive since my brain injury, and what I actually hear is him pointing out how annoying my personality is....

Once when I was looking for someone at this location, the same leader said, "He is hiding from you" (and then he giggled). Again – that irritated me, because I interpreted that to mean that other person wanted to get away from me. Remember, this leader was filled in on how to speak carefully to me. He's book-smart, but he lacks the skills to take care of others who need his help the most.

I've lost sleep over the decision to include these examples here for others to read, because some folks in my life who have listened to me report my feelings after these episodes will know who I am referring to here (though I never stated his name or job title). That may not sit well with them, but I obviously decided that was okay because the reason I'm writing this book is to help others take better care of the brain-injured.

So, please, stop teasing, kidding, giggling, etc., at someone who has a hard time accepting those behaviors. Show compassion, love, and warmth. That's what God has instructed us all to do. Remember a brain injury is not always easily recognizable.

As one of my doctors stated, "It's a shame that you go to that place for support and this is what you get."

Another public place where I am often triggered is restaurants. For some unexplainable reason, I have EXCELLENT hearing nowadays. Unfortunately, that means I overhear things I truly wish I had not.

One thing that far too many people do that really grosses me out is when we're all seated near one another eating our various menu selections at a restaurant, diner, or even fast-food place, certain families find it acceptable to discuss disgusting subjects such as "Aunt Mary's surgery" with all the blood, guts, and gory details, as I'm trying to enjoy my forkful. I would "love" to join in their conversation and tell them they're not in their own kitchen or dining room, so could they please stop discussing bodily functions while the rest of us are trying to enjoy our meal. But, I don't say anything, and then I just get angrier and angrier. I've stormed off to the restroom many times so I don't create a scene for all of the people there – many of whom are oblivious to what's going on. I just wish others would think of others instead of just themselves…. [Ironically – as I was writing about this trigger, a group of my own friends did this about someone's hospital stay. I rudely interrupted my friend who was speaking and asked her to stop. When I explained why, another friend at our table said no one could hear us. I vehemently disagreed. Please stop talking about medical issues when people are eating!]

Another conversation I overheard at a restaurant was about a suicide. This family had gone out to eat to discuss what had recently taken place in their family. Of course, this conversation shouldn't have been listened to by anyone else, so I asked the hostess if Aiden and I could move to another table in the back so that they would have their privacy.

None of my doctors have been able to explain, to my understanding, why my hearing is so pronounced since the surgery. All I do know is that I've definitely heard things that others would wish I hadn't. And then, there are folks who say mean things about me since my brain surgery who don't care if I hear it or not. Once, I heard a lawyer call me a "wacko" at someone else's court appearance. This tortured me for days and days! This superb hearing has only been the case since my brain surgery. (My editor and I discussed the possibility that it is not hearing, but attention, which has changed.)

To digress for a moment, one time my excellent hearing actually helped a feuding couple. I was out celebrating a friend's birthday at a very noisy restaurant. A few booths away from our large table, a couple was arguing about menu selections at Panera Bread (where she wanted to go for lunch the next day). I heard her stating what she wanted to order at Panera Bread the following day, and I heard his emphatic retorts about how wrong she was, and that that place did not serve that particular item. I knew she was correct, because I had eaten there earlier that same day.

Instead of minding my own business, I left my table, walked a few tables away to this couple's booth and said that I couldn't help but overhear their conversation about Panera Bread's menu. I told the man his wife was correct, and she smiled at me and said, "Thank you very much."

After the husband stopped staring at me (probably because who does that: walk up to strangers and interrupt their discussion?), the two of them stopped fighting, giggled at my bizarre behavior, and as I watched them for the rest of their time there, they enjoyed talking. So – sometimes my good hearing is helpful.

But, now let's get back to what triggers me....

Back to that place where I'm supposed to go to feel better, I actually get teased by others, too, though I've been frequently verbal about my brain injury and my inability to deal well with teasing. These are just some of the sentences that others there have said to me [I've explained what some of these were in reference to. Some do not need an explanation. I'm sure you can figure out why they bothered me]:

- "Aren't you embarrassed by how many Mickey Mouses you own?"
- "You should use your brain."
- "You have too much stuff."
- "Why do you carry all those bags?"
- "Where's your baggage?" [She's mocking me for often bringing bags of stuff for kids there. The same person told me to go back to my car to get my bags when she saw me empty-handed. I told her they were inside already. She giggled at her teasing. I fumed, since in those bags I carry toys for little ones.]
- "Let's have Janet be our union organizer." [When some of us were told that some volunteers are actually paid for what they do. This woman who said that thinks she's being funny, but I don't. I'm no one's boss and teasing me about that hurts. Remember – I used to have one to six teacher assistants and/or aides in my classrooms, so I USED to be in charge. Now all I get to do is volunteer. I do miss the responsibility of leadership. I love being with the children. Children are my favorite people. Some of the adults, though, really get under my skin….]

In other settings where I think I should be loved unconditionally, or, at the very least, be understood, I still have to make my way through hurtful comments. Here's a small sample of some of those:

- "Let me see if you have a screw loose."
- "You're so very busy that you can't pick up the phone?"
- "You put baked goods in your Mickey Mouse container to make it look like you baked?" [No – I go to bake sales, wait on lines, spend my money and then bring the goodies to this meeting for us all to enjoy. I'm very candid that I don't bake. Why can't you just be grateful?]
- "Sarcasm isn't necessary." [This was her response when I was

asking a texted question when I didn't understand her words. This should have been my final text, since I threw my cell phone, broke it one more time, and then the doctors told me no more texting after I fixed my cell phone.]

- "You should be happy to be alive. Why do you get so upset over the littlest thing?" [Would you ask someone in a wheelchair a question like that? We all have some different burdens to carry.]
- "You don't know how to use your own camera?" [I have a hard time remembering instructions.]
- "I thought you were on a diet." [I was buying a cupcake, and a woman on the line overheard the person in my life who said that to me, and this stranger retorted, "How rude!" Thank you, lady-who-likes-cupcakes!]
- "Not all of us celebrate birthdays." [I wished "Susan" a happy birthday, since the next day it was Susan's and no one in Susan's family mentioned it, and so someone else from that family had to point their non-celebrating of birthdays out to me. Ironically, the next day, the person who was quoted here, "Sally," asked her relatives for a purse for her birthday. So much for Sally's "theory" that they don't celebrate birthdays, huh?]
- "You don't sound brain-injured." [Said by someone reluctant to accommodate my needs.]
- "You wear baggy pants."
- "That's ridiculous." [I was scared to pick up a dead mouse on the floor of the church I visited for a workshop.]
- "I wish I had meds to help me like that." [I don't appreciate someone laughing off my need for a controlled substance. I'm not proud when I have to take these meds to help me stay calm. I know tons of people who do calm themselves without needing help from a pill. God and I talk about this every time I go to swallow one. I pray for the day that I will have "thicker skin" and don't get so hurt by the thoughtlessness of others….]
- "Your Mickey Mouse clothes are strange."

- "You dominated the last meeting." [The saddest part about this sentence is that it was stated at a support group. I didn't remember talking too much at our last meeting, but, in her opinion, I did. I was mortified when it was pointed out this way. For the rest of this meeting, I only spoke when spoken to. I took a break from that group, so I could re-group.]
- "The last time I saw you, we talked about that. Why don't you remember?" [Because I have memory problems! Why don't YOU remember that?!]
- "I'm just kidding with you." [Usually – that's a masked expression for teasing.]
- "You are too young to wear a bib." [I have bibs at my house, had one at Aiden's house, and in our cars. In restaurants, I use a napkin tucked into my shirt. All of this is because half of my upper lip has no sensation in it whatsoever since the brain surgery. I dribble food and drinks each time I eat, so I use the bibs now because I always got stains on my clothes. When I'm spoken to this way, I'd love to ask that person if they've ever had anesthesia do damage to their lip! I assume they say it because some elderly people use bibs???]
- "You're over-reactive." [Yes – I am, but since you've been told that by my doctor and me several times, you really don't need to point it out one more time. I got it!]
- "You're here for the food? I thought you were dieting." [By the way – staring at desserts doesn't make you a cheater on your diet.]
- "Aren't you almost done with that book?" [Said to me teasingly only eight months after I began writing. Have you ever written a book? It takes a lot of time!]
- "Your dog is a real pain." [No – you are. My dog is my lifeline!]
- "I don't know if you are capable of learning."

I've heard of the following words being insensitively said to other brain-injured people's families. I believe these are very rude:

- "Your daughter can't think." [Yes, she can!]
- "Your husband is I.P." ["I.P." stood for "incapacitated person," which is not true!]

And here are some more things that also bother me:

- Various songs on the radio. [They bring me back to a place and time that wasn't good. For example – there is a group called "One Direction" that my niece G. loved. Any time their song, "The Story of My Life," comes on, I weep. It's a beautiful song that reminds me of what I don't have – a relationship with either of my nieces....]
- Running over an animal when driving, a bird flying into the windshield when someone else is driving, stepping on a worm.... [I am hyper-sensitive around all living creatures now. I'm not saying I didn't care about these situations before, but nowadays, I cry out loud if I run over a squirrel or a bird hit Aiden's windshield when he drove, or I step on a worm while I'm walking my dog, Happy. All of these examples are natural parts of life, but since my brain was injured, these situations take on a whole new category of things that are "odd" about me.]
- The behavior of others gets under my skin way too easily. I wish there were a "pill" to grow thicker skin. But, in the meantime, I have to learn to ignore: the folks stealing sugar packets galore (bag loads) from my coffee stop; some workers at grocery store registers who talk so fast about my bill and then get annoyed with me when I can't answer them right away; people who enjoy playing board games, invite me to join in, and then get annoyed with me when their chosen game triggers my emotions (since some board games use vocabulary that unsettles me too easily, but I try to play along because I want to be around

others); the rude, fresh words of others way too often; people who allow their cell phones' ring tones to disturb others nearby anywhere out in public; staff at some doctors' offices who clearly could not care less about the feelings of their patients and are just there for a paycheck....

Once, a woman who turned her cell phone on more than once in a movie theater was asked (politely) by Aiden to please turn it off when she did it the second time (he ignored it the first time). She did, but then used it one more time anyway. After the movie ended, I heard her call Aiden an "idiot" when she was telling her movie companion that she only had it on for a few seconds (no — it was on longer than that.)

I flipped out! I can't stand people who break the rules and then blame the person who called them on it. She kept saying to me, "I'll pray for you," sarcastically, as I told her off.

No honey, I'll pray for you that you learn how to behave better.

I had heard of adult bullies before, but this incident reminds me of name-callers on the playground years ago. She was confronted and then turned on the person who did nothing wrong. Sad.

How about when you go to the movies you "leave the world behind" and turn off your cells, so we can all enjoy our few hours away from it all?

At another time, on Christmas Day of 2016, I went to church very early to set up a table with crayons and coloring sheets for the little ones so they would have something to do during the service since their class was cancelled due to the holiday.

After I did that, I was about to set up the sometimes-weekly donation I bring of goodies to eat after church. Because it was Christmas Day, I brought a bit more for the folks to munch on after the service (peppermint Oreos, mini candy canes, and bake sale cookies.)

As I was about to unload it all, I noticed the coffee wasn't being set up as it usually is. So, I asked a greeter if we were having our Community Fellowship Hour (as it was written in the bulletin).

Her response was with an unfriendly tone of voice: "No! It's Christmas."

I said, "I know, and that's why I really thought we'd have it. That's why I am different than others," something I'd rather not have others point out.

She then said a sentence that rocked me to the core, to the point that I had to take meds before church even began. Her words made me feel really lonely. "You're single. These families here have to hurry out of here to celebrate with their families."

That was an upsetting thing to point out. I KNOW I'm not married. I KNOW I don't have children or grandchildren. I KNOW my family lives in Florida and they probably won't be calling me today like they haven't for other Christmases. I DON'T need it pointed out just because I asked a simple coffee question.

Words can really hurt, can't they?

Friends at church came to my aid. One offered to drive me home. Others sat with me and let me vent so I could focus on the music and sermon.

[By the way, people DID linger the usual amount of time after that Christmas morning service, 20-25 minutes, and ALL the cookies and candy canes were eaten except one!]

This list could go on and on for a very long time. I'm quite sure that I trigger others, as well. What one doctor has told me to do (which I'm still working on) is: when I'm triggered, either leave the situation or shut up. I actually have a sign on the back of my front door that reads, "Shut up!" I look at it each time I exit. I hope someday reading it actually works for me....

And some people can be kinder towards me. A woman at my condo said, "You get a free pass for not getting everything right." Amen!

Chapter 27

⁓

FORTUNE COOKIES

I KNOW THIS may sound silly, but I actually take to heart some of those words printed on tiny slips of paper that you get in a fortune cookie after a delicious meal at an Asian restaurant. I take some of them home with me and post them on various walls in my home, so I can read them again and again. Here are some of my favorites, with the punctuation as it was [along with an occasional comment from me] that have actually helped me think better:

- An exciting journey awaits you with your first step in a new direction [Teaching is over – brain injury advocacy has begun.]
- Don't be afraid to take that big step
- People are just as happy as they make up their minds to be
- Yesterday was a dare to struggle. Today is a dare to win
- Your talents will be recognized and suitably rewarded
- Complaints are like bee stings but compliments are like butterflies
- You can't stop the waves but you can learn to surf
- You will be called to fill a position of high honor and responsibility
- Don't be afraid of fear

- Security is not in having things; it's in handling things [Handle things better, Janet.]
- The most difficult thing to be is what other people want you to be
- Happiness depends upon ourselves
- Better face danger than always be in fear
- Your love of life can carry you through any circumstance
- The most beautiful views have the hardest climbs
- When life hands you lemons, exchange it for cookies [Chocolate chips with nuts are my preference.]
- You can't start a new chapter if you're stuck at the table of contents
- You will be the sign someone was waiting for [I hope this book helps families dealing with brain injury. Then all this work was worth it!]
- You show your true face to people that really matter
- Moments are best when you live in them
- Laugh often, laugh hard, eat and repeat [Why I so often enjoy the restaurant I got this at.]
- Do not give up – the beginning is always the hardest
- You have the ability to touch the lives of many people
- A person is not wise simply because one talks a lot [I need to talk less.]
- Honesty will reward you well
- Settle a dispute you've been having – be the bigger person and let it go
- You will be well rewarded for your hard work very soon
- If we do not change our direction, we are likely to end up where we are headed
- Don't let anyone tell you how to walk in your own shoes [Unless you have been through brain injury, please don't think that you know what it is like.]
- Enjoy yourself while you can

- Be braver today than you were yesterday
- Adversity is the first path to truth
- Patience is something you should never leave home without
- Your life does not get better by chance – it gets better by change
- Common sense will get you further than GPS [And it is quieter.]
- Make your words count – don't count your words
- Being wiser sometimes means being quieter [Amen!]
- You can't erase your past, but you can write your future
- Don't be grumpy – be grateful
- Quirkiness counts for something – embrace your uniqueness
- Don't hand out advice like candy [Stop correcting everyone, Janet.]
- Don't be a worry wart because who wants a wart?
- Who you are and who you can be is a work in progress [A sign I made for one of my classrooms told my students that.]
- The closest distance between two people is a good laugh
- The sooner you accept it, the sooner you'll get over it
- The simplification of life is one of the steps to inner peace
- Look around; happiness is trying to catch you
- Expect much of yourself and little of others
- Q. Why do some people have headaches? A. They never used it before. [Or – in my case – they have an undiagnosed brain tumor.]
- Music is the soul of language
- If you want to win anything – a race, yourself, your life – you have to go a little berserk. [Sometimes I go more than a little.]
- It is good to let a little sunshine out as well as in
- Listen to yourself more often
- Do not let what you cannot do interfere with what you can do
- The issue isn't what you're saying; mostly, it's the way [Yup!]

- Self-confidence is the first requisite to great undertakings
- Something spectacular is coming your way. [Perhaps it is that my book helps somebody else.]
- Plan to be spontaneous tomorrow. [A real struggle for me.]
- Our greatest glory is not in never falling but in rising every time we fall
- You will be graced by the presence of a loved one soon. [Really?]
- Forgive the action, forget the intent
- Smile! A smile will make you young forever
- You have a strong and sensitive personal nature. [I sure do!]
- Nothing is a waste of time if you learn something from it
- You feel restless – change is just around the corner
- You are not a person who can be ignored. [That's for sure!]
- To have joy, one must share it
- To build a better world, start in your community
- School is a building which has four walls with tomorrow inside
- Fear drives you and makes you better
- Stand tall! Don't look down upon yourself
- Our first love, and last love is…self-love
- A great man never ignores the simplicity of a child. [I never ignore children, just some adults.]
- The hours that make us happy make us wise
- Stuff happens. It is your response that counts
- Learn to listen, not hear
- A simple kindness today will soon bring you unexpected rewards
- Pick a path with heart
- Don't spend your time stringing and tuning your instrument. Start making music now! [Do you like that one, Maggie?]
- May your faith always exceed your fears – no price is too great to go through life afraid. [!]
- Romance comes to life this year in a very unusual sort of way. [Nope!]

- Welcome each day as a fresh new beginning
- One must know that there is a path at the end of the road
- A family reunion in the coming months will be a tremendous success! [I pray this one's true.]

[I'd like to give a big round of applause to the Mid-Hudson Buffet in Kingston, NY, that not only was a great field trip for my students, back in the day when we celebrated Chinese New Year, but also my favorite all-you-can-eat place nowadays. Their food and fortune cookies cheer me up!]

Chapter 28

Ms. Corrector:
There, Their, They're

Is it just me or are THERE too many people screwing up THEIR grammar? I unaffectionately dub myself "Ms. Corrector" because I catch (and then correct) so many others and THEIR mistakes. Of course, I am corrected also by people who like to catch me in a mistake I've made.

I remember my favorite elementary school teacher of the Red Hook Central School, Mrs. Meyerhoff, teaching us about "there" and "their" and "they're." I wish she could have taught so many others – even reporters from our local newspaper, who had a title in bold-face print that got it wrong: "It allows us to showcase our animals in a form that THEIR not usually seen." I wanted to call that paper one more time to inform them that the correct version for that sentence should have been "THEY'RE," for the contraction of "they are."

I think this correction stuff I do so often now is because I used to have to do it when I was a teacher. Back then, I was allowed to, and supposed to, use my "little red pen," which was actually purple. But those days are over, so now I do it at church. Our church secretary, Julie, is such a sweetie-pie who giggles when I show her typos in the bulletin each time I find them. I also do this in restaurants, as menus often have misspellings, and I even do it during doctor's appointments.

Recently, I corrected my brain surgeon when he sent out a fundraiser letter and spelled "neurosurgery" wrong. He laughed, apologized three times, and said he'd fix it for the next mailing, which so far has not happened; I got another letter from him after that appointment, and it was still spelled wrong. I still cannot believe I corrected a brain surgeon!

I know I used to mention other people's mistakes even before I experienced my brain damage, but it wasn't as heightened as it is nowadays. I still remember certain staff I worked with over the years who were fine when they were corrected, but there were others who got a little annoyed by it.

When I spoke to my NYU brain surgeon about the tumor right before he took it out, he told me that where my tumor was located probably affected my personality a lot. I laughed and said apologies were necessary to my family and to those at Ulster County BOCES. He asked me what a BOCES was, and I explained it. He told me he would speak to my family (which he did) but that I was on my own with my former BOCES colleagues.

At the time of this writing (summer of 2015), I had recently been to two Ulster County, NY, BOCES retirement parties. It was more than obvious at both functions that I had upset several people when I had worked there several years prior. Only a few people were friendly. When I shared that with a doctor, she said that I have to remember that I worked there with an unrealized brain tumor and that causes fear in them about their own unknown health issues. Also, it could be my strong personality that was exacerbated by the brain tumor led me to say things that offended people that they have yet to let go.

To this day, I see people that I did used to know way back when – I am not good at names anymore – but I can tell from THEIR faces that I once knew them. I have apologized to so many. Some people tell me what I did back then wasn't as bad as I thought it was. [And even if it was, thank you, Edna, for accepting my apology. That meant the world to me.] Others either walk away or pretend not to see me coming. When that happens, I just talk to them in my head with God's help. I mentally say I am sorry and then I "change the channel" (a neurofeedback expression) in my head. Disney's movie *Frozen* said it best: "Let it go!"

My problem is – I haven't let it go. I hold on to too many bad memories from long ago. Then, too, there are chunks of my life story that I have forgotten. Someone will come up to me and tell me they know me and how they know me. They'll share a story from long ago. Sometimes, I'll remember what THEY'RE talking about, but other times, I am completely lost. What's really upsetting is that many of the stories I can no longer remember are the positive ones. For some reason, I can recall the more painful stuff. I wish it were the other way around.

I've hurt people that I actually care for, by correcting them. One recent example is when someone spelled the word "your" incorrectly (they meant "you're"). Instead of just leaving it alone in the email, I pointed it out. The person got very upset, and I skipped a function I was supposed to attend with her, because I felt so bad about hurting someone who had been so nice to me. We are on the mends now, but I have not forgotten how this took place.

Well…at least I'm honest. I know one thing very well about myself – I correct "mistakes" every chance I get. This is something I used to get paid to do (teaching) but I think I do it now because I can't teach anymore. I think it helps me fill that gap. However, not everyone enjoys my "help."

Luckily, I am also able to be corrected, sometimes. I pray for the day that it will be all times. But, for now, let me share the various situations I "play teacher" even though I no longer am in the teaching profession.

I correct the grammar of others when they speak. For example, if someone says, "Me and Tom went to the store," I tell him or her that the correct way to state it is, "Tom and I went to the store." This usually does not go over well with others. I also correct pronunciations. For example, the word "frustration" is often mispronounced without the "fr" sound at the first syllable. It is incorrectly stated, "fustration." Who gets frustrated with me is the person I point it out to.

I go to restaurants and comment on misspellings on THEIR menus. Recently, I pointed out the incorrect use of the word "you're" on a sign in a restaurant's parking lot. A trip to that place at which I love to eat THEIR delicious lobster rolls has a sign in THEIR lot that reads, "If YOUR not eating at ___, you will be towed" – the "your" should be "you're" for "you are." Some staff enjoy my corrections. Others…not so much….

In a doctor's office, there's a sign that reads: "If you know your contagious, you must notify the Nurse immediately." What I notified them was that THEIR "your" should be "you're."

I also correct spelling mistakes. This happens a lot, and I notice tons of them. I can't believe how many mistakes are in newspapers. For a while there, I called the papers and told them about THEIR misspellings, but after quite some time doing that, I had better things to do than make these calls, because it was too often! [And I really had to refrain when I read someone was "chocked" (vs. "choked") in the Law and Disorder section of my local paper!]

One thing I finally made progress with at a newspaper office was the use of the words "maybe" vs. "may be." They were advertising the use of a flag picture in an obituary of a member of the armed forces. They incorrectly wrote it, "A flag maybe used…." After MANY calls, and even an in-person conversation with a newspaper employee in a social setting, they changed it to the correct way, "A flag may be used...." Wow! Every time I see that ad written correctly, I smile about my victory.

Besides "Ms. Corrector," I also have some other nicknames for myself. One, "The Bag Lady," has its own chapter here. A second is "Drama Queen." I actually had a bumper sticker that said that.

Another name I call myself is "Chatty Cathy." I vaguely remember having a doll with that name as a little girl, but it's true even now. I always talked a lot. One example I remember is a sign that colleagues at Ulster County BOCES used to hold up at meetings: "S U S," which meant "Shut Up, Schliff," which I found humorous. A couple of years before the tumor was discovered, I barely talked, but when I did, it was mostly about germs. But now, I'm back to talking too much. Sometimes, I catch myself, and other times, I don't. I've been informed by many people about this annoying habit, so I'm working on it....

I read in one of the advice columns in the newspaper that at least it's good that it's noticed by the individual doing it, so she can reduce it. I was relieved to read someone else has a similar problem.

Another nickname I call myself now is "Abby Normal." That's my humorous way of pointing out some of my abnormal behaviors. Some people find my "weirdness" endearing, but others shy away. That's okay.

Another one is "Nervous Nellie," because I'm fearful of so much now. My doctors tell me not to watch the news because of how scared I become over the horrible stories there. But, people talk about the news in lots of places I go, and I become frightened. Many times I've had to leave to calm down and think "happy thoughts" instead of blood, guts, and gore.

Aiden had a few accurate nicknames for me also. The ones that are fit for print are: "Talk-a-Lot" and "Sarge." I've given examples of the over-talking here, but the other one is because he felt bossed around by me sometimes. Kiddingly, he called himself "The Colonel," because that outranked me.

A funny story I can write in this chapter is that I should check my own spelling too.

A local grocery store (that will remain nameless) has a school district's name spelled incorrectly on a sign near the cash registers. I've told the management there several times about it, but, with nothing done, I gave up.

But, here comes the humorous part: once, a long time ago when I was speaking at various schools to other teachers about the Whole Language approach to reading, I added this same, incorrect, spelling to my resumé. I didn't notice that until writing this book! So, here I am, correcting a store, when it's wrong on my own paperwork. Are you smiling yet?

Once, I wrote the year "2015" when it was months and months into 2016. When the person I wrote the check to noticed that mistake, he was kind and not rude the way I can be sometimes when I correct others. I wish I could do it his way more often. As I've heard it said many times, "Can't we all just get along?"

Two funny stories that happened at my church when I was decorating for the VBS (Vacation Bible School) in July 2016 that fit perfectly here were as follows....

I was hanging the bulletin board to welcome the little ones to our cave-themed experience. But, when I was hanging the letters to "welcome" I hung it like "WELCME." I made a church lady, Jean, and myself laugh when we simultaneously noticed that I forgot the "O."

Then, I was using washable crayons to decorate the doors into our church. As I tried to write the word "vacation," I began to write "Vatican." I know my church should not have that on the doors. This example is my aphasia problem in writing (versus how it usually takes place – in my speaking).

So, I really need to be careful how I correct others, because I screw up too. I'm just so happy that I was truly able to laugh these two errors off.

The one thing that happened that same week which is not laughable, but actually mortifying, is that I called this pregnant woman "fat," when I meant to say "pregnant." That word just impulsively slipped out of my mouth when I was telling her a cute story from my own book-writing. This young woman is so gentle, she just laughed it off. I find it truly ironic that I'm the overweight one, but I mistakenly said that about someone who has a natural baby belly bump.

I wouldn't be as much of a sweetie-pie as she was if someone, brain-injured or not, used that "F-word" with me! I felt so much guilt about this mistake, I gave her a card the next day letting her know how much her forgiving personality is a blessing to me. [What's so ironic now, since she's given birth, is that she is back to looking thin, and I'M still the fat one!]

Because people use "interesting language" when they text, I steer clear of that a lot! My doctors have told me to only text once in a while. That's why I seem out-of-the-loop many times, because I don't understand hashtags (#), Twitter, apps, and oh, so much more! But, that's okay.

Sadly, I correct others about THEIR word choices way too much. Once, a friend I was talking to over the phone said, "behind your door." I had no idea what she meant and told her so in a rather rude way. She explained that she was referring to the back of my door. I would have said, "the back of your door." Looking back on that example, it's like in the category of who cares???

Once, when I was filling out the annoying paperwork before a yearly check-up, one of the questions on the form irritated me so much, I mouthed off to the poor receptionist. The form's question was: "Your age when you delivered your first child?"

Hey – remember – there's some of us women who, for various reasons, never gave birth. How about making it a bit more general? Like: "IF you've delivered a child, what age were you?" That way those of us who didn't have (or couldn't have children) don't have to feel "different."

I actually correct a museum I've been to several times, because of an incorrect date they have displayed. They tell me each time I'm THERE that several other teachers (and others) have commented on THEIR mistake, but that it's too expensive to correct, so they leave it be. Whenever I'm THERE, I verbally correct it, which sometimes amuses others around me, and sometimes it does not. That's okay – I enjoy setting the record straight even if I sometimes irritate others.

I met a lovely young lady named Ana who took my correction so well, she should teach a class on how to be nice to someone who finds your mistake.

She makes these excellent, funny-worded handbags. Many of her bags were on display at one of the many craft/artisan fairs I attend.

When I showed her that one of her bags had a misspelling on it, she gave me the bag for free (though I kept telling her I'd pay for it). She laughed at herself and was not offended at all that I had pointed to her writing on the bag, "I need a six- month vaction twice a year," and noted that "vacation" was missing an "a." She said she makes mistakes like that and she laughs about it. I told her I'd be glad to check her spellings before she makes a bag. I also told her my free bag would go on my book tour with me for when I spoke about this chapter. [I find it humorous that Ana and I both screwed up "vacation," she on her bag and I in church.]

If you want to see more of her funny bags, see Pipicucunewyork. com.

There's a term "Doo-Wally" I learned at a Dutchess County Scottish Society meeting; it is a word from Scotland – my heritage – that sort of means "out of it," so... I'm a bit Doo-Wally at times!

These Ms. Corrector stories could be a book all by themselves. I really work each day on being careful who and how I correct. I'm grateful for the folks who have done that for me.

I also want some credit for when I have the common sense enough to NOT correct someone or some place.

I needed to complete a form from our town clerk's office. On the sheet was an attached form that the Police Department would have to sign off on. On that second piece of paper is where the typo mistake, that I spotted but did NOT tell the officer, was. Where the officer was supposed to sign, it had a line asking for his singature [*sic*].

On an official document, the word "signature" was misspelled. When I noticed it, I kept silent because I know enough to not laugh when turning in paperwork to an officer.

So, even though I correct a lot, I also know when not to.

"Set a guard over my mouth, Lord, keep watch over the door of my lips." (*Psalms 141*:3)

Chapter 29

MOVIES AND MORE

MY EDITOR WANTED me to list the movies that, in one way or another, have helped me cope. Here's a short list. Because of my memory problems, I'm quite sure there were many others. But, these celebrate the ability to overcome all types of adversities. I've added an asterisk (*) when the movie relates to brain injury.

*50 First Dates** [The beginning of this film is a bit vulgar, and the facts are not actual, but hang in there; it has an excellent story about helping someone cope with a head injury. And I think the ending song is the best version of "Somewhere Over the Rainbow" I've ever heard.]

90 Minutes in Heaven

As Good As It Gets [Jack Nicholson's OCD behaviors in that restaurant were EXACTLY like mine! I used to bring my own plasticware, too.]

Baby Boom

The Bucket List [John Mayer's song at the end of this excellent movie is listed in my Music chapter.]

*Concussion**

A Dog's Purpose [Though this movie got some "bad press," I believed the folks affiliated with the film who stated there was no bad treatment of any dog while filming. This touching movie gave me a helpful mantra that I repeat daily: "Be Here Now."]

Eddie the Eagle

Finding Dory

Flashdance

God's Not Dead 2 [I wish I had seen the original. Maybe I will someday when I put this pen down.]

The Goodbye Girl

*A Heavenly Christmas** [Hallmark Movie Channel]

Hope Floats [A great quote from this movie is, "Beginnings are scary. Endings are usually sad. But it's the middle that counts the most...."]

Ice Castles

It's Complicated

Lion

Mary Poppins [This was the first movie I ever saw, and I even still have the album that came out with that movie.]

Message in a Bottle

*Miracles from Heaven**

Mystic Pizza

Rain Man [A lot of Dustin Hoffman's character's personality matched my first student, Cliff.]

*Regarding Henry**

Saturday Night Fever [Lots of scenes in this John Travolta film were shot in Bay Ridge, Brooklyn, NY, where I lived as a young child. Every time I watch it, I see stores and places I used to go with my family.]

Serendipity

The Shack [A powerful message about having God in your life.]

The Sound of Music

Stepmom [I'm not positive, but the hospital in that movie for Susan Sarandon's illness sure looked like "my hospital" (NYU). If so, little did I know when I watched that great film numerous times, that one day I'd be there myself. Also – it has an excellent Hudson Valley, NY, poster in her character's house that you see you when she's having fun with "her" kiddies. I love living in the Hudson Valley.]

Sweet November [A lovely film about love that highlighted my birthday, November 1st, and began my love of calendars.]

Sully

Terms of Endearment

Tootsie

A Walk to Remember [A great quote from this movie is: "Maybe God has a bigger plan for me than I had for myself."]

War Room [This stars Priscilla Shirer, who is an excellent author and speaker.]

When a Man Loves a Woman [This movie has the best quote: "You're not alone, honey. Never. Never." How I wish that had been said to me!]

When Harry Met Sally

The Wizard of Oz ["A heart is not judged by how much you love, but how much you are loved by others." I sometimes agree.]

Wonder [The BEST movie I have seen in a long time! It even has a favorite place of mine, Coney Island, in it.]

Working Girl

You've Got Mail

Now… Even though this part of the book was about movies, to wrap this chapter up, I HAVE to do a "commercial" for an excellent TV show on the A&E Channel entitled *Born This Way*. It's all about adults with Down syndrome and how they navigate the world.

It is so true-to-life and honestly poignant. Since I'm not writing a chapter about the television shows I watch (though some have been mentioned in here), this show I'm adding to the end of this chapter about movies because of how much I admire it.

As a former teacher of many students with Down syndrome, I just love watching every episode (sometimes more than once, thanks to my DVR abilities). If you haven't caught it, check it out. I wish I could meet all of the people on that show to tell them face-to-face how wonderful they are!

They tell it like it is, and I so appreciate that. The show covers lots of real-life examples of getting along in the world. Kudos to whoever got this show on the air!

Steven, a star on this show, said it best when he said, "Don't dwell on the past. Don't think about the future too much. You've just gotta be in the present right now."

Chapter 30

SEPTEMBER 1, 2016

THE DAY AFTER my mother's 79th birthday, I was absolutely distraught. Something went wrong with the mail that week – I never received my weekly manila envelope from my editor with all the writings I turned in to him the week before. In the two years we've done this process, not once has a package from him gone missing. Now it's "crunch time" (the home stretch of writing this book before it goes to the publishers), and I'm lost without that work.

On the phone with various people to help me find it, I became more and more upset. Aiden is sometimes not able to help me calm down, and actually, usually upsets me more with his *blasé* attitude about life's problems.

I became so bothered, I began to talk about quitting writing for a while, to take a break and "move" (temporarily) to Florida to help my aging mother.

My editor has told me stories of other writers who quit when it gets close to the end. That's exactly where I was and had become too overwhelmed by all of the deadlines, decisions, opinions, and so forth.

Talking to my mom a day earlier, I could not stop thinking about how she needed more help than I could give from NYS.

So, I had pretty much decided to go to my already-scheduled appointment the next day with my editor, but not to go over more writing, but to tell him I was going to put a hold on this venture until further notice.

I decided to go for a calming drive with my dog, Happy, so I could clear my mind of all the nonsense over the phone earlier in the day with the post offices and Aiden. Beautiful landscapes in the Hudson Valley always help me feel better.

No sooner had I left home, a particular song came on the radio. It was Simon and Garfunkel's "Cecilia," the song I wrote about here in my first chapter.

It's the song that "brings me back" to decades ago, dancing with my cousin Heather. That relationship was the main reason I became a special education teacher. It's the reason I have so many long-ago memories of teaching.

I knew as soon as I heard it, that God was speaking to me loud and clear. He was telling me not to give up, keep working on the book, and when it's done, it's done. The deadlines are only suggestions, they are not requirements.

So – I went home and tried to get back to work. As soon as I did, my friend Marla, who wrote for me here, called to invite me to a party and that cheered me up.

Right after that, I called my mom to tell her that, on top of all the pressure from this book, I had just been told by my dermatologist that I needed surgery on my face because of skin cancer. She also cheered me on and told me to get back to the book. So, a song, a friend, and my mom came through for me when I needed them most.

The envelope was "discovered." It had been sent back to the editor with one of those "Return to Sender" stickers. I had to drive back to our usual meeting spot (about an hour away), and I picked it up from him. When I brought it to the Kingston, NY, Post Office to find out why that happened, they stated, "Post Office error."

What's so great about its being found is that it was the "Businesses That Have Helped Me" chapter. I would have been devastated if I left someone out, because if I had to re-write it, I probably wouldn't have done it as well. I have notes all around my condo about what to include, but someone might have been left out. Glad I'm back on track....

Chapter 31

Music, Music, Music

Music has been such an important part of my life. It started when I tried to play the flute, but my elementary music teacher, Mrs. Van Ness, said my arms were not long enough, so I played the piano for a while. Mr. Chupay, a neighbor, taught me.

When I became a teenager, I played the bass drum and the xylophone in the percussion section of my high school band. Basically, I wanted to be in Mr. Van Ness's band so I could be near my high school sweetheart who played the saxophone. When I had to carry that bass drum in parades, I practically fell over because I think it weighed more than I did. Those were the days...to be that thin!

[As I was compiling this chapter, I learned a new thing about the marching I was once able to do. I was at a church choir rehearsal and our director, JoAnne, asked us to march in place as we rehearsed the song so we could get the beat better. I tried to march, hold my sheet music, and watch her. I lost my balance, almost hit a pregnant soprano next to me, grabbed the chair in front of me, and felt my back snap. I hid the pain because I've caused enough drama in this setting, and so

I didn't tell anyone then except Aiden what had happened. I ended up at several chiropractic appointments and needed both a back brace and a cane. So – my doctors tell me – no more marching for me. My brain can't do that much at one time!]

As I've written about here, I've met a few musicians. I was never very good at playing the piano, xylophone, or drum, but I know good music when I hear it, so that's why I'm thankful for meeting musicians.

I thoroughly enjoy going to my friend Maggie's gigs when she's hired to play her guitar at restaurants and such. Her music has such a calming effect on me.

She sings from her soul and that's so obvious. She plays requests so I get to hear John Denver, Judy Collins, and more. Keep it up, Maggie!

Recently (spring 2016), I went to hear Boz Scaggs play at the Ulster Performing Arts Center in Kingston, NY. The UPAC has a lot of great shows and concerts. Boz's warm-up singer was an excellent guitarist, Jeff LeBlanc. When I had only heard him perform three songs, I climbed over others in my row to go buy his CDs. His music touched me. He sings so articulately. His songs resonate well about things we all have to overcome in life, which is very therapeutic. He was humorous on the mic, and though he had gone to college to be a middle-school teacher, he's touring with Boz Scaggs. Because of how tall and handsome he is, I doubt any teenage girl would have paid attention in his class. Go listen to him or get his CDs – he's extremely gifted.

The music that we sing at my church, that is selected by a wonderful woman, JoAnne Schubert, helps me quiet my brain and get closer to God. Though I actually can't read music anymore, when I join one of her choirs, I listen carefully to whatever soprano sits near me, and I copy her. I know it seems funny that I can't read music because, as I said, I played instruments and I sang in school choruses and other church choirs for many years. But, reading music is very hard for me now due to my brain injury. There's a lot of words and symbols on sheet music!

So, I mark up whatever sheets I'm given with lots of arrows and words to remind me how JoAnne wants it done. If we're to sing quietly, I write "sh!" in that section. If we're supposed to hold some notes for a long time, I draw a big, long arrow to remind me to do that. I bring the sheets home with me to practice (instead of leaving them in the pile with everyone else's). If she requires our attendance at three rehearsals but offers many dates to choose from, I try to attend all of them, because I need to. There is a list of some of these excellent songs and others at the end of this chapter. (Thanks, JoAnne, for all of your help compiling this list!)

Once, when I rehearsed with our church choir, I was seated near Marian R., a sweet woman who sang with us that time. She called herself my "therapy dog," because I told her how much my dog keeps me calm. Marian was able to help me keep calm at choir rehearsals, but even before that, she helped me at Growth Groups (Sunday school classes). If I over-talked at G.G., I asked her to say, "duct tape" (or "DT" for short), and when she did, I gave someone else in our group a chance to speak. Her cues helped me a lot. [I miss her gentle nature SO much now since she moved away.]

In lots of the books I've read about brain injury, music is stated to be a real helper to our brain. When my friend Maggie goes to nursing homes to sing to the elderly there, families tell her what songs their loved one enjoyed and so she learns them, and plays them for the patient on her guitar. Many times, people with memory problems sing along with her. That is such a tribute to the brain and its connections to music. That's probably why my neurosurgeon wanted me to listen to music right after the operation and try to remember the words of the songs I selected.

The three months that I was not allowed to drive right after my brain surgery, Aiden and/or my parents drove me everywhere, and I sang along to whatever song was on the radio. Once, my parents were busy visiting friends, and Aiden couldn't drive me one day, so I took a cab to the post office to pay some bills. The cab driver looked amused as I belted out the song on her radio as she drove me around.

I read somewhere (maybe a church sign?) that music makes life a symphony when God is the Conductor. I think that saying helps me remember that God is the One in charge, and music helps us get through "it." (Whatever any of us is going through.)

I love to watch old movies to help me remember music better. *Mary Poppins, The Wizard of Oz,* and *The Sound of Music* come to mind for that.

A radio station near my home called "The Sound of Life" plays excellent Christian music that helps me as well. That station also has inspiring quotes that I write down and then post somewhere to read over and over. My favorite one is this: "Your past is a place of reference, not of residence!" Thanks for that one!

Certain songs on other radio stations really help me feel better, too. Pharrell Williams's "Happy" does just that every time I hear it on the radio. My dog Happy loves it too because she hears her name in it over and over again (as I sing along).

Once, when I was at a BIANYS (Brain Injury Association of New York State) Conference, a facilitator of one of the groups I attended played this song as we sat in a circle to try to work on feeling better about our new lives.

One participant, Angela Leigh Tucker, author of a book, *Me Now— Who Next?,* about her brain injury, was giggling so much in her chair she looked radiantly happy. I kept thinking, as I watched her wiggle and giggle, that I hope someday I can get over this life change as well as she apparently has. Her book is very inspirational. Her personality is helpful to be around because she's not negative like I am. She's much more appreciative of surviving. I hope and pray I get to that same "happy place" someday....

The song "I Hope You Dance" by Lee Ann Womack has also been a big help to me for many years (long before I even knew that a brain tumor was growing inside my head). The words, "When you come close to selling out, reconsider," really saved me one night. I'm not going to go into too much detail here, but suffice it to say, that one line from that song saved my life one dark and rainy evening on the Kingston-Rhinecliff Bridge in the year 2000.

One more breakup had just taken place in my very-messed-up love life, and I was totally "gone." I have a cousin named Drew, and his girlfriend-at-the-time helped me through this dark place by getting that song to me so I could hear those words. Thank you, Mo'! Your love and concern for me has NEVER been forgotten even though other important things have been.

Now, back to a happier subject – a wonderful organization that I so enjoy being uplifted by is The Singing Songbirds. I try to attend a couple of their performances a year, held at The Fountains at Millbrook, a retirement community in Millbrook, NY.

The Songbirds bring together people with disabilities, families, seniors, and/or anyone who loves to sing. The ability to read music is not necessary because they are excellently guided by their director, Peter Muir, and his wife, Judith. When I learn of the dates for their winter and spring performances, I am excited if I'm able to attend. They sing with such enthusiasm and joy, it's a wonderful evening. The ride there is beautiful (on New York's Taconic State Parkway) and reminds me of days gone by when my family drove on it to visit relatives in Brooklyn when we lived in upstate New York. These performances remind me of when my students sang for various audiences. If I had more time, I'd join their group. They seem to be a fun bunch of folks!

As I stated in the chapter about meeting Aiden, I met him at a karaoke night. I learned to sing to him the KC and The Sunshine Band's song "Give It Up." I had mysophobia, so I held the mic with napkins (which took a lot of prodding by others for me to even do). I rarely hear that great song on the radio anymore because it was popular so long ago. But, when I do, it reminds me of my karaoke performances when that tumor was "alive and well" in my brain.

Another song that I only hear every once in a while, but brings me back to a happier time in my life, is the song "Saturday Night" by the Bay City Rollers. I still fondly remember prancing around my parents' house in Florida with my relatives mimicking the song like the Scottish guys who sang it.

A song that I hope someday to be able to sing solo in my church is "Amazing Grace (My Chains Are Gone)." The version I cry over each and every time it is sung there includes the words: "my chains are gone; I've been set free…. My God, my Savior, has ransomed me." I've told JoAnne many times that I'll know when I'm ready to ask her to help me do it solo. I know that those "chains" are still there, but maybe this book's publication will help somewhat with that. This is just one of the many songs we sing in church that I've listed here. I hope they help someone as much as they have helped me.

Speaking of that, another thing I've witnessed in my church that is pure pleasure for me is when these two little girls, who sit near me, get up and dance together in the aisle as our songs are being sung by our worship team and congregation. Watching these girls enjoy the music that way always makes me feel better emotionally. The "free spirit" of little ones is so helpful to me.

So, to wrap up the chapter about music (though there are tons of songs and artists I adore but didn't write about), I just need to end by saying that all schools should make music an important part of the curriculum. Bands, choruses, plays, and other events that incorporate music are so worthwhile for a child's well-being.

Remember – immediately after my brain surgery, I wasn't told to name objects or people. I wasn't told to remember or count numbers. I wasn't told to read lots of books. I WAS told to listen to music and sing immediately to help my brain function optimally again. That right there shows how important music is. It's therapeutic.

One of the books I have listed in my Recommended Books section is *The Brain's Way of Healing* by Norman Doidge, M.D. He stated in this book that brain scan studies have shown that when the brain is stimulated by music, the neurons begin to fire in perfect synchrony with it. He goes on to write that since neurons fire in unison to music, **music is a way to change the rhythms of the brain.**

He has much more in his excellent book, some of which I've noted in my Recommended Books section. Throughout my book are stories about how I used music in my classroom. I also put on some "great productions" at various schools I taught in, with using music as the focus of what we performed. One example I remember vividly is a group of students from Pine Plains CSD singing Whitney Houston's version of "The Greatest Love of All" with photos of the kids displayed behind them as they performed. I have this recorded, and though this old VCR tape from the 1980s has faded, I still can see a little bit of it and hear my students sing this beautiful song about loving yourself. I also vaguely remember a performance we did there to the song "The Living Years" by Mike and the Mechanics.

To this day, I get very weepy when I attend local schools' play productions, because they remind me of a happier time in my life. Recently, I had to leave *Mary Poppins* at the Pine Plains, NY, high school and then *The Beauty and the Beast* performance at another local school because I was so upset, I began to cry too loudly. These are supposed to be fun events, and my demeanor ruins it for any family sitting near me, so I exit way before the play ends.

I have discussed this with my doctors, and we all agreed that I have to work on enjoying the here and now versus missing the past so much that I need medicine to calm down.

I "tested" myself at a third show. It was another local school, performing *The Lion King*. I was able to sit and stay for the entire event and needed no meds to do so. I even went up to the director and told him how thrilled I was with his show AND how pleased my doctors will be to hear that I stayed for all the songs.

So, use music to get better, whether it's at your church, your stereo, your school, or wherever. It helps your mind, body, and soul.

Here is a list of songs and hymns that I've heard sung at my church and elsewhere. They are truly inspirational, and I've been scribbling down their titles and their performers' names for three years so I could add them here.

Their words are displayed on big screens in my church for us to sing along with our worship team. Sometimes I have to just stand and listen to others around me sing the words because I'm too emotional to belt them out.

The power of God's music is such a gift. To quote a publication I read daily entitled *Our Daily Bread,* "music washes from the soul the dust of everyday life." So true!

Another publication entitled *Scientific American Mind: Behavior. Brain Science. Insights* also discusses how music feeds the brain through its power to lift moods and build connections.

To try to reduce some of my OCD behaviors (on doctor's orders), I have just named my personal favorites here in random order, not alphabetically. I'm really trying to learn how things in life don't have to be in "perfect order" to be useful and helpful. I hope you too hear this musical list and truly listen to the messages the words deliver ["by" means "sung by"]:

- "Grace Wins," by Matthew West
- "Forgiveness," by Matthew West
- "Unfinished," by Mandisa
- "Overwhelmed," by Big Daddy Weave
- "Eye of the Storm," by Ryan Stevenson
- "Victor's Crown," by Darlene Zschech
- "Write Your Story on My Heart," by Francesca Battistelli [I've done just that in this book.]
- "Bring the Rain," by Jonny Diaz
- "Amazing Grace (My Chains Are Gone)," by Michael W. Smith
- "How Great Thou Art," by Stuart K. Hine [This hymn makes

me tear up each time I sing it, because I think it's been sung at most of the funerals of my family members.]

- "I Wanna Go Back," by David Dunn [I do too!]
- "Even If," by Mercy Me [This song makes me sob, but crying can help me feel better.]
- "Control," by 10th Avenue North
- "The God I Know," by Love & the Outcome
- "We Believe," by Newsboys
- "Sometimes I Cry," by Jason Crabb
- "Everything That Has Breath," by Parachute Band
- "In the Garden," by C. Austin Miles
- "You Found Me," by Passion
- "It Is Well," by Matt Redman
- "East to West," by Casting Crowns
- "Tell Your Heart to Beat Again," by Danny Gokey
- "Dear Younger Me," by Mercy Me
- "Redeemed," by Big Daddy Weave
- "Breathe," by Jonny Diaz
- "This Is Amazing Grace," by Phil Wickham
- "Cornerstone," by Hillsong Live
- "Mended," by Matthew West
- Any song by Chris Tomlin
- "All Things Possible," by Mark Schultz
- "Walking Her Home," by Mark Schultz
- "Remember Me," by Mark Schultz
- "Back in His Arms Again," by Mark Schultz [Can you tell I like Mark Schultz's music? While working on this book, I met him at a concert at my church. He touched my shoulder as he walked past me after the performance and asked, "How are you?"

I said, "Better now," as he kept moving with the crowd so he could sign autographs. I was better because sitting quietly to hear him sing, tell us stories, show his videos, and even make us all laugh, did make me feel better. I encourage you to listen to his music or see him in person. It's worth it!]

Then, of course, there are songs on the radio that are not necessarily spiritual, but also have a very helpful message. Here are some of my favorites, with their singers:

- "It's Over," by Boz Scaggs [A humorous story is that, even though I attended a concert of his, and had written about him in this chapter, I had to ask the crowd at one of my friend Maggie's gigs who sang this song.]
- "Hold On," by Wilson Phillips
- "You're the First, the Last, My Everything," by Barry White
- "Both Sides Now," by Judy Collins
- "I Hope You Dance," by Lee Ann Womack
- "The Heart of the Matter," by Don Henley
- "I Will Survive," by Gloria Gaynor [And yes, I did!]
- "Dancing Queen," by ABBA
- "So Far, So Good," by Sheena Easton
- "The Locomotion," by Grand Funk Railroad
- "Hold the Line," by Toto
- "You Took the Words Right Out of My Mouth," by Meat Loaf
- "Maggie May," by Rod Stewart
- "Rhythm of My Heart," by Rod Stewart [A funny family-story about this artist that I told during my Grandpa McColl's eulogy is that once, because my grandfather was the president of a Scottish society, he was supposed to introduce a man he called "some Rod guy" at a concert in Florida. Our family had a good chuckle over Grandpa not knowing who this famous singer was.]
- "Out of Touch," by Hall & Oates
- "Release Me," by Wilson Phillips

- "Say What You Need to Say," by John Mayer [That song helped me re-connect with my family once upon a time.]
- "I Think I Love You," by The Partridge Family. [This is a childhood favorite that a DJ just played on the radio and brought me happy memories. I prayed that David Cassidy would be able to read my book and remember this song because of his diagnosis of dementia. David — we will ALWAYS remember you! R.I.P.]
- "You Could Have Been with Me," by Sheena Easton
- "Home," by Michael Bublé [I'm praying for his young son who was diagnosed with cancer as I was putting the "finishing touches" on my book.]
- "Believe," by Cher
- "Jive Talkin'," by The Bee Gees
- "Forever Young," by Rod Stewart [The theme song when I chaperoned a senior prom for my elementary school first student, Cliff. The other chaperone who was with me was Bobby Jacovino. R. I. P., Bobby!]
- "Don't Stop," by Fleetwood Mac
- "Piano Man," by Billy Joel
- "Country Roads," by John Denver
- "Don't Go Breaking My Heart," by Elton John and Kiki Dee [This song was played constantly the summer my family and I were in England, 1976.]
- "Follow You, Follow Me," by Genesis
- "Ride Like the Wind," by Christopher Cross
- "All Right," by Christopher Cross
- "Last Dance," by Donna Summer [This song was played at a dance each last night of the campers' stay at Ramapo Camp in Rhinebeck, NY, the summer of 1981. That camp helped me get my first teaching job, because I learned how to work with special ed. kids. I loved it!]
- "How Sweet It Is (To be Loved by You)," by James Taylor
- "Steal Away," by Robbie Dupree

- "You're a Friend of Mine," by Clarence Clemons and Jackson Browne
- "I Got You Babe," by Sonny and Cher [A song Aiden and I used to sing together at karaoke nights.]
- "Never Gonna Give You Up," by Rick Astley
- "Together Forever," by Rick Astley
- "Heaven Knows," by Donna Summer
- "Cold As Ice," by Foreigner [The "theme song" for my FINAL relationship!]
- "Against All Odds," by Phil Collins
- "Baby Hold On," by Eddie Money
- "You Don't Know What I Feel," by Annie Lennox
- "I'm Still Standing," by Elton John [The words in this song were so poignant for me when I heard it on the radio during a tumultuous spring of 2017….]
- "Treat Me Right," by Pat Benatar [My theme song for the rest of my life!]
- "Mr. Know It All," by Kelly Clarkson [Did she sing that about my love life?]
- "Amie," by Pure Prairie League
- "Can We Still Be Friends?" by Todd Rundgren
- "You Make Me Feel Like Dancing," by Leo Sayer
- "She Drives Me Crazy," by The Fine Young Cannibals
- "Is This Love?" by Bob Marley and the Wailers
- "Build Me Up Buttercup," by the Foundations
- "September," by Earth, Wind & Fire
- "Cecilia," by Simon and Garfunkel
- "Waiting in Vain," by Bob Marley and the Wailers
- "Same Old Lang Syne," by Dan Fogelberg
- "Keep on Loving You," by REO Speedwagon
- "Thinking of You," by Loggins and Messina
- "I'll Be There," by The Jackson 5
- "Black or White," by Michael Jackson [I tearfully watched his

funeral, the day after it took place, since on the funeral day, my brain was being operated on. I watched the funeral over and over in re-runs as I lay in my NYU hospital bed. I cried each time I saw it, alarming the hospital staff, who thought I was in physical pain, rather than sometimes in emotional pain over losing him. I miss him!]

- "Spirit in the Sky," by Norman Greenbaum
- "Sugar, Sugar," by The Archies
- "The Sweet Escape," by Gwen Stefani
- "This Love," by Don Henley
- "Close to You," by The Carpenters
- "Maniac," by Michael Sembello
- "Shannon," by Henry Gross
- "Thunder Island," by Jay Ferguson
- "Nice to Be with You," by Gallery
- "God Only Knows," by The Beach Boys
- "Doctor's Orders," by Carol Douglas
- "I Won't Give Up," by Jason Mraz [This was supposed to be my wedding song with Aiden.]
- "Rock the Boat," by The Hues Corporation [One of the many records we had in my family's jukebox in our playroom in the house I grew up in, in Rhinebeck, NY.]
- "You Light up My Life," by Debby Boone
- "Hungry Heart," by Bruce Springsteen
- "Surrender," by Cheap Trick
- "Waiting for a Star to Fall," by Boy Meets Girl
- "Let the River Run," by Carly Simon
- "The Greatest Love of All," by Whitney Houston
- "The Living Years," by Mike and the Mechanics
- Any song by Carole King [I heard her *Tapestry* album as a little girl in my uncle Ian's garage-turned-into–a-"Woodstocky"-bedroom, in Hampton Bays, NY, so many times that I learned all the words.]

- Any song sung by KC and The Sunshine Band
- "My Own Way," by Jeff LeBlanc [This is an artist not as well-known as the others listed here, but, believe me, I think you'll love his music as much as I do. I hope his musical career takes off!]

[On one of the worst days of my life, in March of 2017, I heard three songs on three different radio stations that helped me immensely get through it all.

The first was Earth, Wind & Fire's "September," and the next song was by The Foundations, "Build Me Up Buttercup." I've written about both of these in my book, and how they were used in my classes. Hearing them on this "dark day" reminded me of happy days long ago in my classrooms.

The third song was "Day One" by Matthew West. I had to move on from a terrible experience. The words in this song got that process started for me.

I believe God is in charge of everything, including songwriters, singers, and DJs....]

Chapter 32

OTHER THINGS THAT HELPED ME (HOLISTIC AND MORE)

I RECEIVED MUCH help from various people whose professions aided me in calming down, behaving more appropriately, and becoming less agitated. That's not to claim that I'm all better. I have a long way to go as far as appropriate behavior. But I have made headway.

One person who has been treating me every three-four weeks, and I so enjoy what she's brought to my life is, Debbie Burklund, my reflexologist. She works for no less than one and a half hours each session (and many times longer than that) to help "ground" me. Instead of the stereotypical psychiatrist's fifty-minute "hour," I get this reflexologist's generous ninety-minute "hour." Debbie listens to whatever is upsetting me, and then she does her thing: not only manipulating my feet but also physically massaging my cranium. Debbie is one of the best listeners I've ever met. Also, she detected a liver problem that I had and helped me remember to contact my doctors about. I will be eternally grateful to her for all she's done for me, including accompanying me to someone else's court sessions.

According to Lauren Yanks of the *Poughkeepsie Journal*, "Reflexology is considered an alternative health treatment that links each organ in the body with an area on the foot – and sometimes the hand, face and ears as well. Massaging these specific areas helps to unblock the body's energy and heal the specific corresponding organ."

Ms. Yanks quotes Debbie Burklund: "Reflexology is so very effective, and I can influence somebody's health so quickly," she said. "When there's disorder in your body, it forms metabolic waste in the reflexes. My job is to remove waste so your body can heal itself. It also happens to feel really wonderful." [Yes, it does!]

Another health field that has helped me enormously is neurofeedback. This helper's name is Debbie Burdick. She calls herself, "The Brain Lady," and that is so very accurate. I worked with T.B.L. at a couple of different locations, and even though they were quite a distance to drive to from my home, those appointments were well worth the trips.

The Brain Lady hooked my head up to what I referred to as her "bells and whistles." She had to put gunk into my hair so that her electrodes would stick to my head to read my brain waves. I had to stare at computer images, then report different things.

Dr. Norman Doidge has some excellent quotes in his book *The Brain's Way of Healing* (that I've written about in my recommended books and literature chapter). Here are some of his neurofeedback quotes:

- "Neurofeedback…trains a person whose brain rhythms are off to control them. So, it is excellent for people with…a noisy brain in general."
- "Neurofeedback is a sophisticated form of biofeedback…. It also has been approved for the treatment of…many other conditions, including…brain injuries…. It is a neuroplastic treatment but is not better known because it was pioneered before neuroplasticity was widely understood." [I attempted to make politicians in NYS aware of it when I spoke to them in the fall of 2015 at a hearing (see appendix).]

- "A conventional neurofeedback session involves hooking a person up to an EEG, a noninvasive way to detect brain waves, then displaying the waves on a computer screen."
- "A quantitative EEG (QEEG) is a test that can indicate if a patient has a 'noisy brain.' This study is often done by advanced neurofeedback practitioners, and must be interpreted by an expert who has actually met with the patient, not simply run the information through a machine." [I have a "lovely" picture of myself in my pictures section of this book, having one of the QEEGs I had done after my surgery.]

It's all mumbo-jumbo to me, but suffice it to say: it worked! I **always** felt better after time spent with The Brain Lady. Like my other Debbie in this chapter (is there something special about that name?), she helped me deal better with society. During the time I spent with T.B.L., I went to a couple of specialists for QEEGs ("brain mappings"). When the results of these tests were shared with specialists to analyze my condition, these doctors were shocked that I was as high-functioning as I am, given the brain damage I have suffered.

One specialist asked if I had been arrested or had a drug or alcohol problem after the brain injury. He was told **no,** though I have to admit that I have at times "talked" to police officers…but luckily, I was able to calm down.

Another specialist said that from the damage I had, he was surprised that I wasn't in a nursing home. When he looked at my brain's image on his computer, he said, "Wow!" I asked him if that was a "good wow" or a "bad wow." He replied it was a "good wow" and said I must be a fighter. I told him he didn't know the half of it!

Another therapy that helped me was Craniosacral Therapy. For this I saw Heidi Washburn, and she was excellent at helping me to relax. To and from her Bearsville, NY, appointments, I had to drive through Woodstock, NY. On my way to see her, I felt quite stressed driving through that very busy little village. On my way back, after therapy, I smiled and enjoyed the unconventional sights one only sees when visiting that unique community.

Heidi Washburn describes her therapy as follows: "Craniosacral Therapy is a gentle hands-on technique that works with the nervous system to help release restrictions that impede a person's ability to function fully. We focus specifically on the soft tissue, fluids and membranes affecting the sacrum, spinal cord and brain…. Because of the positive effect on the nervous system, Craniosacral Therapy is particularly helpful for diseases and injuries of the brain, as well as PTSD and traumatic brain injury."

The only negative aspect of these non-traditional services is that they are not cheap, and they are not covered by insurance. At this writing, I have spent most of my life's savings on techniques to help me chill out. This is what I reported to those politicians at that hearing in October of 2015. The treatments are worth every penny, but when you're on disability support, you need money for extra things, and so I tapped and tapped and tapped some more into the savings I had accumulated since my first job in 1977.

To diverge a bit, that first job was when I was sixteen. I worked at Four Brothers Pizza Inn, in Rhinebeck, NY. I also worked at a restaurant named "The Fox Hollow Inn." Then I worked at the Greig Farm in Red Hook. Mr. and Mrs. Greig were very sweet to me. I picked berries, worked the check-out line, and served as their granddaughters' nanny sometimes. I even lived in their house with them one summer. To this day, I put syrup on my strawberries and blueberries, eating them just as Mr. Greig taught me to, so many years ago.

The money from these jobs as well as my earnings from being a teacher are unfortunately long gone now, but I knew I had to do something to get grounded if I were to make anything of myself after the life-changing brain injury I suffered.

I want to wrap up this chapter with two excellent quotes from my FAVORITE brain expert, Dr. Marian Diamond:

"Never learn bitterness, because you are the only one who suffers."

"What plasticity reveals is that we are the masters of our own minds. That each one of us, as individuals, has the potential to change our brains, to become the person we want to be. What we do, day to day, minute to minute, grows and builds our brain. What a gift, and what a responsibility as we literally create our personal masterpiece – our mature brain."

Thank you to everyone in this chapter who has helped me feel better.

[And, I have to add that a generous woman named Ann Capozzoli taught me, and a group of other people, meditation practices, at the Kingston Library. Then, she even came to my house, for free, to help me learn how to calm myself down when I became unusually agitated, at the beginning of my recovery. Thank you, Ann!]

Chapter 33

BUSINESSES THAT HAVE HELPED ME

SOME OF THE businesses and names I've listed below, I've already mentioned in this book. Others are listed here for the first time. All of them have helped me in one way or another, and they deserve to be recognized for just that.

I deliberately listed them in random order (vs. my usual everything-has-to-be-alphabetical order) just to "mix it up" a bit. All of them are explained as to how they've helped me along the way, and I encourage you to patronize their business if possible; they deserve your support because they take care of others, besides selling their goods.

Rite-Aid Pharmacy's (on Flatbush Avenue in Kingston, NY) pharmacist Bob. He is incredibly gentle and listens very well. He's an excellent medical resource.

Adams Fairacre Farms' (in Kingston, NY) employees Rebecca, Amanda, and Paul. Rebecca helped me try to stay in touch with my family – by ordering flowers each year when hardly anyone kept in touch with me. She helped me write warm notes to them. Amanda is a very patient cashier with me (and others) when I'm very slow counting out my owed money. [And Paul is written about elsewhere here.]

Enzo's Ristorante and Pizza, in Kingston, NY. It not only has delicious food, but its restrooms are fabulously clean, and I could actually eat at this location when I was afraid of germs, because I saw how well they did with cleanliness. Taso and Lora Giannoulis's ristorante is fabulous, and I highly encourage you to try out their excellent cuisine.

Another place that I was also able to eat at, because it is clean and serves yummy food, is the Broadway Lights Diner, also in Kingston. Litsa Chasin's diner is well worth a visit!

Stop & Shop [now TOPS] in Rhinebeck, NY. Several employees there helped me when I was at my absolute darkest time with the mysophobia. They witnessed the tons of items I purchased to "stay clean" with. Their eyes showed sympathy for a woman who arrived at their store week after week and spent thousands of dollars on the same items. One name that I remember is Tammy. Thanks to her, and all the others, for showing love and concern.

Ice Cream Castle in Kingston, NY. The owners, Sandy and Jay Juliano, took such good care of me when I would go through their drive-thru for chocolate milkshakes. They learned, when they first opened, that my shakes had to be thin or I couldn't suck them through a straw (part of the left side of my face is partially paralyzed). Every time I was there with Aiden and Happy, all of the coworkers knew how to take care of me. Sweetness there wasn't just in their ice cream! [Sadly, this business is for sale. So, I found another place that does the same for me. It's called Zoe's Ice Cream Barn in LaGrangeville, NY. Its food and ice cream are delicious, and this distant restaurant takes care of this customer's thin-milkshake request each time.]

Red Hook, NY's "Historic" Village Diner has wait staff that took such good care of me when I was sick, told me they prayed for me, and after my surgery, they were all thrilled to see me come back. My first meal with my parents after they traveled from Florida by train to help care for me after my brain surgery was at this diner with friends.

P. S. Their daily specials are delicious.   [Some of the magnets attached above the window where the waitresses order our food to the cooks in the kitchen were donated by me from my classrooms.]

Lisa Smith – haircutter extraordinaire. When I first met her, she worked at J.C. Penney's in Kingston, NY. She styled my hair nicely after some of it was shaved off for the surgery. Since that store has closed, I now go to see her at C & C's Hair Salon in the Hudson Valley Mall. She's a sweetheart, and I love my appointments with her.

Waitress Susi Santa Anna who helped me in different diners (and at my church's women's *Bible* studies) – just by her kindness and thoughtfulness.

Lotus – a wonderful store in Woodstock, NY. The owner that I met (Jamie) is so gentle and helpful. I would like her "style" even if I didn't adore her mother (my friend Suzi). Jamie's shop sells signs, jewelry, chandeliers, pottery, cards, spa items, candles, and many other home accessories. Some of those signs are part of my collection. I have gone there when I get some time to "breathe." [And a specific story about Jamie is elsewhere here.]

The Mid-Hudson Valley Federal Credit Union's Irma L. She was so kind and patient with me when I would become completely overwhelmed at the bank counter when I couldn't handle money very well at all. She took it nice and slow with me so I could leave with my transactions completed correctly. As many people became (and still become) impatient with me because I forget to do something necessary, Irma always just smiled and helped me get it done.

Pillow Talk owner Aleda Stamboulian of Saugerties, NY. She creates unique pillowcases. Of course, I've purchased her Mickey Mouse ones, but she has quite the variety! She sells at various craft fairs and probably at other places too. I used her pillowcases a lot when I was going for neurofeedback and QEEGs because of the sloppy stuff put in my hair to watch my brain waves. I'd come home exhausted and would plop down on my pillow with yucky hair. When I woke up, I'd take off the pillowcase that specifically matched the sheets and put on one of

Aleda's, so when I went to bed later on after I washed my hair, I'd have a fun, clean pillowcase to sleep on.

Krause's Chocolates in Saugerties and/or Rhinebeck, NY. Chocolate is so comforting, and theirs is the best!

Bear Cave Gifts [Great signs!]

Duck Tape Jax [A young girl, Jaxon-Lily, "duck-tape artist," made me a beautiful Mickey-Mouse-themed duck tape wallet that I decided to use for my business cards.]

Two other young girls (who are friends) have businesses also. Hannah makes dog and cat treats (and my dog, Happy, loves her peanut butter and bacon pig-shaped treats) and Hannah's friend Ashley makes homemade soaps (my favorite is her Hollyberry).

Way to go, all three of you young ladies!

Art in Heaven (Ruth and Joe Breitenbach): this husband and wife team creates the coolest jewelry – earrings, pins, and more. I used to buy from them at craft fairs I attended long ago when I still taught, to wear to school. Nowadays, I still buy adorable earrings just for fun. Here are some of my favorite earrings: fortune cookies, hamburger with fries, sandwiches, doggie paw prints, popcorn, donuts, pizza, hot dogs, pencil with eraser, bacon strips, monkeys, bubbles, ducks, lighthouses, cameras, garlic cloves, lollipops, and so much more. Wearing them reminds me of teaching days gone by.

Some may think it's silly that a grown woman wears these fun earrings outside of a classroom setting, but I don't care. And once, when I was at the Dutchess County Fair in Rhinebeck, NY, a former, retired kindergarten teacher was doing the same thing – purchasing earrings from Ruth and Joe that she will no longer wear to school, but will enjoy wearing out and about like me. She and I smiled and chatted about missing teaching so much. Those of you still in the classroom – remember, someday it will be all over for you too. Get through the stress of it to have fun helping your kiddies enjoy learning.

Panera Bread in Kingston, NY, was so very helpful with me when it first opened, and I was at the worst time of my life with the myso-phobia. I'm not good with names from back then, but I do remember a female manager and another employee (Pam?), who helped me touch money and keep me calm when I ordered and then ate my food. Helping a customer's fear of germs was probably not in their job descriptions, but they did it very well. For that, I'm truly grateful.

I used to go to the Village Apothecary in Woodstock, NY, to purchase lots of items to help me remain as calm as possible after my brain was injured. An employee, Josh, couldn't have been more helpful. I explained to him what was going on with me, and he'd direct me to try this or that. Everything he recommended helped in the ways I needed it to. He was an absolutely excellent employee, and I wish him well wherever he works nowadays.

Go to the local soup sales near you. Their homemade, delicious soups (and desserts sometimes, too) are so enjoyable. Church meals, too, are often yummy!

Computer Gear & More: Fun Stuff for Your Tech Buff [This is a catalog I order some of my best, most-talked-about T-shirts that I wear often. Though I stink at computers, I love the catalog's selection of grammatical sayings. They're funny, yet get their point across.]

Hallmark [The stores, TV programs, and movies are excellent! I love attending the early morning shopping sprees when it's time to buy their Keepsake ornaments. It disappoints me when people trash that wonderful company.]

This example is not a business *per se* but it's about an employee at the doctor's office, and she is worth a mention here: her name is Haley Andrews, and I met her at my gynecologist's office. These appointments are never enjoyable, but for me they are very upsetting, as I sit in a waiting room with happy pregnant women, and little ones running around with their parents supervising, and me, not a mommy or a grandma-to-be ever. I pretty much feel sorry for myself that my life turned out different than for the majority of women.

And that's where Haley comes in. Instead of coldness, she exudes warmth. Instead of treating me like just another patient, she makes me feel welcome. Too many receptionists forget how to be nice to the person waiting to see the doctor. They could learn a thing or two from Haley. [I was sad to learn she has changed jobs. Whatever business she has joined, they are lucky to have her.]

Back when I was so sick with the tumor, there were many times I could not fill out forms correctly. Something as simple as an envelope at Target to mail away my film to be developed (remember when we did that?), I couldn't even remember my own last name or phone number.

There was this sweet, young girl who worked there, named Kristel, who helped me each and every time I went in. It must have been strange that someone as young as I was (mid-40s) could not state such simple information about herself. But, she helped me gently each time.

Fast-forward to late fall, 2016. I saw Kristel's picture in the local paper with her husband, Craig, and their baby daughter, Leah.

Leah was born with multiple health issues. The expenses for all of her medical help were astronomical. So, a hair salon was holding a fundraiser to help with their mounting medical bills.

As soon as I read this touching story in the early morning the day it was in the paper, I remembered how sweet this young woman was to me years ago, though she was just doing her job at that store. She did it with such kindness!

I decided to pray all day about it. After praying, I decided: If my book does well, I'm going to donate a large portion of the profits to this family.

This is a way to repay this one young woman's kindness towards a store customer.

Her kindness to me created a ripple effect. Can you help someone who has helped you, even if it was long ago? Food for thought....

So, I'm quite sure that there were many other businesses that have helped me, some I probably even told that I'd write about them someday. Here are the ones I remembered, or scribbled down before I forgot their help. Thank you, all, for making my "now life" a bit cheerier.

Chapter 34

───≈≈≈───

HONESTY

HONESTY HAS ALWAYS been important to me. A classroom motto I had on a sign and repeated over and over with my students was, "Tell the truth, all the time." When I told my editor there would be a chapter on this, he said that honesty was important to him too.

As one husband said at a brain-tumor support group about his wife, who had a brain tumor after I did, "the tumor removed her filters. She has truth serum now." That is exactly true about me also.

As I was gathering examples for this chapter to point out how honest I really can be, I remembered a recent story about when I pulled up to an ATM at my bank. The person who departed as I arrived, inadvertently left his account open, and the screen asked me if "I" needed another withdrawal. I closed his account by pushing a "no" button. Instead of just then beginning my own withdrawal, I drove out and followed him to a place where he had pulled over.

I told him what had just happened by saying, "Sir, you're lucky I'm the one who pulled in after you or possibly your account could have less money in it." He thanked me over and over and told me he'll be more careful next time.

I know a lot of people would have closed his account like I did. Sadly, I know there's a lot of people who would not have.

I also know that if someone at a register gives me too much change, I return the money that is not mine.

When I visit my doctors regularly, I tell them the honest, true stories about my behavior. When I've taken too much of my controlled-substance meds due to stress, I'm complimented for telling the truth.

One doctor said, "You're so honest."

I pray for the day that I don't need to turn to meds to deal with the stress everyday life brings.

A movie that I went to see with Aiden that covers this very topic was *War Room*. It's a Christian-based film on the trials and tribulations in relationships due to dishonesty. Since viewing this film occurred when we were working diligently on our own relationship, I thought we got a lot out of viewing it together. [Unfortunately, our relationship failed anyway.]

I know we all tell "little white lies" from time to time, but the huge lies, like ones about theft, infidelity, adultery, drugs, alcohol, or pornography addiction, and so on, can tear a family apart. God wants us to confess our sins, so we can be forgiven. I ask God to forgive me, each night when I pray at bedtime, for anything I did or said that day that hurt someone else.

But, to be perfectly honest, I'm not that patient with others nowadays. As a special ed. teacher for so long, I was very patient with my students. Sometimes, I lost my patience with my co-workers who didn't do as good a job as others could or did. I know lots of staff that I used to work with liked me, but there are some who did not. I'm okay with that.

I truly believe in that old saying, "Honesty is the best policy." It hurts to hear the truth sometimes, but at least it means something is not being covered up or changed just to keep you content.

Another example I have of my own truth-serum behavior is the picture taken for this book's cover. In February 2015, I was sitting at a diner and saw an old boyfriend who didn't even recognize me, and I'm sure that's because I weighed 70 pounds more than when he last saw me in the year 2000. I ran out of the diner and began a diet so I would look better for my book's picture.

I lost 40 pounds by the holidays, but, unfortunately put 10 back on from Halloween candy, my birthday celebrations, Christmas parties, and New Year's fun times. Then, my dog's surgery caused so much fear, I ate 5 pounds of comfort food in those two weeks.

Then my editor commented that it looked like I gained back some weight, and that caused more upset, so another 5 pounds went on. So, I lost 40, but gained 50 back! The diet "roller coaster" happened once more, and it probably will again....

Someone said I could get my picture "Photoshopped" for the book cover. I laughed because I knew there was going to be a chapter about honesty, and so how would that make me believable? I'm actually one weight in real life and another in that picture, but believe me anyway? So, when the picture is taken, whatever weight I am, I am. I'm doing the best I can and exercising, too; we'll see.... [We ended up using one taken in 2013.]

I usually look sloppy because I just don't put the effort in that I once did. I look at pictures of myself from my 20s, 30s, and even some of my 40s, and I really looked "put together." Now, I only apply mascara (still too much, right, Mom?), blush, and run a brush through my hair. That's all I do to appear presentable.

I had to be honest, since that's what this chapter is all about.

[And – to add a bit of wisdom at the very end of writing this book.... If someone lies to you about their age, their marital status, their "hobbies," know that they will lie about other stuff, too. Dishonesty destroys relationships. Leave before your heart is broken.]

Chapter 35

JANETISMS

BRAIN INJURY OR no brain injury, there are things that take place in everyday life that really bug me. As I often say, "it's NOT the world according to me" (but, I really wish it were).... My editor and I discussed the need for this somewhat conceited chapter (including that title up there) a few times. Here it is, so I guess you can figure out who "won" that debate. Since I'm quite sure I will NEVER write another book (this is exhausting work – kudos to all authors), here's my list of unique thoughts/opinions which represent my "award-winning" personality. I just need to "say" these once and for all:

I have expressions that I've gathered over the years. Some of them are:

- "heebie-jeebies" [when something grosses me out];
- "hoity-toity" [snobbish];
- "babbler" [someone who talks too much, like me];
- "gazillion" [millions and millions and millions];
- "mucky-mucks" [politicians, since I can't remember their exact titles, like "senator," "assemblyman," etc.] This particular

expression produced some giggles when I spoke at a hearing about brain injury in our state capitol (Albany, NY) in October 2015, as I looked at these politicians' faces [see the appendix on the hearing.];

- "ready, Freddie?" [when I was shopping with Aiden, to see if he was ready to leave. Aiden reminded me of my father sometimes. My dad's name was Fred.];
- "chilly-Willy" [when it's cold];
- "hyper-diaper" [when someone is all wound up];
- "mushy-gushy' [the way I describe cards I want for Valentine's Day, birthdays, etc.];
- "mumbo-jumbo" [for someone saying something that I don't understand];
- "gobbledygook" [what I say in reference to lots of words I don't understand anymore.]

Besides expressions, I have other examples of things that I just need to say:

- While I am paying at a cash register and the clerk is counting out the money I just handed over, someone interrupts and asks that same clerk a question, so then I have to wait for his or her response to the rude interrupter before my transaction is completed. Sometimes their banter goes back and forth while I just stand there. Couldn't the non-emergency question have waited its turn? Almost worse is when other store personnel interrupt for trivial reasons, as just happened to me as I wrote this chapter.
- Smokers who throw their cigarette butts everywhere except in the correct spot. I live near a nursing home that provided a place for their employees to extinguish their butts, but the ground all around was still covered anyway. It looks like a giant ashtray, just like many other places do. Also – smokers, who at an outdoor event like a concert, ruin the fun time for the rest of us by smoking while we try to breathe in the clean air.

- Folks in grocery stores who don't know how to read the signs that say, "10 items or less," so they back up the rest of us who do know how to read. Some store employees tell those with too many items to go on these lines, which defeats the original purpose.
- Coupons being cut out while in the line vs. being organized ahead of time. It's also a bit of "fun" with the buyers arguing with the clerk about saving a few pennies when a coupon isn't used the way they expected.
- Movie theater patrons who ignore the announcements about turning off cell phones. I've had to sit through MANY movies, trying to enjoy what I paid money for, while someone near me uses the cell phone, and the bright light and the sound are distracting. Also, stop talking during the movie, you're not in your living room. I really "love" patrons who arrive late, and even though there are plenty of open seats, they pick the ones right in front of me, blocking my view, though I planned the timing correctly. And finally, how about you open that candy wrapper during a loud movie scene vs. during a quiet portion, so that we all get to hear the important dialogue?
- Neighbors who are so self-absorbed that they pull in and out of the parking areas in a condo setting (thus, lots of others to be disturbed at the same time) with music blaring so loud from their car's stereo system that it's deafening! They're the same narcissistic bunch that blare their horns or beep their car locks at any given time of the day or night. If they are awake, they don't care if they wake you up. And, when their dog (or dogs) poops in the shared lawn area, they leave it there whenever they don't feel like cleaning it up. The disturbances from all of their family feuds bring lots more noise – the screaming vulgarities, the doors being slammed, the sidewalks cluttered with household belongings thrown outside during fits of rage, the many police visits, etc. What's so unbelievable is that all of the examples that I just wrote about are from ONE family only.

I'm sure there are readers that could add to this list because of their own neighbor stories. I know the *Bible* says, "Love thy neighbor," so that's the only reason I have never talked to them about these items. I once wrote a letter to them about how a dog of theirs traumatized my dog, but that's the only contact I've ever made, since I don't trust myself enough to behave the way God instructs us to.

- Drivers who run through stop signs and red lights, text while driving, handle cell phones while driving, tailgate, don't turn down high beams, cut me off, and on and on and on…. I think my tolerance of these selfish behaviors has diminished greatly because of how frequently they occur.

- Noisy patrons in restaurants sometimes really agitate me. It's not just my hyper-sensitive hearing. They talk so loudly, they can be heard from across the room! Once, in a lovely breakfast spot, I had to listen to an entire large family discuss the blood, guts, and gore stories of their loved one who was in a hospital. And recently, I was in a fancy restaurant and had to listen to a husband and wife discuss with their waitress why the husband looked so thin (diarrhea and vomiting stories). Isn't all of that really appetizing? Once, when I was out at a diner with a group of my friends at a very long table for 11 of us, someone at the other end of that table started talking about bird poop on her car, while we were all eating our lunch. I put down my sandwich, and while I was grossed out, I listened to others join in the conversation with her, not bothered by it at all. I was thinking, *Is it just me who thinks restaurants are not the place for disgusting subjects?* A day or so later, I read in an advice column that others would appreciate it if these types of discussions did not take place. I felt better then. It isn't just me.

I'm sure other people have some of their own "isms." What are yours?

Chapter 36

———

ME, ME, ME

I'm not really sure if the behaviors I'm about to list in this chapter bother me so much because of my brain injury or if they would bother me anyway. I wonder, as I gather these thoughts, do these examples drive anyone else, other than myself, crazy??? I do know that each and every day that I venture out into the world, more and more selfish behaviors by others are noticed by me. I work desperately hard NOT to comment each time they take place! Here are some comments I haven't made to the people involved, but they still need to be expressed:

- Stop touching food with your hands at any sort of buffet line, and then put it back. I've witnessed this disgusting habit in restaurants, church events, and parties. If you touch it, take it! Don't leave it for someone else to eat unknowingly. [Also – stop double-dipping anything, unless you are home.]
- Stop giving "quizzes" as a way of introducing a topic in any social gathering. It's an automatic turn-off for people who don't know the correct answers, while others sitting near them are

squirming with delight about what they know and thus, shouting out the answers.

- Stop coughing/screaming/sneezing, etc. into the phone when you're speaking to someone. This is very painful to hear. Cover the mouthpiece, if possible, and speak in a lower volume if you want to be listened to. [I know I have to work on my loudness too.]

- Stop talking about other patients within earshot of patients sitting in the doctor office's waiting room if you are a receptionist. What do you say about us when we're not there???

- Stop printing incorrect times for plays, special events, etc. in the newspapers. Many times I've arrived at what was printed, only to find out I'm very early, very late, or there on the wrong date. I show the printed information to whomever, and all I usually get is a shrug. Please check your work.

- Stop getting mad at me because I actually stop at a stop sign. I am the one following the law. And while you're at it, stop waving me on to breeze through it when I haven't even stopped yet.

- Stop putting me on speaker-phone without my permission, since I think I'm speaking only to you, but I actually can be heard by others.

- Stop texting, mommies and daddies, at the restaurant table when your kiddies are being ignored. Once, as I was compiling this chapter, I actually played peek-a-boo with a little one as her parents "played" on their cell phones and didn't even notice this stranger (me) involved with their child!

- Stop being phony. I can't stand it when certain people act all warm and friendly when it's just the two of us, but when others are around, I get the cold shoulder.

- Stop expecting me to be all warm and friendly to you when someone else has told me what you said about me behind my back. I'll be polite and say, "Hello," but I'm not going to be friendly with a, "Hi! How are you?"

- Stop walking your dog but then leaving his/her poop to be cleaned up by someone else (or worse yet – being accidentally stepped on). As a dog owner, please be responsible and clean up after your pet.
- Stop racing your car through parking lots so those of us walking with our coffee, groceries, children, pets, etc. do not almost get hit by you. [Actually – as I was practically finished with this chapter, I heard a story about a store employee who got hit by a car in the parking lot right after she clocked out. She had to go to the hospital. Slow down, everyone. You'll get there soon enough!]
- Stop filing your nails at restaurant tables. Also: stop taking off your shoes or boots there, brushing your hair, *etc.* Too many people these days think they're home when they're not.
- Stop screaming, cheering, clapping (or anything else that's loud) in restaurants. I know too many eating establishments have TVs nowadays, so you can watch whatever instead of actually communicating with the folks at your table, but some "old-fashioned talkers" like myself actually enjoy conversations vs. TV entertainment. I try to limit taking my patronage there. [Thank you, Vinny, for the help you gave me that fun time we had dinner together.]
- Stop telling all the gory details of a movie you just went to see, while the rest of us are within earshot. First of all – maybe we don't want to hear it all before we go ourselves. And second of all – just because you can "stomach" those nasty, violent scenes, maybe some of us just can't. [This example happened at a diner as I was completing this chapter. But – then, ironically, something happened another time I visited at that very same diner. As I walked in to eat breakfast, I hit my head on the electric box outside. I was bleeding from the right side of my head. Blood was on my hands. The wait staff there helped Aiden get me cleaned up and on ice. Thanks, Kathleen and Nick!]

- Stop being rude. If someone takes the time to hold the door open for you at a place of business, the least you can do is say, "Thanks."
- Stop littering!
- Stop criticizing those of us who arrive early. Again, as I was compiling this chapter, I arrived 10 minutes early for an appointment. The woman at the counter said, "You're really early!" Really?!! 10 minutes isn't that early!
- Stop talking during the church service about things going on in your life when the organist, the pianist, or other instrumentalists are playing the music they have taken time to practice. Some of us want to listen to the beautiful music instead of how it went at your doctor's appointment, etc. [This has happened at every single church I have ever attended. Sometimes I've been the culprit.]
- Stop tailgating me when there is bad weather causing dangerous road conditions, and, therefore, I'm driving slower.
- Stop passing me on double yellow lines because of my above-mentioned slow driving.
- Stop lying! Eventually, the truth will come out.
- Stop "forgetting your manners" when a "please" and/or a "thank you" is in order; please remember to communicate them.
- Stop leaving your chair out when you get up – someone might trip over it.
- Stop minding everyone else's business. Mind your own.
- Stop coughing and sneezing all over everyone out in public. If you are sick, stay home. Some of us have compromised immune systems, and your germs make us end up at a doctor's office or in the hospital.
- Stop finishing my sentences. I'll say what I want, not what you think I should.
- Stop telling me how to do something. Unless I've asked for your opinion and/or your help, I want to learn on my own.

- Stop breast-feeding with your breast completely exposed in public. Some of us are uncomfortable with that. Once, I was at a restaurant when many men were staring at a woman baring her entire breast as she fed her baby, while the women with those men were obviously upset with them for gawking. Thank you to the mommies who use those covers to do this beautiful thing. [I'm not the only person who feels this way. Many have written to advice columnists about this very subject and express their similar feelings.]
- Stop talking during someone's performance. If you don't want to watch, leave so the rest of us can enjoy the show. At concerts, plays, or any other public performance, it really irks me how many people talk throughout the much-rehearsed performance. Once, I was at Radio City's Christmas Spectacular, and two women right behind me talked about their boyfriends, nail salon appointments, etc., throughout the show. What was "Spectacular" was that I bit my tongue! [Kudos to Director Lisë Landis Hopson for telling her audience to please be quiet during the performances at her shows at Kingston Catholic School.]
- Stop noisily clearing snow, leaves, etc. at the crack of dawn. Some of us want to sleep, read, or have quiet time in the early morning. [As I wrote this, snow was being cleared from the sidewalk, by not a snow blower but a loud leaf blower, at 5:55 A.M.!]
- Stop ignoring others. Turn your cell phone off. You'll live without it for a few minutes as you walk on sidewalks, in malls, etc., and then you won't keep bumping into those of us who actually don't need to behave like that for validation. [I heard on *Good Morning America* as I compiled this chapter that pedestrian deaths are up 10% according to a recent study.]
- Stop being so selfish. When you attend a concert, ballgame, etc., try to get your drinks ahead of time. [I actually observed

a group of drinkers yell at this nice older woman, at the end of their row at an indoor concert, because she got tired of moving to the aisle for their umpteenth trip for more beer.]

- Stop leaving doggies outside in bad weather with no food or water. If I see that, I call the authorities. I always will.

- Stop hovering by the coffee dispensers at a function when there are others waiting to get their cup, creamer, and sugar. Get yours and then move away to chat somewhere else.

- Stop letting your kiddies kick the backs of seats at a performance. This really can ruin the enjoyment of the show.

- Stop talking so loud in libraries. I know it's allowed in many of them nowadays, but when you're doing that, some of us can't concentrate on the work we are there to do. [I just met with a librarian who told me it's OK to talk loudly in some libraries because they are "social gathering places." I'd still prefer quiet.]

- Stop looking at newspapers in stores and then putting them back instead of purchasing them, with all of the sections mixed up or missing. Some of us actually pay for them and then return home with less than we paid for. I've watched people remove coupons and sports sections without paying for them!

- Stop parking in handicapped spots when you're not handicapped yourself or not driving for someone who is. People that use those red or blue tags because someone in their family gave it to them, but are not along for the ride, are wrong. Those parking spots are there for a reason – not for your convenience. On the September 2, 2016, ABC show, *What Would You Do?*, there was an episode where this topic was presented: parking in handicapped spots. I LOVED the folks, not knowing they were being filmed, who were scolding the girls (actresses) for taking up one of these spots. I love it when people defend what's right! I knew as soon as I watched this episode, I'd be adding it here. If you're not handicapped, get out of the way for those who are! [My friend Marian loves to tell the story about how I once went into a restaurant and yelled at someone for doing this. I don't remember that, but I believe her.]

- Stop parking your big SUV in a spot labeled for compact cars. There's a woman who does this at a doctor's office I go to regularly. She's lucky I haven't said, "Can't you read?"

- Stop using the word "retard." It truly hurts the feelings of some people who are developmentally disabled or who love someone who is. As a teacher, I've witnessed this first-hand too many times to count! Once, a famous person said this word on a talk show, and two families I used to teach years ago left messages on my answering machine telling me about it. I sent a letter to the star's manager asking the celebrity to apologize, and I explained why. I never heard back. I still boycott all of this star's TV show reruns and movies. Once, when a relative of mine used "retard," I flew off the handle. Recently, I was at a Mother's Day tea, and I was shocked when a retired teacher said, "Are they retarded?" when we spoke about mistakes in newspapers. Name-calling really hurts.

- Stop taking my money for services you provided, then you do not provide a receipt but then say, "You could have asked." Really? That very sentence infuriated me once when I paid for service as I wrote this chapter.

- Stop walking up to two people talking and then rudely interrupt their discussion so you can speak to one of them. Wait your turn!

- Stop teacher-bashing: I will NOT tolerate anyone bashing the teaching profession. Some people think it's okay to criticize teachers just because once upon a time, they attended school. Guess what? Unless you've done the job, you're no expert in the field! There are a few teachers who give the rest of us a bad name, but overall, teachers do an exemplary job of helping our youth grow into adults. They put in countless hours of overtime. The relentless state testing and mandates are grueling. I used to spend much time on Sundays writing lesson plans. I brought many piles of things to correct, look over, plan, *etc.*, on countless vacations and holidays. I went in early and stayed late. And, I'm not the only teacher who did all this. Many teachers, like myself, had jobs in the summer also. So many people comment about our vacation time. Those breaks are well-deserved because of how tiresome our jobs are…. These women and men deserve that much-needed time off to recharge. Teachers deserve more respect for how much they do! Unless you've done that job, you have no idea how hard it can be. [And by the way – many teachers need second jobs to help pay the bills.] Please, please, please thank a teacher instead of criticizing. It means all the world to hear a compliment instead of something negative. That lousy expression, "Those who can, do – and those who can't, teach," could NOT be more inaccurate. It takes a very special person to be in charge of a classroom. Thank you to those of you that do that every day! I know many of you put your heart and soul into your profession.

- Stop writing this, Janet! You could go on and on forever….

Some may wonder why I included this list of selfish behaviors in my book. I figured that this creation of mine will probably be the only chance I get to immortalize my opinions. I seriously doubt I'll be an author again (this took a LOT of time and effort), so I will probably only get one chance to "tell it like it is" in writing.

I just pray that our society becomes nicer to each other. I know that I need to work on that. What about you?

Chapter 37

DANIELLE AND CATHERINE

AND SPEAKING ABOUT our society becoming nicer to one another, here's a chapter about two people who do just that....

Danielle was a little girl when I first taught her at Ulster County BOCES in my special ed. Life Skills classroom. She has Down syndrome and she has been an absolute joy in my life to this day!

When she was in my class, she paid attention and followed the rules – most of the time. Sometimes, I had to send her to "time out" to pull herself together.

Classroom work was hard for all of my students. One day when Danielle was particularly stressed out, she asked if she could take a break from her math worksheet. I said she could, and I turned on the radio for music to calm her. The radio station was playing "Build Me Up Buttercup," sung by The Foundations. Danielle just got up and danced. When others saw her, some of them danced, too. They all stopped working for the three minutes the song played.

After the song ended, I turned off the radio, and Danielle, and all the other students, went straight back to work without me telling them to. I decided right there and then that this song would be ours forever to help us calm down about our struggles.

I went to the store and bought that song and had it available each day for the rest of my teaching career. Each new year, I explained to the students about a former student, Danielle, who got that idea started. Many classes years after that had a three-minute "buttercup break" so they could chill out and then get back to work.

Danielle invited me to her 30th birthday party that she held in a nice restaurant with lots of guests, some of them students in classes from way-back-when with her. I asked the DJ to play that song and a couple of others that my students used in my classroom all those years ago. We all danced at her party, and I cried happy tears on the dance floor, remembering when they all were small. Now they're all adults, and I LOVE being around them.

A bunch of former students went out to lunch with my then-boy-friend Aiden and me once or twice a year. When I first got out of the hospital after my brain surgery, we met a lot more often. But nowadays I have less time because of all the other things I'm involved in to get better: support groups, holistic/alternative therapies, church functions, etc.

One of the "lunch buddies" is Catherine, another student whom I taught a long time ago. Catherine also has Down syndrome and has remained friends with Danielle all through their adulthood.

Catherine leaves hysterically funny messages for me nowadays on my answering machine. It's almost like she has radar for detecting my bad days from far away and calls. When I get home feeling terrible about one more embarrassing meltdown somewhere, Catherine is on my machine, and her words make me laugh and momentarily forget the nonsense that took place that day.

Throughout my career, I taught many students with various dis-abilities. The population that I feel I was the most effective with was the Life Skills students. The fact that I am still in contact with some of them over 20 years later supports that point. [I still love the time I spend with Danielle, Catherine, and Erick and their families. I love their stories from our classroom long ago.]

The time I spend with these "kids" of mine is truly a blessing. They are the sweetest people I know!

From *IN FOCUS, FALL 1997*, Ulster BOCES Special/Alternative Education Programs Newsletter:

Two Young Olympians Take Home the Gold in Friendship

New Paltz - After competing against approximately 50 adult competitors, two young female contestants were presented with bronze medals in the annual Special Olympic softball competition held this fall at Cantine Field in Saugerties.

Catherine, 10, from Lenape Elementary School and Danielle, 13, a student in the Ulster BOCES Special Education program at Lenape, both accompanied the torch and helped carry the Ulster BOCES banner during the opening ceremony of the Special Olympics. The students then went on to place in the contest, which evaluated batting, fielding, base running and throwing skills.

Janet Schliff, an Ulster BOCES special education teacher at Lenape Elementary, coordinated the event. Rich Smith, coach for the summer school program and a summer school teacher at Ulster BOCES, was responsible for training both girls for the competition. Candice Goldstein, speech therapist for the New Paltz school district, was also on hand to lend support to the competitors.

United by their victory at the games, these two students are also friends who met in Ruth Backenroth's special education classroom a few years ago. Although Catherine is now a student in a New Paltz inclusion class, the girls' friendship remains strong. The opportunity for friendships between Ulster BOCES students and New Paltz students is encouraged by the design of the integration of the Special Education program at the Lenape school. Interacting with one another on a daily basis, Ulster BOCES and New Paltz students have lunch together, share the playground and library, and are mainstreamed for music, art, and gym classes.

Among the many benefits of mainstreaming and integration are that Ulster BOCES students get out of the small settings of 1:12:1 or 1:6:1 [teacher:students:staff] and become part of a larger group where they can learn socialization skills. Also, the Lenape Elementary school students learn diversity and acceptance. Ulster BOCES special education teacher, Janet Schliff, summed it up by saying, "It doesn't matter what you look like on the outside, it is who you are on the inside that counts."

The girls' parents also help nurture their friendship by making arrangements for the girls to play together regularly. Catherine and Danielle call their time together the "Friendship Club." Weekly, their play time together is planned to include coloring, exercise, and even making applesauce. Asked to describe their favorite joint activity, the girls simultaneously sang out, "Eating pizza." The girls also shared their thoughts about each other. Giggling, Catherine explained her appreciation for Danielle's sense of humor, "She's so funny, she always makes me laugh." Danielle credits Catherine's helpful nature as her best quality, "She even helps me clean my room!"

[This article was written long ago, but I saved it because Special Olympics is very dear to my heart. Here and elsewhere, I have used the children's names only when I have had parental permission.]

So, to end this wonderful chapter, I need to tell you what Danielle said to me when I told her that Aiden and I broke up: "That's men for you."

She couldn't have said it better!

Chapter 38

~~~

TRIBUTES & THANKS FROM STUDENTS, PARENTS, & OTHERS

[These are as written, except with some names abbreviated.]

Dear Ms. Schliff,

My wife and I would like to thank you for the wonderful work you and the BOCES staff at Lenape have accomplished with J. over the past five years. We only hope that his next teacher will be as diligent with him as you have been.

The job of teacher is hard enough, but it takes a "special person" to be a special ed. teacher, and we are and have been always thankful that you were that special person and teacher for our special son.

God bless you.

Sincerely,

Mr. and Mrs. J. L. [parents]

P.S. We will keep you updated on J.'s progress and let him write often, if he does not see you.

Dear Janet,

We want to thank you for all your hard work, dedication, and caring that you have done. You are an outstanding teacher and we have greatly appreciated your going above and beyond your basic duties! Danielle has truly benefited from being in your class. We can only hope to have her with a teacher 1/2 as good as you. Danielle and the rest of us will miss you – thank you.

Love,

Doreen and Gary [parents]

Just thought I'd pass this along: I was talking about B. with his mom, A., and she said you are the best teacher he has ever had! We are not the only ones who feel that way about you. We will MISS YOU.

Doreen [parent]

Thank you for being a wonderful teacher and person to B.

You're welcome about basket and really you deserve so much more.

If his next teacher is 1/2 teacher you are, I'll count my blessings!!!

The F. Family [parent]

6/20/04

Dear Janet,

Roses are red and violets are blue, and sugar is sweet and so are you. Keep on smiling. You make us all happy, and now we don't have you for a teacher, and it's time to let go, and it's time to cry and to say good-bye to a wonderful teacher to have for six years, and you sure will be missed, with tears or cries to say good-bye, but stay as sweet and kind, and we hope other kids will see it the same way we do. It's hard to say good-bye without a tear, but we need to move on, and it sure won't be the same.

If no one can see how sweet and kind you are, then they are missing out on a friend, not only a teacher, but one who cares about what you do, as a sweet teacher that you always will be. So did you shed a tear? And please don't forget us.

Love always,

The Y. Family [parents]

Bye, bye, bye

6/2/04

Dear Ms. Schliff,

Hi! I'm really glad that I found time to write a letter to you before the end of the year. I've been so really glad that you have been my teacher for the past Six years.

I have learned so much from you and the other teacher between better behavier and health to reading writing and other classes. this is why when I go on to the High School I will miss seeing you in class every day, but I will never forget you and you will never me.

Your friend,

R. [student]

June 2005

Dear Ms. Schliff,

I an glad you are my techer and you are the best techer in the hole world and you helpt me with everything this year

Love,

S. [student]

Hi, we had a great time last night. Your classroom is such a fun and positive place for kids to be! Thanks so much! Have a great day.

R. [parent]

September 2002

I was very impressed with how you worked with the kids this morning. We're very glad to have Erick with you another year!

Walter [parent]

["We can't have a party for Erick without Ms. Schliff," Erick's mom, Clara, said at his 30th birthday party, in July 2017, to which I was invited and enjoyed attending.]

2005

"A. was scared at first meeting his new school teacher, you, but he enjoyed the year at the best school and teacher. Have a great summer."

R. [parent]

2004

"I just want to say J. answered every question on the [Christopher Columbus] study guide correctly on the first try! This certainly is a testament to the info he is receiving in school, and how well he is retaining it!"

J. [parent]

[Christmas card] 2006

"Every holiday, I thank God for the help you gave my son, and you know I will never forget you. Thanks."

N. [parent]

MORE TRIBUTES...

[Some corrections have been made for clarity.]

FORMER STUDENT DANIELLE'S TRIBUTE TO JANET

She was the best teacher to me. She is very spical [*special*] person in my life. She cam to my party for my 30th we hed so much fun.

She put me in the tim out charair [*chair*] if I dot [*don't*] behave. She was a very good teacher to me. We hed som good food we hed key fired chkin [*Kentucky Fried Chicken*] it was so good. and we want to the fair in New Paltz we hed fun. The School wase in New Paltz, in Lanpie [*Lenape*].

I hed fun doing the Woter Day play with Janet Schliff. And I like doing the pie eating constes [*contest*].

I like going on fill [*field*] trips wath hir and it was relly fun.

She mad lering [*learning*] fun and I love doing the play the mitten. With hir. And she took us swiming in New Paltz it was fun and my favorite fill trip was [a water park] it was so much fun.

I like the Book of DR Suess I like to eat green eggs and Ham   it was very good and she taught me how to behave in school.

She give me a book it was Love me Forever [*Love You Forever*] I love it so much.

She is a mickey fin [*fan*].

She was my coach for Special Olympice it was relly fun.

Are school was in Lanape Ementary it was BOCeS.

The year was 1997-1998.

We going out somtim with Danielle and Catherine and Erick.

We always have fun.

She is the best teacher I hed.

I am so gald [glad] she is in my life.

FORMER STUDENT CATHERINE'S TRIBUTE TO JANET

Janet Schliff

Janet was my teacher when I was 8 years old to 10 years old Janet teach at lenape

I remember Water Day Janet panit our feet and we walk on a long paper that was fun

Janet take us out to lunches in town of NP [*New Paltz*]

Janet taught us getting along with others you may not like.

I remember play: The Mitten Friend. Danielle was manator [*narrator*] and I remember ice crame sundaes

Janet tought me about living and life

Special Olympics with Janet

Dietz Staduim for track and field softball at Cantine Field

Janet send all the kids cards and I kept them all

Janet tought me math and make change

I had all lot of fun with Janet

Janet class room was fun and fun and fun and fun

Janet is caring and loving and mavolas [*marvelous*]

Janet is so pretty   I love her

Janet have a big heart   Janet is very funny   Janet funniser [*funnier*]

Janet is funnier

Janet is very lovely and wonderful and beauitful   She rock!

She is special to me

She is so special

REFERENCE LETTER FROM FORMER SUPERVISOR, DAN SHORNSTEIN

During my five-year experience at Ulster BOCES, I had the pleasure of supervising Janet Schliff.... Janet was a team player and very involved in the school community.... She was receptive to suggestions and maintained high standards for herself and students. Janet's students consistently made great academic gains.... In closing, Janet is one of the best. She would, in my opinion, be an asset to any school's program. I give her my highest recommendation.

REFERENCE LETTER FROM FORMER STAFF, PATRICIA BRESNAHAN

I am writing to attest to the professional and kind person that I have known Janet Schliff to be.... Throughout my years working with Janet [first as an aide, then as an assistant], I have admired her teaching style working with a unique group of kids and her direct approach in handling the staff she works with. Janet is very forthright and specific when it comes to the directions she gives to the staff.... Janet knows and openly admits that she expects her staff to perform their jobs well (as she should), so she often rewards the staff. I can remember numerous lunches at diners, frequent gifts, and cards that Janet generously gave. Janet wants her staff to know that they are appreciated.... I thoroughly enjoyed my years working with Janet. I have never seen someone who was so dedicated to benefitting and making a difference in her students' lives.

ARTICLE IN SCHOOL NEWSPAPER, WINTER 1992

Janet Schliff – a Teacher Who Cares
Ed Burkhardt and Jesseka Moxham

Janet Schliff is a busy person, but she's a person who has time enough to care. Schliff is a dedicated Special Education Teacher.... Her class is for students who...have behavior problems. Her goal is to teach them to talk reasonably rather than to verbally or physically abuse others. Occasionally, kids get out of control. Many times, Schliff has been bruised from kicks. She was recently bitten.... She was recently informed that her biography will appear in *Who's Who in American Education, 1992-93*.... Schliff recently helped...a student who was hit by a truck and lay in a coma for a month. Schliff played an important role in the girl's recovery, visiting the child regularly...and also...helping the mother through the tragedy.

PRAISE FROM JOHANNA'S MOTHER

[Approx. 2015]

Johanna still talks about how wonderful Janet is, even though she hasn't been to MOPS [Mothers of Preschoolers, a group held at my church] in a year. She would like Janet to consider becoming her kindergarten teacher.

Thank you for making such a great impression!

[Johanna's mom]

TRIBUTE FROM MARY MAYER

"My memories of you....

- Dynamic personality
- Giving person
- Incredible teacher
- Dedicated to helping everyone!"

[Mary is a teacher I once knew. She told her relative (Jeanne Lange, a friend from my church) I was an amazing teacher, "amazing, amazing, amazing." She added "no one could touch her – loved by parents, teachers, and students."]

KAREN SMITH'S EMAIL BEFORE MY ADDRESS
TO ALBANY, NY, POLITICIANS

Wednesday, October 7, 2015

Dear Janet,

I just want you to know personally that I am praying for you for tomorrow's hearing. I pray for everything that comes over the prayer chain, but there's a soft spot in my heart for you and all that you've been through. I feel like I'm the recipient of some of the positive things that came out of your brain injury/surgery experience.

I'm so appreciative of all the help you've been in Hosanna Kids [Sunday school class]! I can easily see how you would've made an awesome special ed. teacher. I've seen you work with the big kids at MOPS [Mothers of Preschoolers] and how they just love coming to your class.

You have a ton of gifts and talents and for seemingly lots of reasons God drastically changed the path you were on for using them. Some of us get to just follow the obvious path with our gifts, but some get to travel whole new roads and help out others in ways they never thought possible. That's you.

It's amazing, and remarkable, and fun to watch you in action. I hope and pray all goes well for you with the mucky-mucks and that you will get to see God himself at work up there, even in Albany!

Love and peace,
Karen
[Karen Smith is Pastor Wes Smith's wife.]

Chapter 39

SIGNS

As I wrote in another chapter, I have over 200 signs in my home. I've selected my favorite signs for you to read here. This list is just a small example of words that help me smile and get through it all…. [And some of my thoughts added in.]

- Happy. Happy. Happy. [My dog's name.]
- I Will Survive [My mother's theme song for me.]
- Keep calm and take a nap
- Laugh! Sometimes it's just the medicine you need
- Remember the day's blessings, forget the day's troubles
- NEVER…miss a good chance to shut up. [Amen!]
- The only thing domestic about me is that I live indoors
- Today may not be good but there's something good in every day
- I hope you dance
- The older I get, the better I was
- Realize how good you really are
- I wouldn't mind having a split personality as long as the other one did the housework

- To save some time: Let's Just Assume That I'M ALWAYS RIGHT!
- Life is too short to be serious all the time
- Peace, love, and sandy feet [I love the beach!]
- You can never have too much HAPPY!
- Go away! I'm reading
- I will be grateful for this day
- Be sure to taste your words before you spit them out [Too many of mine taste yucky!]
- Your day will go the way the corners of your mouth turn
- The first step to getting what you want is having the courage to get rid of what you don't... [A real struggle for me!]
- Laugh as much as you breathe
- Your best days are ahead!
- What you think is what you become...
- My life will improve from the inside out!
- No matter what happens around me, this will be a good day!
- You can't start the next chapter of your life if you keep re-reading the last one [How true!]
- Don't look back – you're not going that way
- I am so clever that sometimes I don't understand a single word that I say
- You should do something nice for someone every single day, even if it means to leave them alone [Excellent advice!]
- Knowledge talks – wisdom listens
- The most wasted of all days is one without laughter
- Stop thinking so much and just get on with it
- Life is short – smile while you still have teeth
- Never put the key to your happiness in someone else's pocket [This sign hangs near my keychains as a reminder to me to NEVER give my house key to a certain someone ever again!]
- It's what you learn after you know it all that counts
- Sometimes my greatest accomplishment is keeping my mouth shut [Very true!]

- Live for today. Hope for tomorrow. Amazing things will happen.
- My heart is at the beach
- When you get there, remember where you came from
- I'm not crazy – I just have less restrictions
- Seize the day [Remember Robin Williams in that movie *Dead Poets Society,* teaching his students to stand on their desks? With permission, I did that with my students one year, and luckily no one got hurt.]
- Just do what you do best
- Vitality shows in not only the ability to persist but the ability to start over
- No outfit is complete without dog hair
- I'm NOT crazy. I'm just moose-understood [With an illustrated picture of the moose in the Adirondacks.]
- Everyone's entitled to their own ridiculous opinion
- You know you're getting old when happy hour is a nap! [Sometimes, when I bump into people I used to party with years ago, I enjoy hearing the stories of our escapades. Nowadays, my fun is hanging out with the kiddies at my church…followed by a long nap.]
- Do what makes you happy. Be with who makes you smile.
- Hangry: an anger fueled by hunger. A cranky state resulting from lack of food, especially sweet things.
- Let no one dull your sparkle
- There are so many beautiful reasons to be happy
- Fathers of girls have a special place in Heaven
- Be with the guy who ruins your lipstick, not your mascara. [My sign should read "ChapStick," since I don't wear lipstick anymore, but the point of this remains the same.]
- Be kind, for everyone you meet is fighting a hard battle
- If you can't see the bright side of life, polish the dull side
- There's ability in every disability [Absolutely!]

- If you are grouchy, irritable, or just plain mean, there will be a **$10 charge** just for putting up with you. [This was in a restaurant, but I thought it was excellent, so I took a picture of it for my house.]
- It is better to find an error to correct than a fault to criticize
- It took all my willpower but I've finally quit dieting. [I did quit trying to look good for this book's cover picture.]
- Surrender to what is. Let go of what was. Have faith in what will be.
- If you can't be kind…BE QUIET!
- I could have been a novel. [Well – I'm a memoir.]
- Be More Rudolph – he always knew he was a little different but he let his light shine anyway
- To teach is to love
- Teachers are never appreciated until it rains all weekend
- Smile like a dog with a new bone
- We find our greatest strength within ourselves
- 100 years from now, it will not matter what my bank account was, the sort of house I lived in, or the kind of car I drove. But, the world may be different because I was important in the life of a child.
- A very large sign I have in my home is entitled: "Meditations For Women Who Do Too Much," by Anne Wilson Schaef. There are several statements on it, but here are my favorites:
    » Sometimes it helps to know that I just can't do it all.
    » Laughter is like the human body wagging its tail.
    » Sometimes we just think too much!
    » Perfectionism is self-abuse of the highest order.
    » No one else will arrange any quiet time for me. I have to see to it myself.
    » When I say no to a request for my time, I'm not going away from that person, I am going to myself.

» I will remember that my illusion of control is just that, an illusion.

[And, I even saw a sign I enjoyed at my editor's home that read: There's a skinny girl who lives inside of me that's trying to get out, but I can usually shut her up with cookies.]

I also had begun to clutter some of Aiden's walls at his house with some more signs. Here are some of those:

- I'm sorry for what I said when I was hungry
- What happens at the beach, stays at the beach
- I'm so miserable without you, it's almost like you're here
- Don't try to understand me – just love me
- It's never too late to live happily ever after
- A Positive Attitude may not solve all your problems – but it may annoy enough people to make it worth the effort. [Believe it or not – I bought this at a church fundraiser, and it made me laugh because I'm too negative!]

[Unfortunately, none of these signs at Aiden's home actually helped us survive as a couple.]

Even though I have hundreds now, in a while, I'll even have more.

Chapter 40

MAGNETS

LIKE ALL THE signs I have around my house, I also have a record-breaking amount of well-worded magnets. I giggle sometimes when I watch a TV show or movie, and I see a refrigerator door that is empty. Mine is so cluttered, I'm lucky I can find the handle! Not only are they displayed on my fridge, I also have many on my dishwasher, the inner side of my front door, my car, and any other magnetic surface I can adhere them to.

Here are some of my favorites [with my add-in comments for some of them]:

- Choose happy
- It's hard to be optimistic when your fat pants are tight
- If a messy kitchen is a happy kitchen, mine's delirious!
- I wish I was as trim as I was when I thought I was fat
- Without bacon, life is just lettuce and tomatoes [I LOVE BLTs!]
- The way to a woman's heart is through the door of a good restaurant
- Me + Chocolate = Happiness

- A clean house is a sign of a wasted life [Go have some fun!]
- Let go or be dragged
- Life's challenges are God's way of teaching us to trust Him
- Don't you dare call me ma'am [Waitresses and waiters get a better tip from me when they call me "Miss" or "Ms."]
- If you're not happy with what you have, imagine not having it
- When things go wrong, go right to God
- Book junkie
- God adores the sound of your voice – talk to Him often
- Crazy dog lady
- God is everywhere – even at your wit's end
- As a matter of fact – the world does revolve around my dog
- I am in great shape – and the shape is round
- Keep calm and wag on
- I know I'm in my own world… it's okay – they know me here
- I understand the concept of cooking and cleaning – just not as it applies to me
- Danger! Disaster area
- No, my window isn't dirty. It's the dog's nose prints
- It took a lot of willpower, but I finally gave up dieting.
- Teaching: Not in it for the income, in it for the outcome
- Health food makes me sick. [I love my nutritionist, Ingrid, who is trying her hardest to get me to enjoy healthier food.]

So, you can see by these last couple of chapters, my possessions are not just for their normal use, but also for inspiration. Here come more examples….

Chapter 41

My Wardrobe and More...

YEARS AGO, I actually took time and effort into dressing up and looking good. Nowadays – my favorite thing to wear is sweatshirts and T-shirts with funny sayings on them (when I'm not wearing my Mickey Mouse "wardrobe" or attending a special event). The day I handed this chapter in to my editor, Dr. Cooper, I wore the T-shirt that said: "Grammar Police: to Serve and Protect the English Language," because my nicknames for him are "Comma King," and/or "Dr. Comma." I have learned how infrequently I used commas before I met him! (I write like I talk: run-on sentences.) Here are some of my favorite shirt sayings [with my add-in comments]:

- Careful, or you'll end up in my novel [Lots of folks ask me if they're in my book.]
- Dinner is ready when the smoke alarm goes off [Purchased when I actually cooked years ago.]
- Listen and silent have the same letters – coincidence?
- Messy hair – don't care
- Peace. Love. Books.

- Book Nerd
- I'm the crazy aunt everybody warned you about [Aiden scolded me if I packed this when we went to Florida to visit my family.]
- I need my reading time
- Lord – keep your arm around my shoulder and your hand over my mouth
- I have CDO. It's like OCD, but all the letters are in order like they should be
- There and Their – They're not the same [Like a chapter here in this book.]
- Warning – Extremely Annoying [Worn on days when I'm very agitated.]
- God is good all the time [front] All the time God is good [back]
- Keep calm and eat bacon
- What if I don't want to keep calm
- Sassy Lassie [In memory of Grandma McColl, who called me that.]
- I gave him the skinniest years of my life
- Red Shirt Fridays – Support Our Troops – Land of the Free Because of the Brave

I also have great aprons with funny sayings (which is humorous in itself since I don't cook). Here are some of what they have to say:
- The last time I cooked, hardly anyone got sick!
- I kiss better than I cook
- Feast today – shop tomorrow [A Thanksgiving apron.]

Besides clothing and aprons, I also have bracelets, buttons, soap bars, mugs, pillows, blankets, and oh, so much more of things to read each day to cheer me up. Here are some of those…
- Laugh [A purple bracelet I wore for five years to help me enjoy life more.]

- Laugh, laugh, laugh… [On a mug to help me the same way the bracelet did.]
- You are a woman of wisdom, courage, strength, compassion, and creativity
- Amazing Grace [I sing this song when I sip my coffee or tea from the mug.]
- Think big!
- Got milk? [On a mug with a picture of a chocolate chip cookie. It's my personal law that I need milk each and every time I eat chocolate.]
- Dog MOM
- breathe in. breathe out.
- Professional Marshmallow Roaster [I love s'mores!]
- Keep your big mouth shut [On a luxury soap bar.]
- Super Sunday School Teacher [Receiving recognition is so sweet.]
- Trust in the Lord with all your heart
- Enjoy the little things and the big things take care of themselves
- Here lives a wild, wacky, wonderful woman
- Those who can, teach. Those who cannot, pass laws about teaching
- I will not obsess! I will not obsess! I will not obsess!
- God keeps His promises
- Teachers rule
- I make grown men cry
- So many books…so little time.
- Jesus. Coffee. Bacon. Naps.

Almost everything I own sends a message.

Chapter 42

A Tribute From
My Friend Marla

Janet asked me to write a piece for her book. She didn't give me too many specifics regarding content, so I have had difficulty getting started. Janet told me to feel free to say whatever I want to say. Of course, if there were negatives, I would not include them, but there are no negatives in Janet's story that she would not hesitate to tell you herself. Janet is a very interesting person who is in love with Mickey Mouse. A smile comes across my face as I type.

I first met Janet when she took over teaching my special education class for the summer session. This was not an easy summer job. There were only six students in the class, but they all had severe behavior problems and serious learning disabilities. As my replacement, Janet had the lucky opportunity to work with my dedicated teacher assistant, Beverly K. Following the summer session, Janet was hired full-time by our school district and became my colleague.

I was awed by Janet. She was extremely capable, hard-working, dedicated, energetic, and seemed to master the job with ease. Janet loved all her students and did her best for every single one of them. She was creative in her teaching. One of my memories from way back then was a weekly assembly program Janet and her class was responsible for. Janet had her girls dressed as a current rock-and-roll group. She taught them to lip-sync and do accompanying choreography. Janet turned this activity into a reading lesson using the "whole language approach." [Ed.: The whole language approach favors having children recognize whole words as such rather than using the "phonics" approach, which has the students break down the words, analyzing them phonetically.] Janet gave every child in her class a world-class Disney-themed birthday party. She went out of her way to make each child feel special and loved. (Most of our students came from troubled families. Many of them had never experienced a birthday party given in their honor.)

Way back when, probably in the very late 1980s or early 1990s, Janet was a very fast talker. To this day, she continues to be able to squeeze more information and words into thirty seconds than almost anyone I know. I love to teasingly ask her to "please repeat that a little faster." Along with her ability to be a faster-than-fast talker, Janet lacked a filter. There were many times back then when I was stunned at the things Janet would say to authority figures (the school principal, site supervisor, or even the superintendent of schools). Janet said exactly what was on her mind and never seemed to suffer any negative consequences. My mouth would hang open listening to Janet, while feelings of jealousy grew inside me. Janet would say things I wanted to, but I would not dare. I was amazed at how she got away with it.

Janet was a dynamo of a teacher. She was the school district whole language expert and taught many workshops in which she trained other teachers to use the whole language method of teaching reading. Janet made reading fun for kids.

I remember Janet's classroom being overloaded with beautiful books of all shapes and sizes. "Big books" were a large part of the whole language approach. Janet purchased the majority of them with her own funds, usually spending up to $6000 per school year on books and classroom supplies. (The government only allows teachers a $250 per year tax deduction for classroom expenses.) To supplement the student desks, Janet equipped her room with a comfy couch, bean-bag chairs, and rugs.

Some people may have described Janet's classroom as cluttered. The walls were covered with colorful posters, and the shelves were full of manipulative learning materials as well as books and supplies. Educators often have different opinions on what the best learning environment should look like. Some people might say that Janet's room was too stimulating for hyperactive, attention-deficit students. Other teachers might view it as a highly stimulating environment that makes children want to learn and tweaks their curiosity. Janet would have special activity days devoted entirely to reading for pleasure. (I doubt any teacher would dare to attempt such a thing in today's classrooms.)

As far as I know, Janet started having a fear of germs after she changed school districts. I didn't realize how serious and debilitating that fear was for her. I remember meeting Janet for lunch at a diner one day after school. Janet pulled out her bottle of [hand sanitizer] and wiped down the salt and pepper shakers, as well as the utensils. She told me she was seeing a therapist and a psychiatrist. I knew life was rough for Janet, but I don't think I fully understood how much she was suffering. I suppose her fear of germs greatly interfered with her ability to do her job. At that point, I knew Janet had a very serious problem.

My memory fails me, but I'm sure Janet has explained all the details of exactly what her experience had been. In time, Janet told me that she found out she had a brain tumor. I think it was July when she had her surgery at NYU Medical Center. I hopped on the bus to New York City to visit her.

When I walked into Janet's hospital room, I was shocked. She looked terrible. Her face was swollen; her mouth was not in the position it belonged; her head was bandaged up, but she was smiling and happy. Her two sisters, Joyce and Jayne, stood at the foot of her bed.

They had just returned from going to a cupcake bakery and handed Janet a huge chocolate cupcake. Janet had tears oozing out of the corners of her eyes. She stated something like, "I don't have to wash my hands! I'm cured! I can't believe that I'm not afraid of germs!" Janet wasn't able to eat more than a few bites at that moment. She then proceeded to tell me that the doctor had removed from her brain a tumor that was the size of an orange. Her instant cure from germ-phobia was a miracle.

Janet has had problems getting along with her family throughout the time I have known her. I suppose that the tumor blocked out the "filter" most of us possess when relating to other people. The day I visited Janet in the hospital, she was enjoying a loving, supportive relationship with her sisters. I was told that her parents also journeyed to New York from their Florida home to help and support Janet during her recovery. Months, or perhaps a year or two, after her surgery, Janet again suffered some estrangement from her family. Looking back now, I suppose that the tumor blocked Janet's social filter, and the tumor and her operation have left some residual damage.

The Janet I know today can still talk faster than anyone I know. She works hard at taking good care of herself and managing her life as a brain-injured person, due to the trauma caused by the tumor and the operation. Janet continues to be a dynamo of energy. Janet, Beverly, and I meet once every six months to catch up with one another. It is a time we all look forward to. Janet is an Energizer Bunny. Like the Timex watch claim, she takes a lickin' and keeps on tickin'!

I love Janet and admire her bravery and perseverance.

Chapter 43

―――

My IEP

As I stated earlier in my book, I often wrote a special education student's Individualized Education Plan (IEP) with specific information about that one child. By the end of my career (2007), these once-useful documents outlining goals for the student to reach became "cookie cutter" pieces of paper that I despised. They were computerized and only vaguely personalized.

I never minded writing them in the early part of my career. But, by the end, they were a hideous chore that I could no longer understand or do well. I genuinely missed the "old days" when modern technology didn't get in my way.

Therefore – I decided for this book, I've turned into being both student and teacher and I'll write my own IEP to help me with my behavior and memory. Of course, I'll do it the old-fashioned way and write accurate, specific-to-me goals, so I can help myself improve. This should be fun! Let's see....

The "student" (meaning me) will:

1. Count to 10 when someone does or says something that upsets her

2. Repeat the above goal to a higher number than 10 if necessary

3. Be rewarded for each day that appropriate behavior is noticed [i.e., chocolate]

4. Be given extra time to complete all tasks since she is unable to be rushed

5. Be allowed interactions in spaces with minimal distractions

6. Be respectful of another person's viewpoint/opinion

7. Be less reactive when something is said that is personal and hurtful

8. Be a better listener

9. Rest when necessary to be able to complete tasks later in the day

10. Be able to state, "I'll get back to you" or "no" in a calm voice when asked by someone else to complete a task

11. Decrease the amount of worrying

12. Learn how to take better care of self (i.e., eat more fruits and vegetables/exercise more)

13. Be able to find more positives than negatives in each and every situation and relationship

14. Use communication when agitated

15. Be able to state on the telephone, "I have to go" when becoming upset before saying something that she would regret

16. Be able to be more patient with people who are employees at offices

17. Be less observational of others' mistakes

18. Be less impulsive and think things through thoroughly before taking any sort of action

19. Be less agitated with other drivers who do not drive carefully

20. Be able to smile more often

21. Be more careful with the way money is spent

22. Develop a long list of coping mechanisms to deal with all aspects of life

23. Be able to laugh more often

24. Be able to take "snow days" once in a while to take time off to decompress (as she once did as a teacher)

25. Talk to God whenever she needs to feel better [or the public school version, "meditate"]

An ironic thing about this IEP list that I wrote about myself is that I have more behavior goals listed than I used to have to write for my students. That confirms what I already knew: many of my students were better behaved then than I am now.

Chapter 44

The Bag Lady

I DUBBED MYSELF this title because I carry bags to every place I go (including movies, doctor appointments, church functions, various organizations and support groups I attend, and on and on and on...). The bags contain things I need for each place. This is the way I remember things. Way too many people have either rudely commented and/or questioned me about my bags. They are not purses, but bags of all shapes, sizes, and many with great sayings on them. They now replace the huge L.L. Bean teacher bag I once had when I taught school.

What always cracks me up is when someone who's been rude to me about my habit of lugging stuff forgets or loses something of their own. I want to say, "Well – if you had all your needed items in a bag like mine, you would have what you now have to do without."

But – I just smile and bite my tongue. I've had to bite my tongue so many times. I truly don't comprehend why my bags puzzle others to the point of rudeness.

At one of the many stores I buy decorated bags at (Cracker Barrel), I told the register lady how I have a bag for each doctor I see. That way, when it's time for another appointment, I don't have to look for what I need to share with that doctor. It's all organized right there in that bag. Register Lady told me that was a great idea, and she was going to do it from now on.

Once, when I went to a jewelry party, and we played one of those silly games before looking through the catalog to purchase jewelry, we had to find certain weird things in our purses or bags. I had every single, strange item on the list, so I won lots of prizes!

I have to be careful, though. A few times, my bag has been in the way and someone else, or even myself, has tripped over it. That's not too helpful, so I try to squish the bags out of the way, when I can.

Many bags I own have Mickey Mouse on them, but I also have tons without. Because these other bags are too good to gloss over here, I've included what many of them say. Enjoy! [My own comments are added for some.]

- Teachers have homework too!! [The bag I used each Friday for three years when I went to meet with my editor.]
- Book Nerd [Just like my T-shirt.]
- Don't pretend to understand my problems
- Do more of what makes you happy
- Funny – I don't recall asking for your opinion
- Take delight in the Lord
- A good book has no ending
- Live happy
- Scotland! [I bring this one to my Dutchess County, NY, Scottish Society meetings.]
- Bloom where you are planted
- Where's the beach?
- Once upon a summertime
- Give me some sugar
- Little bag of awesome!
- Every tree has character
- Life is all about how you handle Plan B

- Live. Love. Bark.
- Give thanks to the Lord, for He is good
- My best friend is my dog
- This is the day that the Lord has made
- Mahalo [Which I think means "thanks." A great gift store in Catskill, NY, has this title, and I've bought great bags there. While writing this chapter, I even received a gift bag from them.]
- There's no place like the bookstore.
- Practice Gratitude…. Give More…. Sparkle More…. It's the Little Things…. More Road Trips…. Live Happy [All on one bag!]
- Happy camper
- Random Crap [On each of two bags, one large and one larger, from Stickle's, my mother's favorite store in Rhinebeck, NY.]
- Great Big Bag of Stuff [Another bag, the largest, from Stickle's.]
- Live in the moment
- Positive Mind. Positive Soul. Positive Life.

So, now you know why I love my bags, and I'm proud to be "The Bag Lady." Sometimes what's important is not so much what's IN the bag, it's what's ON the bag….

Chapter 45

FAVORITE QUOTES

THESE ARE AMONG my most favorite sayings. I hope you like them too.

"Rescue dogs can make the most incredible pets." *Nat Geo Wild*

"God's plan for our life is bigger than our own." Joel Osteen

"There are two great days in a person's life – the day we are born and the day we discover why." William Barclay, Scottish theologian [Go, Scots, go!]

"The whole purpose of having a life-saving operation is to go back and live life." Dr. Oz

"Forgiveness is not an occasional act. It is a permanent attitude." Martin Luther King, Jr.

"O, would some power the giftie gie us, / To see ourselves as others see us." Robert Burns, Scottish poet [Telling us the value of seeing ourselves objectively.]

"The words you speak become the house you live in." Hafiz

"No matter how difficult the past, you can always begin again today." Jack Kornfield

"The only way you can change the world is by changing yourself." Tommy Chong

"Life can only be understood backwards; but it must be lived forwards." Soren Kierkegaard

"You must do the thing you think you cannot do." Eleanor Roosevelt

"Women are like tea bags. We don't know our true strength until we are in hot water." Eleanor Roosevelt

"I think teaching is the most honorable profession there is." Oprah Winfrey

"…that if you become a teacher, by your pupils you'll be taught." Rogers and Hammerstein's *King and I.*

"I forgive, I love, I learn, and I move on." Marie Osmond [I pray I can do that someday.]

"One person can change things." John Hall, musician, congressman, author

"It's important to keep reinventing yourself." Marie Osmond

"As we express our gratitude, we must never forget that the highest appreciation is not to utter words, but to live by them." John F. Kennedy

"The sooner you accept it, the sooner you'll get over it." Girl teenagers I overheard talking at my church. [So insightful – I told them they'd be in my book.]

"Our words have the power to build up or tear down." *Our Daily Bread*

"Father, please curb my careless speech and put a guard on my tongue today and every day." *Our Daily Bread*

"Don't believe everything you think." Sound of Life, Hudson Valley, NY, radio station

"Getting over a painful experience is much like crossing monkey bars. You have to let go at some point in order to move forward." C. S. Lewis

"The world can only change from within." Eckhart Tolle

"Change your thoughts and you change your world." Norman Vincent Peale

"The trick is to enjoy life. Don't wish away your days, waiting for better ones." Marjorie Pay Hinckley

"Never be in a hurry; do everything quietly and in a calm spirit. Do not lose your inner peace for anything whatsoever, even if your whole world seems upset." St. Francis de Sales

"Happiness is not a station you arrive at, but a manner of traveling." Margaret Lee Runbeck

"Who you are is the sum of all the choices that you make in this life."
Signed, Sealed, Delivered: Truth Be Told [Hallmark movie]

"The way to get started is to quit talking and begin doing." Walt Disney

"Less is more." Robert Browning

"My brain has no off switch." *Cold Case* [TV show]

"Understanding is a two-way street." Eleanor Roosevelt

"Life is what we make it. Always has been. Always will be." Grandma Moses

"I have never felt that anything really mattered but knowing that you stood for the things in which you believed and had done the very best you could." Eleanor Roosevelt

"A little rain can straighten a flower stem. A little love can change a life." Max Lucado

"To strengthen the muscles of your heart, the best exercise is lifting someone else's spirit whenever you can." Dodinsky

"All great changes are preceded by chaos." Deepak Chopra

"In the end these things matter most: How well did you love? How fully did you live? How deeply did you let go?" Buddha

"It is always wise, I think, if you feel something is wrong, to try to stand up for what you believe is right." Eleanor Roosevelt

"Nothing has ever been achieved by the person who says, 'It can't be done.'" Eleanor Roosevelt [In my classroom, I told the kids not to use this four-letter word, "can't."]

"The problems of the world will never be settled unless our national leaders go to God in prayer." Billy Graham

"The more you like yourself, the less you are like anyone else, which makes you unique." Walt Disney

"Tomorrow can be a wonderful age." Walt Disney

"When you believe a thing, believe it all the way." Walt Disney

"No one's invisible pain should go unnoticed." Lady Gaga

"If too many things are planned, there's too much to remember." Harry Connick, Jr.

"Our past tells us that our future belongs to the Lord." Randy Prentiss, Staff Chaplain, Taconic Retreat Center, Red Hook, NY.

"We can be freer if we let stuff go." Randy Prentiss

"If everyone lends a helping hand to those in need, we would take a giant step towards a more peaceful world." Harry Swimmer, CNN Hero

"It's never too soon to be kind." *Our Daily Bread*

"Maybe if you zip [your mouth] up, your wall will come down." Joel Osteen

"I've learned…that I can always pray for someone when I don't have the strength to help him in any other way." Andy Rooney

"I've learned…that sometimes all a person needs is a hand to hold and a heart to understand." Andy Rooney

"I've learned…that love, not time, heals all wounds." Andy Rooney

"Find the good. It's all around you. Find it, showcase it, and you'll start believing it." Jesse Owens, Olympic gold medal track and field athlete

"We're so over, we need a new word for 'over.'" Carrie, to Mr. Big, in HBO's *Sex and the City*. [Even though she told him it was over, she ended up marrying him. I never married Aiden, so it really is over for us.]

"…because it's so easy for, I will say, a man to say you're crazy…." [Taking no ownership of his behavior.] Amber Frey, *Dateline NBC's* "The Laci Peterson Story."

"If you find someone you love in life, you must hang onto it and look after it." Princess Diana [I miss her SO much!]

A whole different level of quotes comes from the *Bible.* Here they are:

"Get rid of all bitterness, rage and anger, brawling and slander, along with every form of malice. Be kind and compassionate to one another, forgiving each other, just as in Christ God forgave you." *Ephesians 4:31-32*

"God will work out everything for our good." *Romans 8:28*

"And the Lord's servant must not be quarrelsome but kindly to everyone, an apt teacher, forbearing, correcting his opponents with

WHAT EVER HAPPENED TO MY WHITE PICKET FENCE?

gentleness." *2 Timothy 2*:24-25 [Appropriately – this was printed on my calendar on my birthday – November 1st!]

"Do not let any unwholesome talk come out of your mouths, but only what is helpful for building others up according to their needs, that it may benefit those who listen." *Ephesians 4*:29

I learn a lot from other people – some famous, some not.

Chapter 46

DR. SEUSS'S HELP

I HAVE LEARNED so much about life from the words of Dr. Seuss – Theodore Geisel. There is SO much more to his stories than just learning how to read!

For many years as a teacher, I celebrated his birthday (March 2nd) with a Dr. Seuss Day. We read all day, dressed up in the cat-in-the-hat's red-and-white hat and just discussed the lessons to be learned from his stories. I know a lot of schools do this each year.

When I couldn't be a teacher anymore, I brought this idea to my church where I volunteer twice a month with preschoolers. We have so much fun looking at all of the books I've accumulated. I post some of the best Dr. Seuss sayings around our little room.

I was going to just quote a few throughout my book, but then I decided they were worth a whole chapter. So – here are my favorite Dr. Seuss quotes. I've starred (*) the ones I've used as a teacher and/or church volunteer. Enjoy and THANK YOU, Dr. Seuss!

- Don't cry because it's over. Smile because it happened.

- Be who you are and say what you feel. Because those who mind don't matter, and those who matter don't mind.
- You have brains in your head. You have feet in your shoes. You can steer yourself any direction you choose! (*)
- Stop telling such outlandish tales. Stop turning minnows into whales. (*)
- This was no time for play. This was no time for fun. This was no time for games. There was work to be done. (*)
- I do not like green eggs and ham! I do not like them, Sam-I-am. (*) [Some years when we celebrated his birthday, we actually made green eggs and ham. It was pretty simple – we just added green food coloring to the scrambled eggs we prepared. The kids, staff, and I loved eating what Sam-I-am in the book wouldn't try until the very end of the story. That's another of the things I miss about teaching.]
- The more that you read, the more things you will know. The more that you learn, the more places you'll go. (*)
- Unless someone like you cares a whole awful lot, nothing is going to get better. It's not. (*)
- You're in pretty good shape for the shape you are in! (*)
- A person's a person, no matter how small. (*)
- Maybe Christmas perhaps means a little bit more! [Thank you, Grinch!]
- Oh! The places you'll go! (*)
- It is fun to have fun but you have to know how!
- You're off to great places! Today is your day! Your mountain is waiting! So get on your way! (*)
- Smile hi! Smile low! Smile everywhere you go! [I wish I would.]
- Try to remember through thick and through thin, when you give it your best... Why, that's when YOU WIN! (*)
- Why fit in when you were born to stand out?
- Today is good! Today is fun! Tomorrow is another one! (*)
- There is fun to be done! (*)

- Do what you love and love what you do. There's no better way to a happier you!
- From there to here, from here to there, funny things are everywhere!
- Oh, the thinks you can think up if only you try!
- Whatever you do, do it well! Do it YOU!
- If you never did, you should. These things are fun and fun is good.

Aren't these great? Dr. Seuss's books are not just for kids, so I hope you enjoy them as much as I do. In that spirit:

Dr. Seuss's rhymes are really fun,
Even if you're not a little one!

At the conclusion of writing this book, I learned that a new Dr. Seuss museum just opened in Springfield, Massachusetts. I can't wait to visit!

Chapter 47

WHY THE TITLE:
*WHAT EVER HAPPENED TO MY
WHITE PICKET FENCE?*

YEARS AGO, AFTER many failed relationships, I had begun writing a book about my messed-up love life. I wrote the stories of all the stuff that had taken place in my life from the early 1990s until when I became too sick to teach (around 2006 or so). One of the many stories I had for that book was when a 1993 boyfriend of mine cheated on me, and because of that, I stopped eating. My family flew me down to Florida to try to help me get better. Grandpa Johnson was particularly concerned and very generous. When I was a child, he had usually given me $5 when we were saying our goodbyes. After this horrible breakup, he slipped a $50 bill into my hand that I didn't notice until I got on the airplane to fly back to New York.

So, to that cheater and you other men whom I was with during that timeframe, consider yourselves lucky that I had a brain tumor, because that book I was writing was airing your "dirty laundry" for all the world to see (with only slight name changes).

The name of that book was the same as this book. I originally was writing about how I never ended up with the husband, babies, nice house, and cozy life that I long ago planned on having. Those three children I wanted (Rachel, Rebecca, and Jonathan – in THAT order) never happened. I married twice – one ended in divorce, and the second one I had annulled.

Now, mind you, there were a few good men in my life that I had dated. In that original memoir, I wrote nothing about "Catholic Boy Jim," "Banker Bob," or "Oregon Greg" (my affectionate nicknames for them) because they were sweet and did not mistreat me. I called Jim that because he was very attached to his church. What he learned there helped me too. I wrote about Jim here earlier. Bob was a nice guy too. He even stored some of my teaching supplies (in his garage) long after we broke up. Another good guy was Greg. I knew him when we both worked for Ulster County BOCES, before he moved to Oregon, that beautiful state. I've remained friends with all three of them to this day. So, those three men were NOT written about in my former "tell-all tale." But, the rest of the men I dated WERE described. Finishing the writing of that embarrassing saga was sidetracked by my brain tumor, you lucky boys.

The day I wrote about here earlier, when I almost missed my first appointment with my editor because I got lost so many times when I had to drive myself, is the day I decided this title would remain. One teenage boy who used his cell phone to help me get back on the correct road to the Orange County [New York] Chamber of Commerce yelled to me as I ran back to my car, "So, what's your book's title?"

As I jumped in to speed away I shouted, "*What Ever Happened to My White Picket Fence?*"

As soon as I drove away, I thought to myself, *Janet, that was the title of your book when you were writing about your screwed-up love life.* But then, the very next thought was this: *Janet, it's the perfect title still! You wanted one life (teaching forever and a happy family life), and you got another (battling disability and advocating for the brain-injured).*

Now, I know that not everyone ends up with the comfy-cozy life they planned on when they were so much younger. Everyone has a story to tell. But, I feel my particular story is unique because you don't see too many middle-aged women recovering from a massive brain tumor with no husband, no children, no grandchildren, and no nearby family members to assist.

Though I've had LOTS of help from friends, my dog, Aiden, church folks, former co-workers, and others, I know that God has orchestrated this all. He had a plan for me, and it wasn't to teach special needs children up until the usual retirement age. He knew that I could write (I was published a few times in educational journals when I was going for my Master's at SUNY New Paltz. My excellent professor there at that time, Dr. Spencer Salend, asked me to be a co-author with him.)

So, as I was saying, God decided I was done teaching. He had a bigger plan. Little did I know that day in June 2009, when the neurologist told me about the size of my brain tumor, that I would "live to tell the tale" and thus, hopefully provide help to others struggling with this "fooler" diagnosis.

I write "fooler" because, as I learned at one of my helpful support groups, MANY of us with brain injuries can appear completely normal, thus no one around us "sees" what's actually going on inside of our heads. I believe I am an excellent "fooler" because I talk fast, remember others' birthdays, arrive on time and so on.... What isn't witnessed by the majority of people, is how HARD I worked to get all of that done correctly and somewhat politely.

I spend hours upon hours planning and orchestrating my day. I have lists everywhere so I can remember the simplest of tasks, as I've written here already. But, just because I look OK, doesn't mean I'm doing just fine.

I find myself to be in many settings where I feel like I'm about to explode due to someone else's rudeness, and so, I talk to God to help me calm down.

I don't know if it's my brain injury or not, but I just witness way too much selfishness everywhere these days. As I was compiling this chapter, a family of four (two parents in their early 40s and their two teenagers) were on a line in a grocery store ahead of me (and also an elderly woman behind me).

I was in a back brace and purchasing one item. The elderly lady had a cane and was purchasing two items. I thought the parents would model for their teenagers how to take care of others. Instead, they placed their MANY items on the conveyor belt even though they saw my brace and her cane.

Wasn't that a teachable moment? Instead, it illustrated one more time how people think of themselves first.

So, we ALL had to wait so the father's beer could be sold by a manager (vs. the under-21 register girl). My back ached, and the elderly lady looked mighty uncomfortable. In my opinion, those parents modeled selfishness, not kindness. Since I've created a scene in the store once before (as I wrote about in my chapter about the things people get right even when I don't), I bit my tongue so as not to create another scene. God does "overtime" with me with that tongue of mine!

I don't really know if it's my hyper-vigilance or what, but I'm sad to observe how often others think of themselves first. Also, as I was compiling this chapter, I observed a selfish daughter on Father's Day, of all days. Guess what, daddy's little girl? It's not all about you! I truly pray that our world will improve and more people will put others before themselves. I strongly believe that that's the only way our world will get better.

I do know that I now have a "bigger" everything: my feelings are stronger on all topics; my emotions are displayed much more often than ever before; my reactions to others' behavior is grandioso; my sensitivity to anything and everything that takes place is over-the-top, sometimes embarrassingly so. This list is just the tip of the iceberg....

And that's why this book had to happen. So many people are experiencing the aftermath of their brain injury but without others in their lives understanding how to: take better care of them more; forgive them more; appreciate their difference more; tolerate their "odd" behavior more; ask how they're doing more; be helpful, just to be kind, more; put the brain-injured person ahead of themselves once in a while more; ask if they need anything, more, and so on....

And remember – no two brain injuries are the same. I actually know people that are offended by me calling myself "brain-injured" when I'm still driving, feeding myself, etc. They think that someone who is not in diapers in a nursing home should not be labeled that. But, guess what?

I may be able to do so much more than others who are also labeled "brain-injured," but I certainly have lost the life I once had when I was completely able to take care of myself physically, financially, emotionally, and behaviorally. As someone stated in one of my support groups, "Brain injury is NOT a competition!" [Exactly!]

And the same is true for many others who, like me, have been labeled "brain-injured" by their doctors, not by themselves. So, instead of treating them badly because they're higher functioning than the person in your realm who has a more severe brain injury, treat them with kindness because their life is altered permanently also.

The best person who could model for you how to do this is Barbara Sickler. I wrote about her in the chapter "Friends," but she needs more of a mention right here and now. Though her sister's traumatic brain injury forced hospitalization and then nursing-home care, which eventually led to an early-in-life death, Barbara treats me with such warmth and love. She sends me cards and notes to cheer me up when she knows I'm experiencing a "rough patch." We met because of the subject of brain injury. But, we will remain friends forever because she lovingly cares about those of us with all degrees of brain injury.

I've experienced first-hand the opposite of her warmth, and it's very difficult to write about because it's so close to home. But, as always, I've prayed to God to lead me, and I have an overwhelming feeling that this has to be stated: take care of the person who had a tumor, stroke, aneurysm, or any other acquired brain injury just like you would the person who had an accident and hit their head. They all have damage to their brain; it just took place in different ways, and in various severities. The only commonality is the life they once lived is now permanently gone. Those of you who treat others badly because of your own self-centeredness are very difficult to be around for those of us who can't keep up the pace any longer. Cut us some slack. We deserve kindness, not phony friendliness.

I need to add that as I was compiling a part of this chapter, I also did this: had three chiropractic appointments for my back that was still in a brace; had a very expensive new mattress delivered so I could help my very sore back; cleaned lots of clutter out of the way so the "mattress men" could get it in the door; tolerated very noisy construction going on for days in the condo attached to mine; had a doctor's appointment, a dentist's appointment (ugh!), a meeting, a funeral, and regular, everyday stuff like walking my dog, etc. I'm proud that I was still diligent enough to get this book work done! Way to go, Janet!

So, it's time to wrap up this book. My editor told me that it takes the average person four to nine years to write a book. I did it in three. And – I did it the "slow" way (handwritten) because I'm slower on the computer. Even though I can use it, I'm very slow-moving so I needed a lot of help. And – my brain is not always up to challenges.

I've already been asked to speak about this book at 20 different locations when it comes out. My editor tells me getting so many invitations while still writing is rare. I'm impressed with that myself.

I now take on God's "Plan B" for my life. **The white picket fence never happened, but so much other stuff did.** And a lot of that was truly good too. My best advice to anyone is to enjoy what you have instead of wallowing in what you don't.

In the spring of 2016, on the last day of a Women's *Bible* Study I had participated in at my church, a "bright light" went off when the book we were studying from, *Jeremiah – Daring to Hope in an Unstable World*, by

Melissa Spoelstra, had a passage from the *Bible* that I realized as soon as I read it, it was going to be put at the end of my book. I started to tear up when it was on this large wall in huge letters as we watched this DVD.

Dear, sweet Ilse touched my arm to ask if I was okay. I said, "Yes – I just figured out how I'm going to end my book." She smiled because she knew how much I was struggling with how to wrap it up.

Writing this book was the hardest thing I've ever done, and with the life I've had, that's really saying something! But, I persevered and never gave up. As Dory says in the Disney/Pixar film *Finding Dory*, "I did it!"

To those of you who need to get closer to God for any reason, know that He's always by your side. The Bible states it better than anyone could. God bless you…here's that passage:

> *I cry out, "My splendor is gone!*
> *Everything I had hoped for from the Lord is lost!"*
> *The thought of my suffering and homelessness*
> *is bitter beyond words.*
> ***I will never forget this awful time,***
> ***as I grieve over my loss.***
> *Yet I still dare to hope*
> *when I remember this:*
> *The faithful love of the Lord never ends!*
> *His mercies never cease.*
> ***Great is His faithfulness;***
> ***His mercies begin afresh each morning.***
>
> *Lamentations* 3:18-23 NLV

The End
of my book!

The Beginning
of the rest of my life….

Recommended Books and Literature that Helped Me

THERE ARE MANY books that I've read as I've prepared this book. The ones that helped me the most are outlined a bit here, but not in alphabetical order. **I've included important statements from some of the books listed that helped either in my own recovery** or assisted me as a writer. I wholeheartedly recommend these excellent resources. I want to thank publicly each of the authors listed here. Your time and effort helped me enormously.

The *Bible* – of course, this has to be listed before all the others listed next. *Psalms* helped me the most at first, but I listened to many other people list other books of the *Bible* that led them to a better life. I just encourage you to read it and learn from it. If it's overwhelming, start in small amounts of time, ask for help understanding it from others who read it, or join a *Bible* study to learn with others. It's the best resource for life, even though it was written so long ago.

Where Is the Mango Princess? A Journey Back from Brain Injury, by Cathy Crimmins

I quoted MANY things from this book because it taught me the most of all the books I read post-injury. I strongly recommend you read this book!

- "He won't be the same man." [The author's husband, Al, suffered a traumatic brain injury. I'm not the same woman since my acquired brain injury.]
- "The brain injury community marks time by asking how long someone has been 'out of' injury…." [According to

a support group I attend for brain injury – I'm a "tween," which explains my pre-teen behavior.]

- "Rebirth after brain injury is slow. Messy."
- "Al is pissed off a lot.... Brain injury patients tire easily and can't concentrate for very long."
- "...one side effect of brain injury is a propensity toward concrete thinking."
- "I leave a Post-it in the logbook, prompting Al to...." [I leave these notes EVERYWHERE to remember stuff!]
- **"A brain-injured person needs a steady routine, a minimal amount of stimulation, and a lifestyle that is not taxing in any way."** [As I was writing this book, I was told by my neurologist that doing this work is **"extraordinary"** for someone with a brain injury like mine.]
- "... the researchers found that people with damage to the temporal lobe, a section of the brain along the lower-left side of the brain, over the ear, often have trouble naming objects. One person might lose the ability to name animals, for example. Another might lose the ability to name utensils." [I get laughed at by others when this happens sometimes.]
- "... getting confused and lost can pose major dangers to brain-injured people in the outside world." [My yellow "Mickey Mobile" Saturn was SO much easier to find in parking lots than my blue Subaru. That's why I don't shop alone in the dark anymore. I'm scared of getting lost in a parking lot.]
- "You wouldn't believe how many people with brain injuries get run over by cars. They get distracted or stop paying attention, and they walk into traffic." [That author is quoting someone who helps her husband navigate life. Aiden told me he had to hold on to me when we saw the sights in New York City because too many times I've stepped off the curb without looking.]
- "In brain injury jargon, he 'perseverates' about the topic. Over

and over and over again, he says...." ["Perseverate" is a word I used to use when teaching, and now I use for myself.]

- **"Brain injury is a tragedy for everyone but a special nightmare for people with intellectual lives and jobs. Our intelligence is our greatest pride...."**
- "First Alan gets extremely tired, and then everything else goes wrong: he loses his...impulse control, and his ability to pick up on social cues and make simple judgments. When tired, Al knocks into walls as he walks. He drops things, and when he does, it makes him angrier...." [Once, I dropped a cup of hot tea into my bag at a Christmas women's brunch at my church. I was so upset, I ran to the restroom to calm down.]
- "He's surly and has temper tantrums." [I act like a child many times.]
- "Alan now has labels for everyone, including himself." [I give lots of folks nicknames.]
- "...three fits a day in which he will rage and throw things around the kitchen or smash the cellular phone because it gets stuck under the car seat...." [I'm under doctor's orders to only talk on my phones when I'm calm, and NO texting with certain people....]
- "As soon as the movie begins.... There's noise.... 'I gotta go. I gotta get out of here.'" [I sit by the door at each and every movie I attend. I've had to leave several times for noisy or scary scenes.]
- "I've read that people with TBI frequently suffer seizures months and years after an initial injury...." [I know more than one person who had seizures years after the tumor was removed. This is one of my fears.]
- "The part of his brain that helped him think before he yelled has been damaged. He can't control his anger." [Said by his daughter. The same could be said about me.]
- "...holidays...extremely hectic. And that's not good for the

brain-injured – the newsletters and magazines about TBI all give hints for keeping the brain-injured from freaking out at this time of year."

- "'If Al were in a wheelchair or had a cast on his leg, people would understand that something happened,' says Crystal Mangir. 'But no one can see a broken brain.'" **[The invisibility of my damaged brain means that people misunderstand what is happening with me quite often.]**

- "Change is very difficult for the brain-injured.... Al had the idea, before his injury, that computers were stupid. He's always been stubborn about technology; now that tendency, exacerbated by his TBI, comes back to haunt him." [That's why my dear, sweet editor had to type this on his computer for me from my handwritten, messy notes.]

Life Amplified: Our Family Touched by Autism, by Karen Skogen Haslem

Even though this book is not about brain injury, this author has very important things to say about God, special education, love, family, and more. [Her son Titus is a God-send to be around. I teared up when I attended his performing with his friends and classmates at Red Hook High School in June of 2017.]

- "… I had tried to stay away from the baby section in stores, it would just make me sad and I'd end up crying all the way home." [Me too.]

- "I was angry and felt cheated. In my grief, God allowed me to be honest. I know He counted every tear and felt my heartache."

- "I had to come to the realization that God had a plan that was better than my plan."

- "… most people who are in special education really do care about your children and want the best for them. Some of the problems within special education ultimately come down to the budget and the people at the top of the ladder who are not face-to-face with your child every day." [You said it, girl!]

- "Embrace someone the way they are, don't just tolerate them." [I scribbled a HUGE "!" in her book when I read that sentence because that applies to so many people!]

- "It's okay to wonder, but not to worry. Enjoy the joyful moments in the journey. Sometimes it's an uphill climb, sometimes one can let go and coast." [Thank you, Karen, for that great "life advice."]

- "The teachers asked us what type of therapy we did with him over the summer. Our response: 'We got a dog.'" [Me, too!]

- "If people could 'see' his disability, they might be a bit more understanding."

- "People who choose to go into the Special Education field are an amazing breed. Like all teachers they work long hours, but at times endure physical abuse and really difficult challenges. Because of this, the burn-out rates in the specialty are high." [A professor I had back in the 1970s at SUNY Plattsburgh, Dr. Flood, basically said that same thing. She told our huge class of students studying to be special ed. teachers that only a few of us would make it to retirement.]

- "As much as we like to think that society has changed in the way we view people with disabilities, there will always be those who choose to believe that those of us who have a disability are somehow less than everyone else. That mentality is so short-sighted. Think of all the greatness to be done in the world if we choose to embrace those with such amazing minds. Instead of living in denial and fear, I hope we choose to welcome these amazing people…." [Better words could not be said, Karen! Thank you!]

The Gift in You: Discover New Life through Gifts Hidden in Your Mind, by Dr. Caroline Leaf

- "You were wonderfully and beautifully made with specific intent and incredible purpose."
- "The frontal lobe (also called the prefrontal cortex) is capable of an impressive display of functions, is connected to all other parts of the brain, and is where all the neural connections converge. It also houses the brain's most sophisticated circuits. This enables the frontal lobe to integrate and manage all the activities of all other parts of the brain." [**And this is one part of my brain that is permanently damaged.**]
- "In fact, God has designed the brain in such a way that as a memory is brought out of the nonconscious mind into the conscious mind, it becomes unstable and has to change – either in a more toxic or less toxic direction: it never stays the same. That's great news for us because we can fix – rewire – toxic memories. **Your amazing ability to use your frontal lobes to stand outside of yourself and observe your own thinking provides the fuel for this change.**"
- "Laughter quite literally dissolves distressing toxic emotions because you can't feel mad or sad when you laugh. When you laugh and have fun, endorphins are released which make you feel so great and at peace, those toxic thoughts can't get out of your brain fast enough. Fun protects your heart because when you laugh and enjoy yourself, your body releases chemicals that improve the function of blood vessels and increases blood flow, protecting against heart attack. Fun reduces damaging stress chemicals quickly, which, if they hang around in your body for too long, will make you mentally and physically sick. Fun and laughter also increase your energy levels."
- "If you don't build relaxation into your lifestyle you will become a less effective thinker, defeating your ability to accomplish your gift. In fact, for the brain to function like it should, it needs regroup consolidation time. If it doesn't get this, it will send out signals in the form of high-level stress hormones

some of which are adrenaline and cortisol. If these chemicals constantly flow they create a 'white noise' effect that increases anxiety...."

- "The neuroplasticity of the brain will grow the toxic unforgiveness an even deeper root and the branches will get ever more pervasive...."
- "Forgiveness is not excusing the behavior, but it is placing the situation into God's hands."
- "God wants to protect our brains and does not want us getting worked up about little things."
- "...with the neuroplasticity God has so graciously built into the function of our brain, you really can achieve lasting change. Never forget: you can change your brain and release your gift. So, plant new seed and walk in confidence that change can happen – we can see it in Scripture, just as we can in science." [**Amen!**]

The Tourette Syndrome & OCD Checklist: A Practical Reference for Parents and Teachers, by Susan Conners

This book is an excellent resource for all teachers because it describes in superb detail how to help the student in the classroom who is distracted with TS or OCD.

It is also very helpful for families to be better equipped at advocating for their child's needs.

As with another book I recommended here (*Life Amplified* by Karen Skogen Haslem), I hope these two books are future textbooks for college classes for educators. They have plenty of information to absorb and then help their students with.

Miracle on Hammertown Road: One Man's Fall and Salvation, by Jim "Bubba" Bay with Mic Ruzich

This book is about a man who fell off the side of the road one night when he was out walking, climbed out of a deep hole, and lived to tell his story about brain injury and many other medical problems because of it. Here are some of the highlights that have helped me:

- "Kids never cease to amaze me. If we could think like kids more often, this world might just be a better place." [Amen!]
- "What doesn't kill you defines you." [Quoted from Geoffrey Talcott.]
- "Jim is now a witness for the Lord and is alive to tell his story. It is the same in each of our journeys during life. We all have obstacles and feel like we're not going to make it at times, but with God's help we can overcome every challenge. Just ask Jim!" [Quoted from Donna Philipbar.]
- "With my brain injury I'm very forgetful...."
- "My memory isn't what it used to be: I forget things if I don't write them down... [I] occasionally say the wrong word – I might say 'bat' when what I want to say is 'hat.' Sometimes I forget words, and gaping holes open up in my conversations as I wrack my brain trying to find the word for what I want to say."
- "Sometimes my life feels like a tennis match, the ball bouncing back and forth between two sides: on one – I feel it a miracle to be here at all; on the other – it hurts to be me... my emotions go back and forth, up and down."
- "When I go shopping, I often give money to a cashier and get distracted by something.... This forgetfulness about money has become something of a problem...."
- "I wish I felt as good as I looked."
- "... No matter how bad you think you have it, there are always many who have it much worse."

Ting and I: A Memoir of Love, Courage, and Devotion, by [my editor] Douglas Winslow Cooper

This is about a husband's deep love for his sick wife. Reading this helped me be a better writer, and here are some quotes that did just that (or that I totally agree with):

- "Staying in the here-and-now is a good way to keep from sadness or worry."
- "Writing a book is a scary task."
- "Our staff has told me horror stories of fist-sized bedsores down to the bone on nursing home patients who received inadequate care. By that stage the sores are deadly. Too many patients, too few staff, poor morale among the staff all can contribute. Once a bedsore starts to develop, it is admittedly a challenge to reverse." [My friend Barbara's sister's bedsore led to her death after her TBI.]
- "If we are to count to 10 before speaking in anger, the quiet person is doing that already."
- "Even if what we do is not as good as it was years before, the years we have left can be quite precious." [I reread the sentence over and over on a paper I wrote it on to make me feel better about the life I've lost.]

Do No Harm: Stories of Life, Death, and Brain Surgery, by Henry Marsh

This book is written from a British brain surgeon's perspective – he has excellent quotes I've listed here, and even told the story of the patient who had the exact OCD behaviors I had (about clean hands) and needed brain surgery also.

- "She probably knew already that the last thing you get in hospital is peace, rest, or quiet, especially if you are to undergo brain surgery next morning." [How true!]
- "Meningioma…. These particular tumours are always benign and usually grow quite slowly…." [The one I had.]
- "Few – if any – of these patients would survive or emerge unscathed from whatever it was that had damaged their brains." [I survived, not unscathed.]
- "… eventually even benign tumours can prove fatal if they grow large enough, as the skull is a sealed box and there is only a limited amount of space in the head." [**My brain surgeon**

said, "Not much" when I asked him how much time I had left if the tumor hadn't been discovered. That was very scary to hear!]

Change Your Brain, Change Your Life: The Breakthrough Program for Conquering Anxiety, Depression, Obsessiveness, Anger, and Impulsiveness, by Daniel G. Amen, M.D.

Though I have not finished reading this book, what I've read so far is excellent! Here are some of the quotes I've highlighted:

- "You cannot be who you really want to be unless your brain works right. How your brain works determines how happy you are, how effective you feel, and how well you interact with others."
- "…the **temporal lobes**, underneath the temples and behind the eyes, are involved with memory, understanding language, facial recognition, and temper control." [Boy – do I have to work hard on that last one!]
- "My research and the research of others had implicated the left temporal lobe in aggression."
- "My colleagues and I have observed that left-side brain problems often correspond with a tendency toward significant irritability, even violence."
- "…top middle portion of his frontal lobes…. This part of the brain allows you to shift your attention from one thing to another. When it is overactive, people may end up getting 'stuck' on certain thoughts and behaviors."
- "Willie found that the 'minor concussion' was wreaking havoc with his life. Normally a friendly person, he found himself suddenly losing his temper at the smallest things. His whole attitude and demeanor began to change. Where he had once been patient, he now had a short fuse. Where he had once been amiable and calm, and he was now always angry. His irritability and constant flares of temper began to alienate his friends

and family." [Remember – even mild concussions can produce brain-injury-like behaviors!]

- "Unfortunately, there are many professionals who lack sophisticated information on how the brain actually works." [**How true! I have been asked to speak at hospitals to help change this.**]

Dr. Amen's research has been broadcast on the PBS channel. It's an excellent way to learn from him!

The Mild Traumatic Brain Injury Workbook: Your Program for Regaining Cognitive Function & Overcoming Emotional Pain, by Douglas J. Mason, Psy.D.

This self-help workbook was wonderful for me to use even though my brain injury was medically labeled non-traumatic. The exercises and activities helped me grow emotionally and cognitively after my surgery. Below I list some quotes and observations that helped me:

- "The exercises have been tested by more than a hundred patients with different levels of brain injury…."
- Excellent warning signs related to brain injury from concussions and other traumas are listed thoroughly.
- Excellent descriptions of all parts of the brain to help better understand behavior changes and much more (for example – damage to the frontal lobes can cause a lack of emotional control).
- Thorough lists of physical aspects of brain injuries such as: headaches, poor balance, fatigue, anxiety, attention deficit (for example: "Things like… simple math problems may seem much more difficult.")

To sum up, this workbook helped me understand and realize a ton about why I do what I do. The best part of the book is the story of "The Meaning of Life" that the author put in his closing. I reread this example repeatedly when I'm having a bad day. Thank you, Dr. Mason, for putting this workbook together for those of us who have suffered a brain injury. You are a present from God!

Fully Alive: Discovering What Matters Most, by Timothy Shriver

This is an excellent book about one of my favorite topics – Special Olympics. Though I attend some games now and then, the coaching and volunteering time has dwindled completely since I no longer teach and therefore, spend my "free time" trying to improve my social skills – a daily struggle. Here are some great quotes:

- "…you can see another view of the world if you turn your lens around. Keep your eyes open, and you will see both what is close and what may seem far away."
- "I needed to be able to use my mind to see the real stuff in the physical world but also to quiet all the distractions of my mind to see the equally real stuff of the heart that lay beneath them."
- "But with a strong relationship, learning is the endlessly exciting process of pursuing the questions and dreams that animate teacher and student alike." [My brain tumor got in the way of my once-animated teaching style. Those students that I taught at the very end of my career really lost out!]

Special Olympics Oath: *Let me win. But if I cannot win, let me be brave in the attempt.*

The Brain That Changes Itself: Stories of Personal Triumph from the Frontiers of Brain Science, by Norman Doidge, M.D.

This was a helpful book and so I read it two times – once in February 2011 and then again in June of 2015. Here are some of the key points for me:

- "There are many kinds of worriers and many types of anxiety.… But among the people who suffer most are those with obsessive-compulsive disorder, or OCD, who are terrified that some harm will come, or has come, to them or to those they love."

- "Obsessive-compulsives, so often filled with doubt, may become terrified of making a mistake and start compulsively correcting themselves and others." [See my Ms. Corrector chapter, for example.]

- "It would seem that the most frightening thing about brain disease is that it might erase certain mental functions. But just as devastating is a brain disease that leads us to express parts of ourselves we wish didn't exist. Much of the brain is inhibitory, and when we lose that inhibition, unwanted drives and instincts emerge full force, shaming us and devastating our relationships and families." [**So true for my life!**]

- "Regression…can be problematic, as when infantile aggressive pathways are unmasked and an adult has a temper tantrum." [I've had too many tantrums to count since my surgery, but luckily, they have decreased substantially.]

- "Sometimes regression is quite unanticipated, and otherwise mature adults become shocked at how 'infantile' their behavior can become."

This is another PBS program based on this doctor's research.

The Brain's Way of Healing: Remarkable Discoveries and Recoveries from the Frontiers of Neuroplasticity, by Norman Doidge, M.D.

Another "brain book" by the author I just quoted. Here's some more:

- "The reader will find cases, many very detailed, that may be relevant to someone who has, or cares for someone who has experienced…traumatic brain injury, brain damage, Parkinson's disease, multiple sclerosis, autism, attention deficit disorder… Down syndrome…." [All of these are part of my life story, in one way or another.]

- "In many brain problems, we now know, neurons are firing at the wrong or unusual rates....and brain injuries, among others: they create a noisy brain because so many of the signals are out of sync."
- "Sound – as is often the case for people with brain injuries – posed a special problem. She was hypersensitive to all sounds, which now seemed unbearably loud. Shopping malls with piped-in music...drove her crazy." [**Once, at a fundraiser walk for brain injury, I went right over to the DJ blaring music from the booth that was one of our sponsors and told (not asked) her to turn it down, because the people there are brain-injured, sound-sensitive, and it's too loud. This is just one more example of people, even those involved with the cause, who don't "get" brain injury.**]
- "Indoors, the flickering, pasty hues of 'energy-conserving' cool-white fluorescents illuminate us with a ghostly glow that is so unnatural that some sensitive patients feel ill when bathed by them." [In some places, I have to wear sunglasses indoors because of this.]
- "He had realized that brain-injured patients, like children with developmental disorders, have energy, sleep, attention, sensory, and cognitive problems." [So, the patience I once had with my students I now must have with myself.]

Write Your Book with Me: Payoffs = Plan x Prepare x Publish x Promote, by Douglas Winslow Cooper, Ph.D.

This is another book by my editor, and here are the quotes that helped me the most:

- "Authors are authorities. Memoirs mold memories. Completing the 'memoir marathon' doesn't quite make you rare, but certainly makes you stand out." [And, it made me exhausted!]
- "...to write a memoir, the story of part of your life, as you

experienced it, it will not be the whole truth, but some of it, and none of it should be false, although nobody's memory is perfect." [I did the best I could with my brain damage.]

- "Nonfiction Books: The Truth, Approximately"
- "Memoirs: Part of the Truth, How You Saw It…. It tells the truth, not necessarily all the truth."
- "…as most books lose money." **[I have never been in this project to make money. If that happens, great. I'll share it with worthwhile organizations and charities. But, the reason I wrote this was pretty simple: brain injury is not understood by the majority of people, and it needs to be, so those of us who have one will be treated better by our caregivers, family, friends, and the world-at-large. That means – please try to: understand us better, rather than avoid or ignore us; not correct us about our mistakes (since we usually know what we've done wrong all by ourselves); don't point out what we once were able to do (we miss it way more than you realize); embrace us with love and warmth (that many of us are starving for since we're so different now).]**
- "Changing minds, thanking those who have helped you, criticizing those who have fallen short…all add to your sense of well-being." [I hope I've changed minds, thanked as many people as I can remember, and I realize I've done quite a bit of criticizing here….]

No Stone Unturned: A Father's Memoir of His Son's Encounter with Traumatic Brain Injury, by Joel Goldstein [I know this author and not only is he an excellent writer, but he is one of the best advocates for brain injury because he speaks eloquently about his family's story.]

Chicken Soup for the Soul: Recovering from Traumatic Brain Injuries: 101 Stories of Hope, Healing, and Hard Work, by Amy Newmark and Dr. Carolyn Roy-Bornstein [There are remarkable stories written by many survivors of brain injury.]

A Guide to Approaching Mild/Moderate Brain Injury: Fourth Edition, June 2017, A Survivor's Guide, by Brent D. Feuz. [This is an excellent resource and notebook to help those of us who can navigate after a brain injury but who still need help figuring out how to deal with our "new normal." I have met this author, and I love how directly honest and well-spoken he is. He "pulls no punches," and he reminds me of me because he tells it like it is!]

The Traumatized Brain: A Family Guide to Understanding Mood, Memory, and Behavior after Brain Injury, by Vani Rao, MBBS, M.D., and Sandeep Vaishnavi, M.D., Ph.D. [I've heard excellent comments about this book, and I cannot wait to read it and then share it with others in my life who HAVE TO understand me better!]

I Judge You When You Use Poor Grammar: A Collection of Egregious Errors, Disconcerting Bloopers, and Other Linguistic Slip-ups, by Sharon Eliza Nichols

More Badder Grammar!: 150 All-New Bloopers, Blunders, and Reasons Its Hilarious When People Dont Check There Spelling and Grammer, by Sharon Eliza Nichols [The "mistakes" in the title are on purpose.]

Instant Happy: 10-Second Attitude Makeovers, by Karen Salmansohn

The Dash: Making a Difference with Your Life, by Linda Ellis and Mac Anderson

I Hope You Dance, by Mark D. Sanders and Tia Sillers **[Inscribed by me to me. Why? "So the incident from the summer of 2000 NEVER happens again!!!"]**

Stop Walking on Eggshells: Taking Your Life Back When Someone You Care about Has Borderline Personality Disorder, by Paul T. Mason, MS, and Randi Kreger

Wishes Fulfilled: Mastering the Art of Manifesting, by Dr. Wayne W. Dyer

Being in Balance: 9 Principles for Creating Habits to Match Your Desires, by Dr. Wayne W. Dyer

Staying on the Path, by Dr. Wayne W. Dyer

Humpty Dumpty Climbs Again, by David Horowitz [This is a children's book, but it has an excellent message for us all.]

Our Daily Bread, pamphlets by Our Daily Bread Ministries

Freedom from Obsessive-Compulsive Disorder: A Personalized Recovery Program for Living with Uncertainty, by Jonathan Grayson, Ph.D. [This book and an episode of *Oprah* with this author helped me understand my fear of germs.]

Heaven Is for Real: A Little Boy's Astounding Story of His Trip to Heaven and Back, by Todd Burpo with Lynn Vincent

The Relaxation Response, by Herbert Benson, M.D., with Miriam Z. Klipper

Head Cases: Stories of Brain Injury and Its Aftermath, by Michael Paul Mason

The Untethered Soul: The Journey beyond Yourself, by Michael A. Singer

Shades of Light: A Spiritual Memoir: A Mother and Daughter's Pathway to God, by Phyllis Cochran

Beyond Head Knowledge: Knowing Christ Who Satisfies Our Hearts, by Naomi Fata

The Language of Letting Go, by Melody Beattie

The Happiness Project: Or, Why I Spent a Year Trying to Sing in the Morning, Clean My Closets, Fight Right, Read Aristotle, and Generally Have More Fun, by Gretchen Rubin

Gabby: A Story of Courage and Hope, by Gabrielle Giffords and Mark Kelly with Jeffrey Zaslow

Here's the Deal Don't Touch Me, by Howie Mandel with Josh Young [This helped me understand mysophobia.]

The Anger Workbook: An Interactive Guide to Anger Management, by Les Carter, Ph.D., and Frank Minirth, M.D.

Proof of Heaven: A Neurosurgeon's Journey into the Afterlife, by Eben Alexander, M.D.

Struck by Genius: How a Brain Injury Made Me a Mathematical Marvel, by Jason Padgett and Maureen Seaberg

The Purpose Driven Life: What on Earth Am I Here for?, by Rick Warren

Laughing in the Dark: A Comedian's Journey through Depression, by Chonda Pierce

My Stroke of Insight: A Brain Scientist's Personal Journey, by Jill Bolte Taylor, Ph.D.

From Flawed to Fantastic: How I Turned My Disability into an A$$et, by Fantastic Frank Johnson [An inspiring guy.]

Laffirmations: 1,001 Ways to Add Humor to Your Life and Work, by Joel Goodman

Spirit of the Adirondacks: A Photographic Journey, by Paul L. Gibaldi [A wonderful example of life after a head injury.]

Chasing Daylight: How My Forthcoming Death Transformed My Life, by Eugene O'Kelly with Andrew Postman

Finding Peace: Letting Go and Liking It, by Paula Peisner Coxe

The Woman's Book of Soul: Meditations for Courage, Confidence, and Spirit, by Sue Patton Thoele

Eat, Pray, Love: One Woman's Search for Everything Across Italy, India and Indonesia, by Elizabeth Gilbert

Perfecting Ourselves to Death: The Pursuit of Excellence and the Perils of Perfectionism, by Richard Winter

Life's Little Instruction Book: 511 Suggestions, Observations, and Reminders on How to Live a Happy and Rewarding Life, by H. Jackson Brown, Jr.

Living Passionately: 21 People Who Found Their Purpose – and How

You Can Too! by coordinating author Maria Blon [Who also coordinated the best book launch party I've ever attended!]

Neurology Now: Your Trusted Resource for Brain Health, published by the American Academy of Neurology and the American Brain Foundation [I learn so much from these publications. They are free, once you complete the form attached in each issue. There are helpful articles about many brain disorders, such as: ALS, Alzheimer's, autism, brain tumors, epilepsy, multiple sclerosis, Parkinson's, strokes, concussions, and much more! I read each one and share things I've read at the various support groups I attend.]

The Challenge! A periodical publication of the Brain Injury Association of America

A User's Guide: Your Brain – 100 Things You Never Knew, a special publication by National Geographic

Healthy Hudson Valley: Healthy Body and Mind, Ulster Publishing [This is an insert in my local newspapers. It has helpful information in the area where I live. Check your local papers for similar inserts. Remember – not all information is on the computer as well as it is in the printed form. I will "defend" printed publications and newspapers till the end….]

Healthy You Magazine, published bi-monthly by the Center for a Healthy You

Battlefield of the Mind: Winning the Battle in Your Mind, by Joyce Meyer [I have many of her books, but this one is my favorite.]

No More Meltdowns: Positive Strategies for Managing and Preventing Out-of-Control Behavior, by Jed Baker, Ph.D.

Me Now – Who Next? The Inspiring Story of a Traumatic Brain Injury Recovery, by Angela Leigh Tucker, as told by Bill Ramsey [I read this one more than once because Angela's enthusiasm for life after her brain injury is truly remarkable. She lifts my spirits every time I see her at brain-injury conferences, meetings, fundraisers, etc. I pray that someday I'll be able to be half as joyful as she is. "Inspiring" is in that book's title, and it is a perfect word for not only the book, but for Angela's personality as well.]

Jeremiah: Daring to Hope in an Unstable World, A Bible Study by Melissa Spoelstra [I referenced this book in the "Why the Title…" chapter of my book. This book and the first six of the others listed below are from various women's *Bible* studies I attended and learned a lot from.]

The Gospel of Mark: The Jesus We're Aching For, by Lisa Harper [Though her style is very different from the other women authors I've listed here for the *Bible* studies I attended, she makes me laugh out loud! Her style of the written word, as well as her unique DVD recordings, make the *Bible* easier to grasp and enjoy. I've never laughed so loud in church as I do when we're listening to her speak. I highly recommend her! Even though she and I have very little in common, I love her style. But, one thing we do have in common is that she uses silly names like I do. For example: "Perky Patty" and "Downer Debbie." Too cute! As some women in my church say, "We're sisters in Christ." And – Lisa rewards her audience with chocolate, so she rates high in my book.]

Fingerprints of God: Recognizing God's Touch on Your Life, by Jennifer Rothschild

Missing Pieces: Real Hope When Life Doesn't Make Sense, by Jennifer Rothschild

The Shelter of God's Promises: Participant's Guide, by Sheila Walsh with Tracey D. Lawrence

What Love Is: The Letters of 1, 2, 3 John, by Kelly Minter

The Armor of God, by Priscilla Shirer [She is an excellent author, speaker, and actress. I was excited to see her playing the lead role in the movie *War Room.*]

Your Best Life Now: 7 Steps to Living at Your Full Potential, by Joel Osteen [I've read many of his books, but this one's my favorite.]

Don't Sweat the Small Stuff…and It's All Small Stuff: Simple Ways to Keep the Little Things from Taking Over Your Life, by Richard Carlson, Ph.D.

Love You Forever, by Robert Munsch and Sheila McGraw [The BEST children's book I've ever known!]

A Laugh a Day! A Daily Dose of Heavenly Humor, Hallmark Gift Books

Put the past behind you and give…The Gift of Forgiveness, by Charles Stanley

Still the One: A Rock 'n' Roll Journey to Congress and Back, by John Hall

The Great American Book of Church Signs, by Donald Seitz

Church Signs (Collector's Edition), by Donald Seitz

Over the Rainbow, by E.Y. Harburg, Eric Puybaret, and Harold Arlen, with songs performed by Judy Collins

AARP Bulletin [There are many helpful articles each month, but one that stood out was in the October 2015 issue. It was titled, "Are Old Head Injuries Fogging Your Brain?" by Mike Tharp. It tells of experts' warnings about the effects of trauma and how they can linger for decades.]

Poughkeepsie Journal [This newspaper has lots of excellent information each day, but the reason I've listed it here is because it has health research documented. One brain-injury example was posted on February 16, 2016. It said, "Stroke or brain injury patients often have trouble making sounds or retrieving words." This quote is from an article written by Lauran Neergaard about a form of aphasia.]

Mindfulness Skills Workbook For Clinicians & Clients: 111 Tools, Techniques, Activities, & Worksheets, by Debra Burdick, LCSW, BCN [This is the best neurofeedback specialist I had! She's written about in my book as "The Brain Lady."]

Healing the Broken Brain: Leading Experts Answer 100 Questions about Stroke Recovery, by Dr. Mike Dow and David Dow with Megan Sutton, CCC-SLP

The Rough Guide to the Brain, Revised 2nd edition, by Dr. Barry J. Gibb

Between You & Me: Confessions of a Comma Queen, by Mary Norris [The author who taught me that the beginning of my book's title should be "What Ever…" not "Whatever…."]

Chicken Soup for the Soul: Inspiration for Writers: 101 Motivational Stories for Writers – Budding or Bestselling – from Books to Blogs, by Jack Canfield, Mark Victor Hansen, Amy Newmark, Susan M. Heim [My three favorite chapters are those by Jessica M. Ball, Diane Nichols, and Phyllis Cochran.]

Breaking the Silence: My Final Forty Days as a Public School Teacher, by M. Shannon Hernandez [This book helped me a lot in various ways!]

You Should REALLY Write a Book: How to Write, Sell, and Market Your Memoir, by Regina Brooks and Brenda Lane Richardson [What a help!]

I am 100% positive that after my book goes to print, I will "dig out" several other books that have helped me through this journey. My condo could be a mini-library (or a bookstore) with the amount of books I have on bookshelves, tables, chairs, counters, and in piles, baskets, bags, closets, plastic tubs, and on and on and on.

I read every single day from multiple books. This love of reading began at a very early age, and it never really went away. One of my favorite pastimes is wandering a bookstore, chatting with personnel there, enjoying their delicious goodies (if available), and just relaxing in a comfy chair, with a book in hand.

More often than not, I buy the books I've "snuggled" with, and so that leads to the clutter I described here. But, that's okay because I enjoy re-reading some of the highlights I've underlined in each book.

I haven't put a yellow highlighter down since seventh grade in Miss Maroney's art class at Linden Avenue School in Red Hook, NY. She gave us papers to read and taught us the importance of "marking them up" so we could reference the important sentences later. This strategy has served me well for over 40 years. Practically every book, article, and so on in my home is marked up!

I hope you read the above-mentioned literature and get as much from it all as I did. These authors are admired by me much more than they ever were before, now that I know how much work it entails to be one!

Appendix 1.
Letter From Dr. Tamai

HEALTHQUEST
Medical Practice
Division of Neurology

July 21, 2014

Re: Janet Schliff

To Whom It May Concern:

Ms. Janet Schliff has a non-traumatic brain injury due to a large meningioma that was resected. This has affected her mood and personality. Due to her brain injury, she is, at times, emotional and quick-tempered. Ms. Schliff may misinterpret how people behave and act around her. She can become easily triggered by seemingly innocent comments or behaviors. Please speak and behave with consideration whenever dealing with Janet, as this will likely be a life-long problem.

If you have any questions, please do not hesitate to contact me at [office telephone number].

Sincerely,

Janet Tamai, DO

Appendix 2. BIANYS Handout (Spring 2014) Acquired Brain Injury

The Brain Injury Association of New York State [BIANYS] presented the following information at a spring 2014 state conference.

ACQUIRED BRAIN INJURY

NON-TRAUMATIC BRAIN INJURY

1. Anoxia
2. Infections
3. Strokes
4. Tumors
5. Metabolic Disorders

TRAUMATIC BRAIN INJURY

OPEN BRAIN INJURY

Penetrating Injuries

1. Assaults
2. Falls
3. Accidents
4. Abuse
5. Surgery

CLOSED BRAIN INJURY

Internal Pressure and Shearing

1. Assaults
2. Falls
3. Accidents
4. Abuse

Appendix 3. Brain Injury Wallet Card

I am a brain injury survivor.   **TRYMUNITY**

Name: _____

Address:_____

_____

Emergency Contact:_____

Emergency Phone:_____

Symptoms of a brain injury include:
- **Poor** coordination, **balance** or muscle control. (Standing, **walking**)
- Blurred speech and/or vision or impaired hearing
- **Impaired** attention, concentration, **memory or understanding**
- **Difficulty controlling anger and/or aggressive behavior**
- Confusion, disorientation, dizziness or distractibility
- Delayed thought processing and response time
- Depression, **irritability, restlessness, impatience, anxiety or agitation**
- Impaired judgment, insight or reasoning and planning skills
- **Inappropriate or compulsive behavior**

- Seizures, **headaches, fatigue or other medical conditions**

I can best communicate in a calm, non-confrontational manner. If you observe the above symptoms please help me by immediately calling the emergency number on the other side of this card.

Thank you for your courtesy and assistance!

BRAIN INJURY SURVIVOR WALLET CARD

A person with a brain injury can carry this wallet card to help avoid misunderstandings with law enforcement, first responders and others. The card includes contact information, common signs and symptoms of brain injury and a request to call a designated emergency contact if needed.

Instructions:
1. Download wallet cards (PDF);
2. Print wallet card.
3. Write information on card.
4. Trim card along edges. Card may be laminated to make sturdier.

[Barbara Sickler, whose sister did not survive a brain injury, shared this notification with me. I have one in my wallet at all times, with the symptoms that I experience **highlighted**. A friend from church, Debbie Vought, allowed me to use her name and contact information, if needed. Luckily, this has never been necessary. I pray that it won't be.]

Appendix 4. Schliff Testimony to Albany, NY, Lawmakers

October 8, 2015

Testimony from Janet Johnson Schliff

Respectfully submitted to the Assembly Standing Committees on Health and Mental Health and the Assembly Task Force on People with Disabilities, in the city of Albany, NY.

Dear Committee Members:

MY BRAIN INJURY STORY

I was a special education teacher for 25 years. I began my career for the Pine Plains Central School District in New York State. Most of my career I worked for Ulster County BOCES. I ended my teaching career working for the Rondout Valley Central School District. I found out in 2009 that I taught for 20 of those 25 years with an undiagnosed brain tumor.

I had retired early (in my late 40s in 2007) because of an inability to function appropriately anymore. I had mysophobia (fear of germs) and I couldn't even hold a piece of chalk in my classroom. I had headaches that were debilitating, but the doctors blamed them on the medications I was on for my fear of germs. It turns out the mysophobia was caused by a latent brain tumor!

As women, we are often "measured" by our ability to run a

household – raising kids, food prep, housekeeping, our job, etc. The only thing I got right on that "list" was my job. I put my entire heart and soul into it. I've never had children; I ate already-prepared foods from the microwave and had others clean my house. But what I did do, teaching, I was excellent at! I won numerous awards because of it. The award that I am most proud of is the Mid-Hudson School Study Council's Excellence Award that I received in October 1992. The New York State Commissioner of Education put a medal around my neck at a special ceremony held at the Hotel Thayer at West Point. I went from that level of excellence down to a fear of touching my classroom's door-knobs, phone, chalk, etc. It was excruciating, but then…it all made sense when a neurologist told me I had a massive brain tumor, the size of an orange, and I had to be rushed to the NYU Medical Center in New York City for brain surgery.

So, from July 2009 (when I survived several hours of brain surgery) to spring of 2010, I was "high on life" (or euphoria, as some of my friends dubbed it). I was thankful that the mysophobia was over. But, then, everything changed! I was furious at the doctors who didn't get this correctly diagnosed. I was hurt that I could no longer teach, since I have permanent brain damage to my temporal and frontal lobes. (See attachment from my neurologist.)

I am now labeled ABI (Acquired Brain Injury) and have both severe behavior and memory issues. I can cite many examples of things I've lost or forgotten since my brain surgery. Some of these examples are very embarrassing when you're only in your early 50s. My "mistakes" are very obvious to others. And – I also have many examples of the behavior issues I now face and have to deal with throughout EVERY single day. I am hyper-vigilant, impulsive, overly sensitive, overly reactive, just to name a few….

Because the only thing I did well at (teaching) was now over for me, I lashed out to anyone in my path (at restaurants, in stores, even at church)! I became aggressive, verbally abusive and so on. The behaviors I once helped my students control, I now had to do for myself 24/7.

I HAD to get a handle on my "crazy" behavior before I was arrested.

So – I learned about many alternative therapies to help me calm down. I began Neurofeedback, Craniosacral Therapy, and Reflexology. All three of them helped me enormously! After approximately 4 years of these appointments, I was able to pull myself together enough to be able to be invited to Assemblyman Kevin Cahill's office to speak about brain injury and thus, other invitations to meet with "mucky-mucks" (what I affectionately refer to politicians as since I can't remember almost everyone's correct title) up at our state's capital. Just a couple of years ago, I would NEVER have been able to sustain the stress from all of it had it not been for those life-changing therapies!

The problem is, none of them (and other therapies I've heard wonderful reports about from other brain-injured people) are covered by health insurance. I used up most of my savings account to cover these therapies. I had a savings account because I was a teacher for 25 years. Many people with brain injury are not as financially secure as I once was. But, now, I only have approximately $3000 left after all of the years I wrote checks to the various therapists. That money spent was one of the reasons I'm calmer now, and thus have not been erratic, or verbally abusive like I once began to be before I started these holistic therapies. I knew enough to get help before I landed in jail.

I firmly believe these therapies should be tested to help prove that they can help others too. I know that will help our society because a brain injury happens every 13 seconds. [**Since this 2015 writing, it has accelerated to every 10 seconds!**]

I realize that this is a huge undertaking. I know change is hard and slow. Just as massage therapy can be covered by health insurances, I think the work to get other therapies approved will be worth it for the people who will greatly benefit from a calming effect these therapies provide.

I know firsthand that people with brain injuries deserve to have the best treatments to be able to adjust to their "new life." I know that I was invited to possibly speak at this hearing because of their success with me. Please consider whatever needs to be done so brain-injured people can become more included in our society.

We, the brain-injured, may not be able to do what we once could, but may be able to do something good after getting the help we deserve. I will never be a teacher again. I hope I can help others in a new way…. Thank you very much!

Respectfully,
Janet Johnson Schliff

Appendix 5. Brain Tumor Vigil

BRAIN TUMOR VIGIL

A Service of Healing, Remembrance, Advocacy and Hope*
created by The Healing Exchange BRAIN INJURY TRUST
©2000-2008

www.braintrust.org

We would be grateful if you would please acknowledge T.H.E. BRAIN TRUST when you use this service we created. We wish you courage, peace and blessings. We send our appreciation for your participation in this special community.

I. Introduction

As we gather together in support of those who need healing, and in remembrance of those who are no longer here, let us join our thoughts and prayers. Our presence as a community strengthens those who are healing, and our words reach out to comfort those who are grieving. May all who are here today be blessed with health and strength, and may all who are mourning find serenity and peace.

II. Responsive reading – a prayer of remembrance

READER: In the rising of the sun and in its going down, we remember them.

TOGETHER: In the blowing of the wind and in the chill of winter, we remember them.

READER: In the opening of buds and in the rebirth of Spring, we remember them.

TOGETHER: In the blueness of the sky and in the warmth of summer, we remember them.

READER: In the rustling of the leaves and in the beauty of Autumn, we remember them.

TOGETHER: In the beginning of the year and when it ends, we remember them.

READER: When we are weary and in need of strength, we remember them.

TOGETHER: When we are lost and sick at heart, we remember them.

READER: When we have joys we yearn to share, we remember them.

TOGETHER: So long as we live, they too shall live, for they are now a part of us, as we remember them.

III. Reading of Names

READER: At this time, we remember and honor those who have been diagnosed with brain tumors. Some of these people are no longer living, but their memories continue within us. Others are living their lives as brain tumor survivors, with all of the challenges that surviving may involve for themselves and their loved ones. We send out hope and healing to each of these gentle spirits and to their families and loved ones.

[Read any names you have collected]

In addition to those names read aloud, we invite anyone here to come forward and speak a name or names, including their own. Each of us can also silently acknowledge loved ones and friends that have been affected.

[at conclusion of reading of names]

READER: Out of the glaring darkness of life's chaos,
      we must struggle for the words
      that will bring light and understanding.
      May we be blessed with clarity of thought,
      mindfulness of the blessings that surround us,
      and a vision of peace.

      Life is eternal, love is immortal, and death is only a horizon.
      A horizon is but the limit of our sight.

IV. Hope and Healing – a prayer for renewed health

READER: Let us send healing thoughts and prayers to everyone diagnosed with a brain tumor. Research shows that prayer can help in healing. Our gathering is powerful.

TOGETHER: Let us focus our loving attention on everyone in our community in need of healing. May they be restored to renewed health.

READER: Each of us can silently acknowledge loved ones and friends, both present and absent ones who are in need of our prayers.

[A moment of silence is observed]

READER: May all who are ill or suffering find peace and comfort.

TOGETHER: May all who encounter challenges – physical or emotional – find their strength and courage increasing each day.

READER: Grant to all who are in need of healing, the consolation of hope.

REFLECTIONS (At this time in the service, gathered members may be asked for additional reflections on healing. Poems, songs or any thoughts are welcomed. This section may be included as time permits.)

V. A Prayer for Our Community
(with opening REFLECTIONS if time permits)

READER: May all who are living with brain tumors find compassion, comfort and support from our community.

TOGETHER: May everyone in a position to make important contributions to brain tumor research, treatment, and prevention be empowered to do so.

READER: May all people affected by brain tumors, their families, friends, and their lay and professional caregivers, be blessed with courage and hope.

TOGETHER: Allow us to find new meaning in the challenges we encounter.

READER: Grant everyone affected by a brain tumor the blessings and strength of a caring, supportive community like the one we have gathered today.

TOGETHER: Grant us the vision to understand how we can work together.

READER: May all whose lives have been changed by a brain tumor find inspiration to adapt to new ways of living.

TOGETHER: May all of us find comfort knowing that we are not alone, as we encourage one another and share our experiences together.

READER: May we all be blessed with health and strength, as we continue our efforts on behalf of the global brain tumor community.

TOGETHER: Amen.

VI. Closing Prayers

READER: Eternal source of life,
      You have called us into life
      and set us in the middle of purposes
      we cannot measure or understand.

TOGETHER: Yet we are thankful for the good we know,
      for the life we have,
      and for the beautiful gifts that are part of our life each day.
      Fill us with hope knowing that
      what is good and lovely does not perish.

ALL: May we go forth renewed in courage and hope. So may it be.

VII. Conclusion and Announcements

---

*Editorial note: the prayers in this ecumenical service have been gathered from a number of sources including prayer books from different faiths. Original text by Nancy Conn-Levin and Samantha Scolamiero, founder of T.H.E. BRAIN TRUST, is also included in the service.
© The Healing Exchange BRAIN TRUST, Inc.

Appendix 6. Jury Duty Waiver Letters Excerpts

My Neurologist, Dr. Janet Tamai, D.O.

November 17, 2011

To Whom It May Concern:

RE: Janet Schliff

The above-named patient has a diagnosis of: S/P Craniotomy.

Ms. Janet Schliff is not capable to serve jury duty.

This condition is: permanent.

My Psychiatrist

November 16, 2011

Ms. Janet Schliff, a retired Special Education teacher, has been a patient under my care for several years now. She has been unable to work since [2007], when a massive brain tumor produced so much neurological and psychological dysfunction that she found it impossible to go on. Surgical resection was necessary; it required removal of part of her temporal lobe, leaving her memory altered. She was too emotionally labile to return to work. Her decision-making processes are currently severely disturbed and can appear arbitrary. The problem often derives from choices transiently informed more by irritation at a word or a behavior rather than by the issues at hand. This could actually represent a danger to the judicial process were she to be on a jury....

In summary, Ms. Schliff is currently not fit for jury duty; moreover, jury duty is contra-indicted for her. This disability may be permanent.

APPENDIX 7. LETTER TO *DAILY FREEMAN* EDITOR: A MIRACLE

10/13/09

Dear Editor:

Amy Kirschner wrote an excellent letter (September 29) about writing positive stories. I totally agree with her and here's mine.

In July I was diagnosed with a massive brain tumor (the size of an orange). When it was removed, I needed 42 staples. The wonderful surgeon and staff from NYU Medical Center in Manhattan took great care of me!

I had been disconnected from my family since 2005, but all of them came up from Florida to help me!

For over three years before the surgery, I had mysophobia (germphobia). I retired early on disability due to it. (I had been a special education teacher for 25 years). I've missed being with my students every day.

Well, the tumor caused the phobia and the surgery cured it! The tumor was benign and I'm invited to Florida for this Christmas! I thank God every day for this miracle!

So that's my positive story! Thank you Amy for a great idea! I hope you read more of them here!

Janet Schliff
Lake Katrine

[What's so ironic about this is that I'm not as positive now.]

Appendix 8. Lois Tannenbaum's Brain Injury Support Group Mindset Handout

When you initially learn something, the pathway or connection is weak. The more frequently you think a particular thought, the stronger the pathway becomes, forming an automatic habit of thinking. We call this brain training.

FRAMING OUT A NEW MINDSET

1. Set an intention
2. Be true to yourself
3. Change your mental diet
4. Beware the monkey voice in your head
5. Upgrade your physical diet
6. Stop comparing yourself to others
7. Create an uplifting environment around yourself
8. Celebrate your successes
9. Be grateful
10. Create a list of your accomplishments and review often
11. Don't take yourself or life too seriously
12. Do something new
13. Stretch your comfort zone
14. Do something nice for yourself
15. Do something nice for someone else
16. Do things you find joyful

17. Do something physical
18. Spend time with positive people
19. Create positive affirmations about yourself
20. Allow yourself to be where you are
21. Remind yourself that you are a perfect expression of life
22. SPEND TIME JUST BEING!!

Appendix 9. Daily Report Sheet

Janet Schliff

Teacher

Ulster County BOCES

Rondout Valley Middle School

DAILY REPORT

_____'s day was:

Excellent   Good   Fair   Set-back

His/Her work was:

Completed   Neat/Well done   Could have been better

Not completed   Messy/Careless   Ran out of time

Homework   _____   No homework

                _____

                _____

Teacher comments:

Parent comments:

_____

Teacher Signature

_____

Date

_____

Parent Signature

_____

Date

Appendix 10.
Operation Christmas Child

To: Freida Wright, Operation Christmas Child Field Representative

From: Janet Schliff, Special Education Teacher, Ulster County BOCES

Re: Operation Christmas Child

Date: 11/17/02

Thank you very much for the books and especially the pin. When Judy Butler presented the pin to me, I was very touched and I wore it all week as my class prepared the boxes for this year's project. Judy said you would like a write-up about how I got so many boxes filled since my class is a leader locally in a public school setting. This was an excellent compliment to get and I'd be glad to share our story....

My class is an Ulster County BOCES special education life skills class located at the Rondout Valley Middle School in Accord, NY. For the six years we've been involved with OCC, we have been in various public schools but the last two years we have been in this one. Because this project starts at my church (Fishkill Baptist), I need to get permission from my supervisor. I have had that granted from various supervisors along the way but most recently from Ms. Anne Kelly. Then, I need to get permission from the building principal of the middle school we are located in (Mr. Ray Palmer). Both of these people are supportive of this idea and for that I am grateful. That is how I am able to proceed.

After that, I write a letter to my colleagues and the parents of my students (see attachment). I decorate a large bulletin board by the office with pictures from the information kits (you'll see pictures I'm forwarding soon). My class decorates large boxes with Christmas wrapping paper and we leave them in the offices in our school for staff to donate their items. We empty those boxes periodically as they tend to overflow due to a generous staff like I am fortunate to work with at Rondout Valley Middle School.

In our arts and crafts lessons this year, we decorated the shoe boxes we were given since we didn't have the usual OCC red and green ones. We used stickers and stamps. This took lots of time and patience to make the boxes look special! My staff was very helpful with this section of the story. Some of my students also chose to decorate boxes during their free choice time.

On the day we call "Operation Christmas Child Headquarters Day" (this year – November 15th), our classroom is virtually turned into what I refer to as "Santa and his helpers." With my guidance, my staff and students sort all of the items donated into four categories (toiletries/school supplies/toys or candies/clothing). But before any sorting can start, we begin by watching the video provided. Since it is a public school, I turn down the volume when Franklin Graham speaks of God since I'm not allowed to teach that. What I speak about through that section (and when it is mentioned other times), is that love for others less fortunate than ourselves is our focus. You need to know that some of my students come from homes that are less fortunate than most, but when they watch the video, they see there are others worse off than themselves. One student in my class who is in foster care asked me after this year's screening, "Ms. Schliff – can I send those kids my money?" which was truly touching and led to an excellent discussion....

The viewing of that video is so moving, it motivates everyone to get to work – and work we did! We filled shoe boxes from 9:45 a.m. until 1:45 p.m. with only a 40-minute break for lunch/recess and then a 10-minute unexpected fire drill. When that bell went off for the drill, we were frantic only because we had so much left to do and it was the very end of the day. But – it all got done and we filled 80 shoe boxes! When we began this project just six years ago, I was proud of the 13 we filled then. We've come a long way! Next, the boxes were loaded into my [small] car (which, if this increased rate keeps us, I'll be car shopping soon) and delivered to Fishkill Baptist on Sunday to be part of the dedication ceremony.

I believe Operation Christmas Child does and can belong in a public school. I do it without preaching to anyone. I teach about taking care of others and colleagues can join in or not. I have never heard anything negative about it, only positive comments ever. I just think our world needs more ideas like this....

Thank you for asking to hear how we did it. I'm thrilled that my class did so much to help those children in other places who have so little.

CC: Anne Kelly
    Marlene Anderson-Butler

Appendix 11.
Invitation to a Party

INVITATION TO A COMPLIMENT PIZZA PARTY

Dear _____,

You have been invited by my class to a compliment pizza party <u>today</u> at _____ to celebrate all of the compliments we've recently been given. You were one of the people who paid us a compliment which we added to our "pizza wheel." Please feel free to stop by for some pizza. <u>Thank you!</u>

Sincerely,
Ms. Schliff & class
(BOCES)

Your compliment was _____, on _____.

APPENDIX 12.
LETTER OF REFERENCE

Ulster County BOCES
Board of Cooperative Educational Services
Career & Technical Education Center
PO Box 601, Port Ewen, NY 12466

July 21, 2003
Dr. Marilyn Pirkle
PO Box 9
Accord, NY 12404

Dear Dr. Pirkle:

I am pleased to recommend Ms. Janet Schliff for a teaching position at the Rondout Valley School District. I have known Ms. Schliff since she started in her teaching position at Ulster County BOCES. I hired Ms. Schliff when I was the Director of Special and Alternative Education and had the privilege of working with her for several years.

Ms. Schliff is a dedicated, committed and caring teacher. She possesses exemplary skills in delivering instruction to students performing at various levels of abilities. She has consistently contributed to creating a positive learning environment in her classroom.

During her tenure at Ulster BOCES, Ms. Schliff received recognition from the Mid-Hudson School Study Council for Excellence in Teaching.

I recommend her for a teaching position without reservation.

Sincerely,
Howard Korn
Director of Career/Technical Education & Adult Services
HK:mas

Appendix 13. Resumé

JANET A. SCHLIFF

Profile

Versatile and passionate professional with significant "hands-on" experience in the Life Skills Special Education field. Particular expertise in implementing techniques targeting individuals' different strengths and learning styles. Positions held have required the ability to create a truly unique learning experience for all my students with a strong emphasis on practical, daily life skills. Highly effective and direct communicator, able to develop trust and build solid relationships with students of varying ages, abilities, and diagnoses. Proven ability to coordinate and link individuals with a variety of community services as a part of a cohesive team.

Professional Experience

Life Skills Special Education Teacher (1:12:1)
Rondout Valley Central School District (2003-2007)

Worked directly with mentally challenged adolescents ages 12-15 in a full range of practical, Life Skills areas… Developed and led sessions in food preparation, budgeting, housekeeping, and personal hygiene… Incorporated field trips to local stores and restaurants to reinforce learned skills… Emphasized proper manners, proper ordering, shopping fundamentals, and cash-flow management with teens… Assisted students with a variety of behavioral and social skills... Trained and supervised teaching assistants and teacher aides.

- Maintained a weekly laundry schedule with class
- Facilitated recipes on food preparation and party hosting
- Organized Christmas caroling trips to a local nursing home

Life Skills Development Program Special Education Teacher (1:12:1; 1:8:1)

Management Needs Special Education Teacher (1:6:1)
Ulster BOCES (1989-2003)

Taught children labeled mentally handicapped and emotionally disturbed ages 6-15 in all Life Skills and curriculum areas... Supervised teacher assistants and aides... Implemented various behavior management plans... Organized field trips throughout Ulster County... Trained in TRIBES (behavioral cooperative learning program)... Conducted several songs sung at concerts and moving up ceremonies... Directed various play productions.

- Coordinated Ulster BOCES Special Olympics Track and Field
- Implemented the BOOK IT Reading Incentive Program for the district
- Instituted the Sparkly Crest Dental Health Program for the district
- Initiated the Ulster BOCES Running Club (Sophie Finn Extension)

Self-Contained Special Education Teacher / Resource Room Teacher
Pine Plains Central School District (1982-1989)

Taught children labeled mentally handicapped, emotionally disturbed, and/or learning disabled, ages 6-14 in curriculum and Life Skills areas...

Supervised teacher aides... Planned numerous field trips throughout the Hudson Valley... Organized and chaperoned overnight camping/ educational trips... Directed various play productions... Conducted several songs sung at winter/spring concerts.

- Coordinated a school-wide fundraiser for the Gannett House of Poughkeepsie, an emergency housing shelter for homeless families
- Initiated the Pine Plains Special Olympics Track Team and acted as Training Club leader for 3 Special Education classes
- Developed a swimming program and conducted lessons for 2 Special Education classes
- Implemented a breakfast and dental program for students
- Coordinated a community spaghetti supper as a classroom fundraiser

Education

State University of New York at New Paltz
Master of Science Degree in Education: Special Education (1985)
- Grade Point Average: 3.97

State University of New York at Plattsburgh
Bachelor of Science Degree in Special Education, K-12 (1982)
- Grade Point Average: 3.67

Certifications

New York State Permanent Certification, Special Education (K-12)

Awards

The 1992 Dean's Award for Excellence in Teaching: Ulster County
State University of New York at New Paltz and Mid-Hudson School Study Council (1992)

Who's Who in American Education
The National Reference Institute (1992-1993 Third Edition)

Publications

Co-authored with Dr. Spencer Salend of the State University of New York at New Paltz an article entitled, "**An Examination of the Homework Practices of Teachers of Students with Learning Disabilities**," *Journal of Learning Disabilities,* December 1989: Volume 22, Number 10, pp. 621-623.

Co-authored with Dr. Spencer Salend of the State University of New York at New Paltz an article entitled, "**The Many Dimensions of Homework**," *Academic Therapy,* March 1988: Volume 23, Number 4, pp. 397-403.
   - Both articles were presented at the National CEC Conference, San Antonio, Texas (4/93)

Activities

Training Club Coordinator/Advisor (1992-2005)
Ulster County Special Olympics; Ulster BOCES Special Olympics — Track and Field, New Paltz, NY

Fundraising Chairperson (1997-1999)
Ulster County Special Olympics, Kingston, NY

Training Club Coordinator (1983-1990)
Dutchess County Special Olympics; Pine Plains Special Olympics — Track and Field, Pine Plains, NY

Superintendent of Sunday School
Third Lutheran Church, Rhinebeck, NY

Whole Language Presentations and Courses Taught

Whole Language for the K-3 Special Education and Regular Education Class
30-hour/15-hour In-service Courses
Fall 1990 to Fall 1997
Ulster and Dutchess BOCES-SETRC Office
Mid-Hudson Teachers Center
New Paltz and Poughkeepsie, NY

An Introduction to Whole Language and the Special Education Classroom
Undergraduate Course Workshop
April 1999
Marist College, Poughkeepsie, NY

Classroom Celebrations
Mid-Hudson Reading Council
Thirteenth Annual Fall Conference
October 1996
Vassar College, Poughkeepsie, NY

Classroom Celebrations
Staff Development Workshop — Brinkerhoff Elementary School
December 1995
Wappingers Falls Central School District
Wappingers Falls, NY

Classroom Celebrations
Staff Development Workshop – Gayhead Elementary School
March 1995
Wappingers Falls Central School District
Wappingers Falls, NY

Evaluation and Assessment in the Whole Language Classroom
Staff Development Meeting
February 1995
Pawling Central School District
Pawling, NY

Implementing Whole Language
TAWL Conference
September 1992
SUNY New Paltz
New Paltz, NY

Implementing Whole Language
Staff Development Meeting
March 1992
Kingston City School District
Kingston, NY

An Introduction to Whole Language
Staff Meeting — Sophie Finn Elementary School
June 1991

Ulster County BOCES
Kingston, NY

Basics of Whole Language — Make and Take — Primary
Ulster County Staff Enrichment and Educational Development
Conference
April 1991
Rondout Valley Middle School/High School
Accord, NY

Reading – An Invitation to Many Worlds
Mid-Hudson Reading Council
Seventh Annual Fall Conference
October 1990
Vassar College, Poughkeepsie, NY

Implementing Whole Language
Superintendent's Conference Day
March 1990
Ulster BOCES
New Paltz, NY

A Look at Whole Language
Superintendent's Conference Day
January 1990
East Ramapo Central School District
Spring Valley, NY

Implementing Whole Language
NYS Second Annual Whole Language Conference
October 1989
Rochester Convention Center
Rochester, NY

[Thanks to Mikaela O'Brien for helping Dr. Cooper and me by typing up this document when he couldn't, because he was caring for his ill wife.]

Epilogue

So, I HAVE to have the last word – I couldn't control myself.

I pray that what happened to me (or the examples of other brain injuries I've written about here) doesn't happen to you or someone you love.

But, if it has or does, I hope all of the work I've done here helps you. I know writing has helped me! Rest in peace, all the loved ones of my readers who have died due to their brain injury.

Thank you, God, for letting me live to tell my tale. I will try to live, to the best of my ability, in accordance with your words from *Galatians* 5:22-23: "But the fruit of the Spirit is love, joy, peace, patience, kindness, goodness, faithfulness, gentleness, and SELF-CONTROL...."

[So, God and I have a **full-time job** with that self-control challenge of mine!]

ABOUT THE AUTHOR

Janet holds degrees in special education and education. She's never had any children of her own, but loved being a teacher for 25 years until a massive brain tumor and the damage that it caused led her to be on disability.

Her main reasons for writing this book are to try to help other families that have experienced brain injury, a difficult challenge that changes the lives of everyone involved, and to help the community at large understand people with disabilities better.

Many of her doctors, therapists, and support groups are surprised at how well she manages life's difficulties. Though she's no longer able to teach, she loves volunteering with children so she can still contribute to society in some way.

Janet lives with her Puggle, Happy, in Lake Katrine, NY.

My first student, Cliff, and me. (Fall 1986)

Foster son, Brian, and me in New York City. (Summer 1990)

I had just received the Mid-Hudson School Study Council Award for Excellence in Teaching, at the Hotel Thayer at West Point.
(October 20, 1992)

Three days after my brain surgery, I look terrible, but I'm out of the hospital, getting to visit my friend Marian. (July 10, 2009)

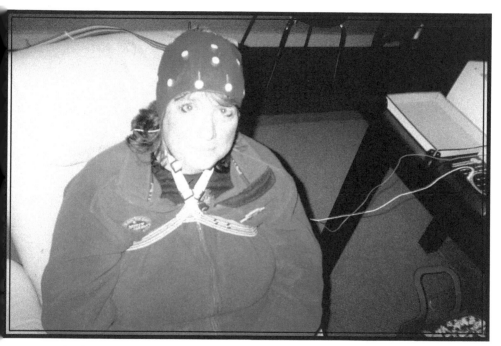

I'm having one of many QEEGs. Yucky hair – don't care! (2011)

Dr. Lois Tannenbaum, BIANYS Board President,
actor Gary Busey, and me. (June 5, 2015)

Danielle's 30th birthday party. (Summer 2014)

Catherine and me. (Fall 2009)

*Little did I know that when this glamor shot was taken of me,
my brain tumor was already growing! (1994)*

CPSIA information can be obtained
at www.ICGtesting.com
Printed in the USA
BVHW02s1314010318
509032BV00013B/6/P